Modern Language Association of America

Approaches to Teaching World Literature

Joseph Gibaldi, Series Editor

1. Joseph Gibaldi, ed. *Approaches to Teaching Chaucer's* Canterbury Tales. 1980.
2. Carole Slade, ed. *Approaches to Teaching Dante's* Divine Comedy. 1982.
3. Richard Bjornson, ed. *Approaches to Teaching Cervantes'* Don Quixote. 1984.
4. Jess B. Bessinger, Jr., and Robert F. Yeager, eds. *Approaches to Teaching* Beowulf. 1984.
5. Richard J. Dunn, ed. *Approaches to Teaching Dickens'* David Copperfield. 1984.
6. Steven G. Kellman, ed. *Approaches to Teaching Camus's* The Plague. 1985.
7. Yvonne Shafer, ed. *Approaches to Teaching Ibsen's* A Doll House. 1985.
8. Martin Bickman, ed. *Approaches to Teaching Melville's* Moby-Dick. 1985.
9. Miriam Youngerman Miller and Jane Chance, eds. *Approaches to Teaching* Sir Gawain and the Green Knight. 1986.
10. Galbraith M. Crump, ed. *Approaches to Teaching Milton's* Paradise Lost. 1986.
11. Spencer Hall, with Jonathan Ramsey, eds. *Approaches to Teaching Wordsworth's Poetry.* 1986.
12. Robert H. Ray, ed. *Approaches to Teaching Shakespeare's* King Lear. 1986.
13. Kostas Myrsiades, ed. *Approaches to Teaching Homer's* Iliad *and* Odyssey. 1987.
14. Douglas J. McMillan, ed. *Approaches to Teaching Goethe's* Faust. 1987.
15. Renée Waldinger, ed. *Approaches to Teaching Voltaire's* Candide. 1987.
16. Bernard Koloski, ed. *Approaches to Teaching Chopin's* The Awakening. 1988.
17. Kenneth M. Roemer, ed. *Approaches to Teaching Momaday's* The Way to Rainy Mountain. 1988.
18. Edward J. Rielly, ed. *Approaches to Teaching Swift's* Gulliver's Travels. 1988.
19. Jewel Spears Brooker, ed. *Approaches to Teaching Eliot's Poetry and Plays.* 1988.
20. Melvyn New, ed. *Approaches to Teaching Sterne's* Tristram Shandy. 1989.
21. Robert F. Gleckner and Mark L. Greenberg, eds. *Approaches to Teaching Blake's* Songs of Innocence and of Experience. 1989.
22. Susan J. Rosowski, ed. *Approaches to Teaching Cather's* My Ántonia. 1989.
23. Carey Kaplan and Ellen Cronan Rose, eds. *Approaches to Teaching Lessing's* The Golden Notebook. 1989.
24. Susan Resneck Parr and Pancho Savery, eds. *Approaches to Teaching Ellison's* Invisible Man. 1989.
25. Barry N. Olshen and Yael S. Feldman, eds. *Approaches to Teaching the Hebrew Bible as Literature in Translation.* 1989.

26. Robin Riley Fast and Christine Mack Gordon, eds. *Approaches to Teaching Dickinson's Poetry*. 1989.
27. Spencer Hall, ed. *Approaches to Teaching Shelley's Poetry*. 1990.
28. Sidney Gottlieb, ed. *Approaches to Teaching the Metaphysical Poets*. 1990.
29. Richard K. Emmerson, ed. *Approaches to Teaching Medieval English Drama*. 1990.
30. Kathleen Blake, ed. *Approaches to Teaching Eliot's* Middlemarch. 1990.
31. María Elena de Valdés and Mario J. Valdés, eds. *Approaches to Teaching García Márquez's* One Hundred Years of Solitude. 1990.

Approaches to Teaching Chopin's *The Awakening*

Edited by

Bernard Koloski

The Modern Language Association of America
New York   1988

Copyright © 1988 by The Modern Language Association of America

Library of Congress Cataloging-in-Publication Data

Approaches to teaching Chopin's The awakening.

  (Approaches to teaching world literature ; 16)
  Bibliography: p.
  Includes index.
  1. Chopin, Kate, 1851–1904. Awakening. 2. Chopin,
Kate, 1851–1904—Study and teaching. I. Koloski,
Bernard, 1937– . II. Series.
PS1294.C63A6433   1988   813′.4   87-31351
ISBN 0-87352-507-8
ISBN 0-87352-508-6 (pbk.)

A version of Suzanne W. Jones's chapter, "Two Settings: The Islands and the
City," appeared in *Southern Quarterly* 25.2 (1986): 108–19.

Cover illustration of the paperback edition: detail of *The Four Elements: Water*,
decorative panel (Julius Klinger, *The Woman in Art Nouveau Decoration* [New
York: Dover, 1985], pl. 5.)

Published by The Modern Language Association of America
10 Astor Place, New York, NY 10003-6981

CONTENTS

Preface to the Series   viii

Preface to the Volume   ix

PART ONE: MATERIALS   *Bernard Koloski*

Paperback Editions and Anthologies   3

Further Reading for Students   9

Further Reading for Teachers

    Background Studies   11
    Biography   13
    Critical Studies   13
    Bibliography   15

Aids to Teaching   16

PART TWO: APPROACHES

Introduction   21

Women's Experience

The Awakening as a Prototype of the Novel of Awakening
    Susan J. Rosowski   26

The Awakening in the Context of the Experience,
    Culture, and Values of Southern Women
    Elizabeth Fox-Genovese   34

Childbirth and Motherhood in *The Awakening* and in
    "Athénaïse"
    Patricia Hopkins Lattin   40

The Awakening and the Woman Question
    Dale Marie Bauer and Andrew M. Lakritz   47

Women's Language in *The Awakening*
    E. Laurie George   53

Backgrounds

A New Biographical Approach
  Emily Toth   60

The Historical and Cultural Setting
  Nancy Walker   67

Chopin's Stories of Awakening
  Mary E. Papke   73

The Awakening's Relationship with American
    Regionalism, Romanticism, Realism, and Naturalism
  Peggy Skaggs   80

Course Contexts

The Awakening in a Course on Women in Literature
  Barbara C. Ewell   86

The Awakening in an Introductory Literature Course
  Ann R. Morris and Margaret M. Dunn   94

The Awakening in an American Literature Survey Course
  Thomas Bonner, Jr.   99

The Awakening in a Research and Composition Course
  Evelyn Sweet-Hurd   104

The Awakening in a Course on Philosophical Ideas in
    Literature
  Jo Ellen Jacobs   107

Patterns That Yield Meaning

Characters as Foils to Edna
  Barbara H. Solomon   114

Two Settings: The Islands and the City
  Suzanne W. Jones   120

Symbolism and Imagery in *The Awakening*
  Joyce Dyer   126

Stylistic Categories in *The Awakening*
  Nancy Rogers   132

Edna as Icarus: A Mythic Issue
  Lawrence Thornton   138

Edna as Psyche: The Self and the Unconscious
  Rosemary F. Franklin   144

A Reader-Response Approach
  Elizabeth Rankin   150

Participants in Survey of *Awakening* Instructors   156

Works Cited   157

Index   167

PREFACE TO THE SERIES

In *The Art of Teaching* Gilbert Highet wrote, "Bad teaching wastes a great deal of effort, and spoils many lives which might have been full of energy and happiness." All too many teachers have failed in their work, Highet argued, simply "because they have not thought about it." We hope that the Approaches to Teaching World Literature series, sponsored by the Modern Language Association's Committee on Teaching and Related Professional Activities, will not only improve the craft—as well as the art—of teaching but also encourage serious and continuing discussion of the aims and methods of teaching literature.

The principal objective of the series is to collect within each volume different points of view on teaching a specific literary work, a literary tradition, or a writer widely taught at the undergraduate level. The preparation of each volume begins with a wide-ranging survey of instructors, thus enabling us to include in the volume the philosophies and approaches, thoughts and methods of scores of experienced teachers. The result is a sourcebook of material, information, and ideas on teaching the subject of the volume to undergraduates.

The series is intended to serve nonspecialists as well as specialists, inexperienced as well as experienced teachers, graduate students who wish to learn effective ways of teaching as well as senior professors who wish to compare their own approaches with the approaches of colleagues in other schools. Of course, no volume in the series can ever substitute for erudition, intelligence, creativity, and sensitivity in teaching. We hope merely that each book will point readers in useful directions; at most each will offer only a first step in the long journey to successful teaching.

Joseph Gibaldi
Series Editor

PREFACE TO THE VOLUME

At colleges and universities throughout the country, Kate Chopin's *The Awakening* has become one of the most often taught of all American novels. An MLA survey taken in preparation for this volume shows the novel being used in no fewer than twenty college courses—on subjects ranging from American literature, women's literature, and women's studies to realism, textual linguistics, folklore, and composition. At a time when some of America's important fiction has gone out of print, *The Awakening* was in 1987 available in at least eight paperback editions and was included in its entirety in three of the four major college anthologies of American literature and in the *Norton Anthology of Literature by Women*.

The Awakening's remarkable revival in the past twenty years has been due primarily to the recognition that this 1899 novel articulates brilliantly an intelligent, sensitive woman's experience of life. For many readers, Per Seyersted's publication in 1969 of Chopin's *Complete Works* provided what Emily Toth calls "an epiphany, a piercing insight into American women's literary past" (Seyersted and Toth 212). Kate Chopin has helped satisfy Americans' suddenly discovered hunger for a classic woman writer who addresses some of contemporary women's concerns.

But classroom teachers have found other reasons for using the novel. *The Awakening* is, as one instructor notes, "triumphantly" accessible to the present generation of university students. Kate Chopin is new to most students. They have probably not come across her work in secondary school. While it is obvious from the first sentences that the book is the product of the nineteenth century, Kate Chopin's language is clear, direct, free from puzzling syntactic convolutions. Students are pleased with this strangely distant, vaguely romantic, yet thoroughly modern prose. And the novel is short. Even second-language students or students with a less than desirable academic background are willing to read it all and to talk about it.

The book is, in fact, something of a teacher's dream—a classic though topical novel that students respond well to after a first reading, yet an exceptionally rich work that rewards close literary analysis in surprising and exciting ways. Even before the full force of the current Chopin revival, Fred Lewis Pattee, Edmund Wilson, Lewis Leary, George Arms, Kenneth Eble, and Larzer Ziff had all praised the book, and all for somewhat different reasons.

Precisely, however, because of Kate Chopin's sudden emergence out of the blue, few people other than specialists seem aware of the extent or the variety of Chopin scholarship and fewer yet of what imaginative teachers across the country have been doing with *The Awakening*. This volume seeks to remedy the latter situation, to make available in one place the essence of the classroom teaching that has helped establish Kate Chopin's reputation as the author of a world masterpiece. It offers new as well as experienced instructors a full spectrum of classroom approaches reflecting the current state of the art in teaching *The Awakening*.

The volume is divided into two parts. The "Materials" section contains a guide to paperback editions of the novel, advice about further reading for students and teachers, and a list of teaching aids. The "Approaches" section contains essays about teaching the novel that are written by instructors working in departments of English, philosophy, history, and women's studies and teaching undergraduates in state universities, liberal arts colleges, community colleges, research institutions, and other settings. Full bibliographical information for the books and articles mentioned is presented in the "Works Cited" section.

The contributors' essays reflect their experience with students as well as with literary studies. Some of their presentations will be most useful for teachers approaching Chopin for the first time or those working with first-year students of varied talents and backgrounds. Some will be more valuable for instructors who have already taught *The Awakening* or those who are teaching advanced students. And some should provide new insights even for teachers well read in Chopin criticism and well accustomed to using the novel in the classroom.

The essays include, but are not limited to, approaches growing out of women's experience. Yet whoever the instructor or whatever the course, *The Awakening* is, for our generation at least, no more separable from women's concerns than is *The Scarlet Letter* from puritanism or *Moby-Dick* from the sea. Teachers might bear in mind Annette Kolodny's conviction that "all readers, male and female alike, must be taught first to recognize the existence of a significant body of writing by women in America and, second, they must be encouraged to learn how to read it within its own unique and informing contexts of meaning and symbol" (60). This volume may help college instructors guide their students toward such recognition and such enlightened reading.

Many people helped bring this book into existence. Thousands of students in the United States and abroad have embraced Kate Chopin as their own and through their excitement have led many of their teachers to reread the novel and reconsider their classroom approach to it. To them must go the primary acknowledgment. Instructors who responded to the MLA Kate Chopin survey or to the announcement of this volume in the *MLA Newsletter* have made possible the "Materials" section. A list of their names is included near the close of the book. And the authors of the essays have been energetic and diligent, making their presentations succinct and accessible to as broad an audience as possible.

I am grateful as well to many individuals who have at various stages helped this project along. Carolyn Heilbrun and Peggy Skaggs wrote generous appraisals of the prospectus for this volume. Joseph Gibaldi has been an enduring source of encouragement, patience, and good sense. Emily Toth has again and again shared with me her encyclopedic knowledge of Kate Chopin and Chopinists. Joyce Dyer suggested several important additions to the manuscript. Tom Bonner and Barbara Ewell offered valuable advice. John May and Judy Diana guided me to useful information about Chopin films. My colleagues Winifred Neff, Dick Walker, Jay Gertzman, Larry Uffelman, and Walter Sanders read parts of the book and suggested changes. The staff at the Mansfield University Library checked various entries in the bibliography, and the university made available a small grant to help me finish the manuscript. Karen Choate, Marie Kopp, and other students were very helpful.

And I must thank the women of my family—Monique, Milissa, Laurie, and Jenny. They have led me to many awakenings.

BK

Part One

MATERIALS

Bernard Koloski

Paperback Editions and Anthologies

Twenty years ago only one paperback edition of *The Awakening* was in print. Today teachers are using the novel in a wide variety of editions and in four college anthologies. I examine here some advantages and disadvantages of the different texts, following more or less the order of their preferred use by teachers and focusing largely on what teachers believe to be important. I begin with a critical edition, turn next to editions containing some of Chopin's short stories, to those containing the novel alone, to a paperback collection of short stories alone, and to college anthologies containing the full text of the novel. Since editions help define or limit classroom approaches to literary works, teachers may find it useful to look through this section before ordering or reordering a paperback *Awakening*. All but one of the paperbacks and anthologies discussed here use as their text either the 1899 edition of the novel published in Chicago by Herbert S. Stone or the text of the novel in the 1969 *Complete Works of Kate Chopin*, edited by Per Seyersted, which, except for two words, is identical to the 1899 edition. The Avon paperback edition appears to draw its text from the Rinehart paperback edition, which (see below) contains some errors.

Margaret Culley's Norton Critical Edition (1976) is by far the most commonly used paperback among respondents to the MLA survey. It was chosen three times as often as the next most popular edition. Teachers like the Norton's inclusion of political and social documents of the 1890s, especially the passages from Dorothy Dix and Thorstein Veblen. Only the Modern Library edition among other paperbacks contains any such documents, and its selection is not nearly so ambitious as is the Norton's (see the discussion below). Teachers like the reprinting of early reviews of the novel—the Willa Cather review, for example. And they like the critical essays, especially those of Cynthia Griffin Wolff, Kenneth Eble, and Larzer Ziff (see the "Further Reading for Students" section of this survey). "The background material is invaluable," one instructor writes. The critical essays are "outstanding," another says. Those essays "push students beyond their immediate responses," still another adds. And more than one person mentions being pleased with the inclusion of critical essays that emphasize psychological issues. The Norton edition is especially popular among teachers who use the novel as a "springboard to research" (see Evelyn Sweet-Hurd's essay in this volume) and among those who teach at colleges with very limited library resources or who deal with excessive vandalism in the library.

But the Norton has some disadvantages. Unlike several other paperbacks, it does not contain any of Chopin's short stories, and many teachers find those stories valuable in approaching the novel. Other teachers are concerned about undergraduates being "overwhelmed or dominated by critical interpretations," as one respondent phrases it, so they refer to the Norton themselves but do not offer it to their students, at least not on a first reading of the novel. "I'd rather have students use it as a possible reference book than wade through its scholarly material as a central experience of the course," one respondent writes. There are, furthermore, problems with the book's text and scholarship. One Chopin scholar complains that it "unfortunately contains several textual errors"—like "Tell me, Mademoiselle, does he knew [rather than "know"] that I see his letters?" on page 80 and "She greeted him with affected carelesness [rather than "carelessness"]" on page 84. One scholar notes that because of the recent swift emergence of work on Kate Chopin, several of the Norton's critical essays are "less substantial than what we now have available." "A lot of fine work has come out since 1976," she adds. And an international Chopin scholar writes that he sometimes uses the Norton text, "even though it represents sloppy scholarship," citing as one example its including a letter on pages 157–58 without noting that the letter is reprinted from Daniel Rankin's Chopin biography.

In fairness to the Norton, I should add that textual or other errors may exist in other editions—there has been no thorough study of *Awakening* paperbacks—though, except for textual problems in the Rinehart and Avon editions and except for factual errors in the introduction to the Modern Library edition (see below), teachers responding to the MLA survey apparently did not notice any. Yet given the Norton's great popularity and given the respect that university instructors have for the Norton Critical Edition series, some changes in the book are clearly in order. The Norton *Awakening* was, it seems, assembled in a rush at the height of the Kate Chopin revival in the mid-1970s. It needs careful revision.

Barbara Solomon's Signet edition (1976) is the most frequently used alternative to the Norton. Teachers surveyed praise the introduction and the notes. Those who think it important that students read some of Chopin's short stories (see the essays in this volume by Patricia Lattin and Mary Papke) are pleased with the Signet's selection of seventeen stories, including the often anthologized "Désirée's Baby," "A Pair of Silk Stockings," and "The Story of an Hour," along with "Athénaïse" (see Lattin's essay) and "At the 'Cadian Ball," with its remarkable sequel, "The Storm." Some teachers who do not assign any stories as part of the course still choose the Signet because they like those works available for students who want to read more Chopin after discovering *The Awakening.* Solomon's is "the best introduction and the best selection of short stories," writes one scholar who has examined all the available editions.

Sandra M. Gilbert's Penguin edition (1984) is one of several other editions that include some of Kate Chopin's short stories. Though recently issued when the MLA survey was taken, the Penguin had already attracted many teachers' notice. "The selection of stories is excellent and Gilbert's introduction is provocative," one respondent writes. Others who had not yet used the book were planning to because they were familiar with Gilbert's coauthorship of *The Madwoman in the Attic* (see the "Further Reading for Teachers" section of this survey) and coeditorship of *The Norton Anthology of Literature by Women*. The Penguin's twelve stories include all those mentioned above, and the Penguin was in 1987 the only available paperback edition of the novel other than the Signet that includes "The Storm."

Lewis Leary's Rinehart edition (1970) contains twenty stories, more than any other paperback (except for Helen Taylor's collection of Chopin short stories discussed below), and includes "Désirée's Baby," "The Story of an Hour," and "Athénaïse," but it lacks "The Storm." Some experienced Chopin teachers use this pioneering edition because its stories let students "place *The Awakening* in the broader context of Chopin's work," to quote one respondent, or because some of the stories are valuable for probing folklore elements in Kate Chopin. But teachers should note that the Rinehart contains some textual errors, like "*coup d'état*" on page 303, and it unfortunately continues to mangle the crucial last sentence in chapter 15 more than ten years after Margo Culley pointed out the mistake in a *Kate Chopin Newsletter* article. In spite of the errors, some instructors like the text and like Leary's introduction. And one person writes that she used the Rinehart because it was "the only edition available in Tübingen, West Germany, where I was teaching," illustrating the severe limitations instructors working outside English-speaking countries usually have on their choice of texts in English. Copies of *The Awakening* are likely to be in especially short supply abroad because new entries into the American literary canon take time to become available in most other nations.

Nina Baym's Modern Library edition (1981) is unique among recent paperbacks because it selects and arranges short stories exclusively as they appeared in Chopin's two published volumes of stories. A few teachers use it precisely because of that orientation or because they are familiar with Baym's scholarship or her editorial work on the *Norton Anthology of American Literature*. The edition includes "Athénaïse," though none of the others mentioned above, and it includes also a few documents of the 1890s—from Elizabeth Blackwell, Elizabeth Cady Stanton, Charlotte Perkins Gilman, and the New Orleans *Picayune*. The edition does not pretend to challenge the Norton, but it offers background readings useful for instructors who want to offer their students some flavor of "the tradition Chopin inherits," as one teacher phrases it; and those readings are made more valuable by Baym's exceptionally lucid and balanced introduction. One scholar, however, objects to factual errors in that introduction. Kate Chopin had six children, she points out, not five; she had no New Orleans kin; reviews of *The Awakening* were not all "unfavorable."

The Bantam edition (1981) contains eight stories, including "Désirée's Baby" and "A Pair of Silk Stockings" but not "Athénaïse" or the others mentioned above. Teachers like its print and praise what one calls its "good, representative" selection of stories. "Some editions," this respondent adds, "emphasize Chopin's more explicitly feminist stories even though they may not be her most characteristic, or even her most successful, work." And some teachers like the Bantam "for aesthetic reasons," as one person phrases it—because it has no introduction or afterword. "I prefer to have no critical apparatus available to students on first reading," this teacher says.

Kenneth Eble's Capricorn edition (1964), the most commonly used edition that contains the novel alone, was the first paperback *Awakening* and, until Lewis Leary's 1970 Rinehart edition, the only one. Eble's facsimile edition "preserves the integrity of the original publication in text and spirit," one respondent notes. And many teachers continue to choose this edition because of its attractive typeface and because of Eble's influential and, as one teacher calls it, "superb" introduction.

The Avon edition (1972), like the Bantam, is without an introduction, and also without any short stories. Teachers should note that much like the Rinehart, which apparently is the basis for its text, it seriously garbles the last sentence in chapter 15. The book continues in use today and represents something of the ultimate text for those who want no academic apparatus at all for students' first reading of the novel.

Helen Taylor's paperback collection of short stories, *Kate Chopin Portraits* (1979), contains twenty-nine stories, including all those discussed above, though, like all the above editions, it does not contain "Vagabonds," a story one widely published scholar thinks deserves to be anthologized. Taylor's collection also does not contain the text of *The Awakening* (its British publisher issued a paperback version of the novel in 1978). Though not easily accessible in the United States, Taylor's is at the moment the only paperback edition of such a large number of stories that is available to teachers who want their students to read more of Chopin's fiction.

I've avoided discussing the bibliographies included in most of these paperbacks because all, except perhaps for the one in Gilbert's 1984 Penguin edition, are somewhat dated as of 1987, and all are somewhat specialized, reflecting the needs of the editors. Teachers seeking a bibliography, especially teachers new to Kate Chopin, might better consult the Chopin bibliographies mentioned at the end of the "Further Reading for Teachers" section of this survey.

I've also avoided discussing the cost of the various texts because prices continue to change, but cost is an important factor for a great many teachers who responded to the MLA questionnaire. Many instructors who would like to use the Norton edition do not do so because of its higher price, although several people argue that it is relatively inexpensive. Many others cite cost as part of their basis for choosing the Signet, Capricorn, Bantam, or Avon edition. Most teachers, furthermore, find that for courses requiring many texts, the cost of *any* individual paperback edition of the novel is too high, and they choose anthologies instead. Instructors who teach Chopin in American literature survey courses almost always use anthologies rather than separate paperbacks.

The full text of *The Awakening* appears in three standard college anthologies of American literature, those published by Macmillan (1985), Norton (1985), and Random House (1985). The Harper American literature anthology (McQuade et al., 1987) contains three of Kate Chopin's short stories ("Désirée's Baby," "A Pair of Silk Stockings," and "The Storm"), but not *The Awakening*.

Teachers were using the Macmillan and Norton more often than the Random House, but mostly because their departments had chosen the textbook for the American literature course, not apparently because of any perceived advantage in the Kate Chopin text or the introduction to it. The Norton anthology does not repeat the textual errors of the Norton Critical Edition, and teachers reported no problems with the text of the Macmillan or Random House. So although some instructors are enthusiastic about the notes in the Macmillan and some find the Norton's *Awakening* introduction especially appealing, instructors are and should be as comfortable working with Kate Chopin from one of the major anthologies as from another.

The Norton Anthology of Literature by Women: The Tradition in English (1985), which also includes the text of the novel, was just appearing as the MLA survey was taken, but the instructors who contributed the essays included here had almost all examined the book, and most were "impressed" or "pleased," finding it "very useful" or even "perfect" for a course in women's literature or some courses in women's studies. One contributor is especially happy with the inclusion of Kate Chopin's novel along with Brontë's *Jane Eyre* and Toni Morrison's *The Bluest Eye* because all three books, she writes, "show the efficacy of anger in compelling women to develop a persuasive internal voice which challenges the dominant values of the cultural order." "All of us who teach Women in Literature courses," another contributor writes, "will have to consider the Norton."

But a few people had objections. "I doubt at this point that I would use it—unless forced into doing so by the absence of any convenient rival," one writes. "I remain a little suspicious of the premature canonization of what we might call the godmothers of the current generation of scholars in women's literature. The anthology is not as representative as it might have been," she adds, "and, above all, it strongly privileges the 'bien pensantes.' Conservative women, anti-feminist women, even women who attempt some gender-neutrality get short shrift." Another contributor complains about the introduction to Kate Chopin. "The interpretative slant" of the book, she says, "as well as the content, at times, I find somewhat narrow." "But in spite of all its faults," she sums up—speaking, perhaps, for others as well —"it's without question a landmark text. And a beginning."

Out of the editions available to teachers of Kate Chopin today should emerge a paperback that suits most classroom needs. The Norton is at the moment the only choice for those who want contemporary reviews and critical studies included with the text of the novel. For those who want an edition containing some of Chopin's short stories, the Signet is the most popular choice, but the Penguin is an attractive alternative and the Modern Library, Rinehart, or Bantam a possibility. For a paperback containing the novel alone the Capricorn is a better choice than the Avon. And any of three current anthologies provides an acceptable text for teaching *The Awakening*.

Further Reading for Students

Many of the teachers who responded to the MLA survey assign no secondary reading to their students because, they explain, "I stress primary works in my course"; I want students "to concentrate on the experience of reading and discussing the novel itself"; I like students "to develop their own analyses rather than leaning on authority"; I am interested in "their unencumbered conclusions—reading criticism tends to make my students stop thinking on their own." Some teachers would rather that their students keep journals or complete other writing assignments than read secondary sources. Some would like to require secondary readings but have found that their students cannot successfully manage such assignments and keep up with a heavy schedule of primary readings.

But most teachers do require additional reading of students, and most of them give a few very similar assignments. First in popularity by far is some part of the materials in the Norton Critical Edition of the novel. Instructors are particularly fond of asking students to read from the Norton either the contemporary reviews of Chopin's novel or the "Contexts" section, stressing especially the excerpt from Thorstein Veblen's *Theory of the Leisure Class* or the newspaper columns of Dorothy Dix. The Norton is the paperback edition respondents used the most, in part because they find the contemporary reviews or the passages from Veblen, Dix, and others so very useful with their classes. "Thanatos and Eros: Kate Chopin's *The Awakening*," by Cynthia Griffin Wolff, is the critical study most likely to be assigned to students, both by teachers who use the Norton and by those who do not. Wolff's 1973 *American Quarterly* article has had a great impact on Chopin scholarship and Chopin teaching as well. It continues to be the single most influential essay written about *The Awakening*.

Per Seyersted's *Critical Biography* is the most frequently assigned book-length study; many respondents call it "very helpful." Teachers who ask that students learn something about Kate Chopin's life invariably turn to Seyersted, as do those who are not using the Norton but want students to sample the flavor of Kate Chopin's times. Some teachers emphasize Seyersted's information about the New Orleans that Kate Chopin knew in the 1870s.

Several of Chopin's short stories are assigned by some teachers. See the discussion of Chopin's other works in the "Further Reading for Teachers" section of this survey. Charlotte Perkins Gilman's short story "The Yellow Wallpaper" is assigned by some teachers to be read as a parallel text with *The Awakening*.

Individual teachers assign a wide variety of other essays and other books as well, and a few respondents provided library reserve lists tied to their own reading and their classroom approaches. See "Further Reading for Teachers" and the references in the articles in this volume by Barbara Ewell (women in literature), Laurie George (women's language), Elizabeth Fox-Genovese (southern women), Dale Marie Bauer and Andrew Lakritz (the woman question in the late nineteenth century), Nancy Walker (the historical and cultural setting), Emily Toth (biography), Peggy Skaggs (American literary movements), Nancy Rogers (stylistic categories), Jo Ellen Jacobs (philosophical ideas on love and will), Joyce Dyer (symbolism and imagery), Susan Rosowski (the novel of awakening), and others. Also see "Aids to Teaching" for ideas about other classroom activities.

Further Reading for Teachers

Respondents to the MLA survey suggest a good number of sources for teachers new to Kate Chopin. Many have very strong beliefs: "I think," one writes, "beginning teachers should be familiar with the literary models Chopin plays with, like *Madame Bovary*." "And they should know," he adds, articulating what many others suggest, "at least some of Chopin's short stories, should know the history of the work's reception (including the initial scandal it caused), should have some awareness of the position of women in late nineteenth-century American culture, and should be familiar with some of the basic concepts in feminist literary theory." Other instructors stress the importance of Chopin's early novel, *At Fault*; of Chopin biography; or of recent Chopin criticism. I list here teachers' recommendations, a few works appearing as the MLA survey was being taken, and a few items of Chopin bibliography.

Background Studies

The Norton Critical Edition of *The Awakening* and Per Seyersted's *Critical Biography* head the list of sources recommended for teachers approaching Kate Chopin for the first time. But instructors offer many other suggestions as well.

Larzer Ziff, *The American 1890s: Life and Times of a Lost Generation*, is cited most often as the best general discussion of the culture and literature of the times. Its chapter on Kate Chopin and other women writers is extremely useful, many teachers note. Other instructors include Warner Berthoff, *The Ferment of Realism: American Literature, 1884–1919*, on their lists of valuable background readings. Thorstein Veblen's *Theory of the Leisure Class* is, one teacher writes—speaking for some others as well—"the most powerful background work I've used" for the novel. Many instructors note that Veblen's discussion of conspicuous leisure and conspicuous consumption and of dress as an expression of the pecuniary culture are especially relevant to Chopin's story. The newspaper columns of Dorothy Dix (Elizabeth Gilmer) in the New Orleans *Daily Picayune* are helpful background reading, several instructors note. Included in the Norton Critical Edition of the novel are Dix's "The American Wife," "Summer Flirtations," and "Women and Suicide."

Some teachers recommend other works of literature. In addition to "The Yellow Wallpaper" (1899) by Charlotte Perkins Gilman, "The Angel over the Right Shoulder" (1852) by Elizabeth Stuart Phelps and "Mrs. Flint's Married Experience" (1880) by Rose Terry Cooke appeal to some teachers as valuable fictional treatments of nineteenth-century married life. Other instructors recommend Ibsen's *A Doll House*, Flaubert's *Madame Bovary*, Tolstoy's *Anna Karenina*, and other European works of the late nineteenth century that, one teacher notes, "share thematic concerns with *The Awakening*."

Five studies of literary women and women in literature draw consistent praise from teachers as being of great help in understanding Kate Chopin's accomplishment. Ellen Moers's *Literary Women* is cited by many teachers as the most useful of all. Sandra M. Gilbert and Susan Gubar's landmark study *The Madwoman in the Attic: The Woman Writer and the Nineteenth-Century Literary Imagination* appears again and again on teachers' lists of valuable background reading. Judith Fryer's *The Faces of Eve: Women in the Nineteenth Century American Novel*, Barbara Welter's *Dimity Convictions: The American Woman in the Nineteenth Century*, and Patricia Meyer Spacks's *The Female Imagination* are consistently mentioned.

Anne Firor Scott's *The Southern Lady: From Pedestal to Politics, 1830–1930*, which provides a very valuable picture of southern women during Kate Chopin's time, and the somewhat newer *Tomorrow Is Another Day: The Woman Writer in the South, 1859–1936* by Anne Goodwyn Jones, focusing on literary women, are both cited by respondents, along with Marie Fletcher's "The Southern Woman in the Fiction of Kate Chopin." And several teachers refer to Eudora Welty's "Place in Fiction," Clement Eaton's *A History of the Old South*, and Wilbur Joseph Cash's still controversial *The Mind of the South* as valuable background sources.

The New Feminist Criticism: Essays on Women, Literature, and Theory, edited by Elaine Showalter, is probably the most useful available guide to feminist criticism. It was new when the Kate Chopin survey was being taken, so only a few teachers mention it, yet with its essays by Sandra Gilbert, Susan Gubar, Carolyn Heilbrun, Annette Kolodny, Nancy Miller, Lillian Robinson, and others, and with its excellent bibliography, it is almost certainly the best place for a teacher who knows little or nothing about feminist criticism to begin reading.

Teachers find useful several other books and articles dealing with women's experience: Simone de Beauvoir's classic study *The Second Sex* and Carroll Smith-Rosenberg's "The Female World of Love and Ritual: Relations between Women in Nineteenth-Century America" (the first article in the first issue of *Signs: Journal of Women in Culture and Society*); also Elizabeth Abel, Marianne Hirsch, and Elizabeth Langland, eds., *The Voyage In: Fictions of Female Development*; Carol P. Christ, *Diving Deep and Surfacing: Women Writers on Spiritual Quest*; Mary Kelley, *Private Woman, Public Stage: Literary Domesticity in Nineteenth-Century America*; Ann Douglas Wood. "The Literature of Impoverishment: The Woman Local Colorists in

America 1865–1914"; and Emily Toth, "The Independent Woman and 'Free' Love." And *Reconstructing American Literature: Courses, Syllabi, Issues*, edited by Paul Lauter, should be useful for almost any teacher exploring ways to strengthen the treatment of women's experience in American literature courses.

Biography

Per Seyersted's *Kate Chopin: A Critical Biography* is without question the source teachers use most often to explore Chopin's life and times. Since its publication in 1969, the Seyersted biography has been the standard work on the subject, and it continues to provide some of the essential data for almost all Chopin biographical work. Many instructors also mention the nonfiction sections in Seyersted's *Complete Works of Kate Chopin* as excellent places to begin exploring Chopin's thinking.

Emily Toth's articles, her contributions to *A Kate Chopin Miscellany* (Seyersted and Toth), and the volumes of the *Kate Chopin Newsletter* that she edited are often cited by teachers as extremely valuable sources. Several instructors stress the importance of Chopin's diary, which is included in the Seyersted and Toth *A Kate Chopin Miscellany*. Many respondents refer to Toth's various "new discoveries" and await with anticipation her forthcoming Chopin biography, which, one respondent writes, will be "crucial" (see Toth's discussion of that work in her essay in this volume).

Daniel Rankin's early biography was found useful by instructors and was especially important to those who sought to offer students a glimpse of how Kate Chopin was viewed before the current Chopin revival began. Barbara C. Ewell's *Kate Chopin* and Peggy Skaggs's *Kate Chopin* were appearing as the MLA survey was being taken, so most teachers did not have a chance to comment on them, but both contain biographical presentations.

Critical Studies

Kate Chopin criticism has blossomed in recent years, and teachers find useful many studies exploring a wide variety of issues in *The Awakening*. Cynthia Griffin Wolff's "Thanatos and Eros: Kate Chopin's *The Awakening*" is the article most often cited by teachers as a valuable background source. Along with Per Seyersted's *Critical Biography* and the other articles included in the Norton Critical Edition of the novel, it has had an important influence on the teaching of Kate Chopin.

Several studies from the 1950s and 1960s continue to be cited: Kenneth Eble's "A Forgotten Novel: Kate Chopin's *The Awakening*"; Edmund Wilson's *Patriotic Gore: Studies in the Literature of the American Civil War*;

Robert Cantwell's "*The Awakening* by Kate Chopin"; George Arms's "Kate Chopin's *The Awakening* in the Perspective of Her Literary Career"; Warner Berthoff's *The Ferment of Realism: American Literature, 1884–1919*; Joan Zlotnick's "A Woman's Will: Kate Chopin on Selfhood, Wifehood, and Motherhood"; Marie Fletcher's "The Southern Woman in the Fiction of Kate Chopin"; and Larzer Ziff's *The American 1890s: Life and Times of a Lost Generation*.

The 1970s produced a great deal of Chopin criticism. The studies found most useful by teachers include Donald A. Ringe, "Romantic Imagery in Kate Chopin's *The Awakening*"; Priscilla Allen, "Old Critics and New: The Treatment of Chopin's *The Awakening*"; Elizabeth Fox-Genovese, "Kate Chopin's Awakening"; Ruth Sullivan and Stewart Smith, "Narrative Stance in Kate Chopin's *The Awakening*"; John R. May, "Local Color in *The Awakening*"; Robert Arner, *Kate Chopin* (spec. issue of *Louisiana Studies*); Peggy Skaggs, "Three Tragic Figures in Kate Chopin's *The Awakening*"; Elaine Jasenas, "The French Influence in Kate Chopin's *The Awakening*"; Cathy N. Davidson, "Chopin and Atwood: Woman Drowning, Woman Surfacing"; Charles W. Mayer, "Isabel Archer, Edna Pontellier, and the Romantic Self"; Nancy Walker, "Feminist or Naturalist: The Social Context of Kate Chopin's *The Awakening*"; Otis B. Wheeler, "The Five Awakenings of Edna Pontellier"; Ottavio Mark Casale, "Beyond Sex: The Dark Romanticism of Kate Chopin's *The Awakening*"; Sharon O'Brien, "The Limits of Passion: Willa Cather's Review of *The Awakening*"; Kenneth M. Rosen, "Kate Chopin's *The Awakening*: Ambiguity as Art"; James H. Justus, "The Unawakening of Edna Pontellier"; Jane P. Tompkins, "*The Awakening*: An Evaluation"; George Spangler, "Kate Chopin's *The Awakening*: A Partial Dissent"; Lewis Leary, "Kate Chopin and Walt Whitman"; Gregory L. Candela, "Walt Whitman and Kate Chopin: A Further Connection"; and the introduction by Barbara Solomon to the Signet edition of the novel.

Among studies appearing in the 1980s, teachers mention Sandra M. Gilbert, "The Second Coming of Aphrodite: Kate Chopin's Fantasy of Desire"; Anne Goodwyn Jones, *Tomorrow is Another Day: The Woman Writer in the South, 1859–1936*; Lawrence Thornton, "*The Awakening*: A Political Romance"; Robert S. Levine, "Circadian Rhythms and Rebellion in Kate Chopin's *The Awakening*"; Suzanne W. Jones, "Place, Perception, and Identity in *The Awakening*"; Joseph L. Candela, Jr., "The Domestic Orientation of American Novels, 1883–1913"; Rosemary F. Franklin, "*The Awakening* and the Failure of Psyche"; and Barbara C. Ewell, *Kate Chopin*.

Many teachers suggest that beginning Chopin instructors familiarize themselves with some of Chopin's other fiction. They most often recommend several short stories (see the essays in this volume by Patricia Lattin and

Mary Papke, and see also the discussion of paperbacks containing stories in the "Paperback Editions and Anthologies" section), especially "Athénaïse" (see Lattin's essay), "The Story of an Hour," "Désirée's Baby," "A Pair of Silk Stockings," "Vagabonds," and "At the 'Cadian Ball," with its sequel, "The Storm." Some instructors find Chopin's early novel *At Fault* valuable background reading.

Teachers find useful the brief discussions of Chopin's short stories in Barbara Solomon's Signet edition of the novel, in Lewis Leary's Rinehart edition, and in Helen Taylor's *Kate Chopin Portraits*. They turn also to Per Seyersted's *Critical Biography* and to George Arms, "Kate Chopin's *The Awakening* in the Perspective of Her Literary Career"; Patricia Hopkins Lattin, "Kate Chopin's Repeating Characters"; Joyce Dyer, "Kate Chopin's Sleeping Bruties"; Peggy Skaggs, " 'The Man-Instinct of Possession': A Persistent Theme in Kate Chopin's Stories"; Robert D. Arner, "Characterization and the Colloquial Style in Kate Chopin's 'Vagabonds' " and "Kate Chopin's Realism: 'At the 'Cadian Ball' and 'The Storm' "; James E. Rocks, "Kate Chopin's Ironic Vision"; Elmo Howell, "Kate Chopin and the Creole Country"; and Barbara C. Ewell's *Kate Chopin*.

For a discussion of *At Fault*, teachers mention Thomas Bonner's "Kate Chopin's *At Fault* and *The Awakening*: A Study in Structure," Lewis Leary's "Kate Chopin's Other Novel," Donald A. Ringe's "Cane River World: Kate Chopin's *At Fault* and Related Stories," Robert D. Arner's "Landscape Symbolism in Kate Chopin's *At Fault*," and Bernard Koloski's "The Structure of Kate Chopin's *At Fault*."

Bibliography

Several bibliographies are available for readers who want to further explore Kate Chopin scholarship. The most recent and the best to begin with is Tonette Bond Inge's essay in *American Woman Writers*, but see also Marlene Springer's *Edith Wharton and Kate Chopin: A Reference Guide* and its update, Emily Toth's "Bibliography of Writings on Kate Chopin," Thomas Bonner's "Kate Chopin: An Annotated Bibliography," and Richard H. Potter's "Kate Chopin and Her Critics: An Annotated Checklist."

Aids to Teaching

At the moment the audiovisual apparatus available on Kate Chopin is less extensive than that devoted to some other major authors. And for a variety of philosophical, pedagogical, and practical reasons many Chopin instructors prefer to avoid audiovisual aids. "I'm bad at this," one writes. Many instructors have nevertheless found or created various teaching materials helpful for approaching *The Awakening*. I describe here what respondents to the MLA survey thought valuable.

Some teachers show students maps of the New Orleans area, noting the position of Grand Isle, where the novel opens and closes, and of the Chênière Caminada, where Edna goes with Robert in chapter 12. Others show maps of the French Quarter in New Orleans, where chapters 17 through 38 take place, or photographs of the architecture in that area. And some teachers show slides they have collected of southern Louisiana. One teacher writes, "Many students have no idea just how extravagant and rich this area is, nor do they understand that the lush tropical climate of the area had much to do with Edna's awakening."

More than one person mentions materials available at the Bayou Folk Museum—named after the title of Chopin's first book of short stories—in Cloutierville, Louisiana, where Chopin lived with her husband. One teacher shows slides she collected in the Cloutierville area, and Emily Toth notes in her bibliography in *A Kate Chopin Miscellany* (Seyersted and Toth) that a microfilm version of scrapbooks about the Cane River country assembled by Mildred McCoy is available through the Archives Division at Northwestern State University, Natchitoches, Louisiana 71497. Several teachers substitute for museum materials the photographs in the Seyersted biography and in *A Kate Chopin Miscellany*.

Some instructors note with anticipation the appearance of Thomas Bonner's *Kate Chopin Companion*, to be published by Greenwood. The book will include a dictionary of characters, places, localisms, plot briefs, and citations from persons and places in Chopin's life, along with maps of Louisiana, New Orleans, and St. Louis. It will also contain a bibliographic essay, eight Maupassant stories translated by Chopin, and a chronology. As this volume was nearing completion, one instructor wrote to recommend that teachers look into Robert Stone's novel *Children of Light*. The book is about the screenwriter and lead actress of a Hollywood production company filming *The Awakening*.

Some instructors use music. One teacher makes available tapes of several Frédéric Chopin impromptus and of Isolde's song from Wagner's *Tristan and Isolde* so students can hear the music Mlle Reisz plays while Edna reads

Robert's letter from Mexico in chapter 21. Another sings for his students, "Ah, si tu savais"—by Michael William Balfe (1808–70), according to Margaret Culley in the Norton Critical Edition—the song that Edna remembers Robert singing to her at the end of chapter 14 and that she objects to Victor singing during the party scene in chapter 30. Still another has taped a student playing Kate Chopin's song "Lilia" (the song is included in *A Kate Chopin Miscellany*) and uses that tape with her class. No one, however, seems interested in offering students the duet from Louis Hérold's opera *Zampa* that the Farival twins are playing as the novel opens.

Several teachers show slides of French paintings. "Manet, Delacroix, Cézanne, Sisley, and Renoir are especially helpful," one says. "Manet and Renoir are the best," another writes. Still another lists several specific French and other paintings she finds valuable: Edouard Manet, *In the Winter Garden* (1879); Edmund Charles Tarbell, *In the Orchard* (1891); Mary Cassatt, *Women Admiring a Child* and *Mother and Child* (c. 1890); Maurice Prendergast, *Revere Beach* (c. 1896); and Thomas Wilmer Dewing, *The Spinet* (1902).

At least four Kate Chopin films are available. Ann R. Morris and Margaret M. Dunn (see their essay in this volume) describe the use of a film of excerpts from *The Awakening* (dir. Paul Lally). "The fifteen minute film offers," they add, "an interesting contrast to the novel in that several vignettes of Edna (sitting on the beach, learning to swim, lying in a hammock) indicate her thoughts through 'voice-over' and these thoughts are the *narrator's* words in the book itself. In an epilogue, Joy Hawkins, the actress who plays Edna, offers her impressions of the novel as a 'journey of self-discovery.' " (Information on rental or purchase of films and videotapes can be found in the final section of "Works Cited" at the end of this volume.)

Several teachers refer to *The Joy That Kills*, a film inspired by Chopin's short story "The Story of an Hour" (dir. Tina Rathborne). Though the film is based on the short story, one respondent writes, "it reflects in its composition and setting the influence of *The Awakening*. It is a good vehicle to explore relations between the two narratives in light of a common theme." And "it is an excellent presentation of the stifling, hothouse atmosphere in which many of Chopin's women exist," another instructor writes. One teacher, however, cautions instructors to note that the film "introduces a whole new story in addition to Chopin's short story," and a few teachers say they have been disappointed by the film and would not recommend its use.

Kate Chopin's "The Story of an Hour" (dir. Marita Simpson) is a filmed version of Chopin's short story. A finalist in both the American Film Festival and the Hemisfilm International Film Festival, *"The Story of an Hour"* has been well received by several reviewers, and one teacher writes that it is a "truer" version of the short story than is *The Joy That Kills*. "It is a dramatization of the story, not a take-off from it," she adds. The film includes a short introduction to Kate Chopin's life and artistry.

Although respondents to the MLA survey had not used it, there is a feature-length film version of *The Awakening* called *The End of August* (dir. Bob Graham). The *New York Times* announced in August 1986 that producer Robert Geller was preparing a new film version of the novel.

One teacher showed the Jane Fonda film of Ibsen's *A Doll's House* (dir. Joseph Losey) when teaching *The Awakening* "in tandem" with the play. The combination of Chopin and Ibsen "was quite successful," she adds. Another has taught the novel alongside of Henry James's *Bostonians* and used the film version of that novel (dir. James Ivory) with some success.

Elizabeth Rankin's essay in this volume has a useful reader-response diagram, and Rosemary Franklin's essay a chart outlining the myth of Psyche and Eros.

Finally, instructors should note that while none of the respondents to the Kate Chopin survey mentions it, there exists a Cliffs Notes guide for *The Awakening*, prepared by Kay Carey. Like other pamphlets in the Cliffs Notes series, it is—despite a denial on the inside cover—designed to be a substitute for a work of literature, rather than a supplement to it. The guide is misleading at best, and at seventy-four pages is not even a time-saver, the novel itself being scarcely longer.

Part Two

APPROACHES

INTRODUCTION

The following essays are organized into four sections, but the groupings are to some extent arbitrary. Teachers may find it best to begin reading wherever they like. Those new to Kate Chopin might start by checking the "Course Contexts" section to see if any of the essays fit their teaching assignments, or perhaps the "Backgrounds" section to give themselves some notion of how to begin constructing their own approaches to the novel. Experienced teachers might turn first to the "Patterns That Yield Meaning" section for ideas to strengthen, expand, or possibly even reorient their teaching approaches. All teachers may at some point need to examine the essays in the "Women's Experience" section.

And all teachers would do well to look beyond what seems implied by the titles of the essays. Patricia Lattin concentrates on the theme of childbirth and motherhood but in the process describes a way to introduce students to intertextuality. Jo Ellen Jacobs teaches an upper-division philosophy course, but her discussion of love and will has implications for instructors of literature, history, or women's studies. Lawrence Thornton and Rosemary Franklin examine two different mythic readings, but their findings speak to those studying the background of the novel or those teaching introductory literature courses, among others. And Laurie George uses "feminist" to refer exclusively to "women who are exploring the connection between women and language," but her linguistic insights have importance for almost anyone concerned with discussing Kate Chopin's novel in the college classroom. Each of the essays has significance for teachers outside its apparent audience. Some of them offer a fresh reading of the novel. Some synthesize traditional or new critical thinking about Kate Chopin. Some describe ways to guide students as they read, ways to organize classroom time spent on the novel, ways to probe connections with other literature. The following overview of the essays may guide teachers to those approaches best suited to their students.

Women's Experience

Susan Rosowski, addressing the issue of how "patterns of male and female experience differ," assigns her students traditional examples of the male bildungsroman and then examples of the female "novel of awakening," such as Flaubert's *Madame Bovary* and Cather's *My Mortal Enemy*. Students begin with Chopin's book as a "prototype of the novel of awakening" and "make connections to one other novel—then another—until they recognize that the pattern Chopin presented runs through literature about women."

Elizabeth Fox-Genovese, determined to "teach the novel with some attention to historical context," encourages students to "distinguish between gender and sexuality in assessing Chopin's notion of female independence." She asks them to recognize that Chopin "may have thought that her attempt to treat sexuality independent of gender relations respected the social values of southern society, but she misjudged."

Patricia Lattin probes the themes of childhood and motherhood by having students read the novel alongside Chopin's short story "Athénaïse," whose heroine is a "tentative, incomplete model of an independent woman." The presence of Gouvernail in both the story and the novel gives students an introduction to intertextuality and "a sample of the dense social reality of Chopin's complex fictional world, a world with numerous repeating characters and places."

Dale Marie Bauer and Andrew Lakritz suggest to students that Chopin "calls into question the ideologies and assumptions about women's place articulated by leading thinkers of her time." Focusing on William James, Thorstein Veblen, and Ward Hutchinson and working with Mikhail Bakhtin's argument that the novel can be a form of social and cultural dialogue, they lead their students to participate in the conversation Chopin "orchestrates" and to "distinguish between competing versions of the real."

Laurie George, following Elaine Marks, uses the word "feminist" to refer to "women who are exploring the connection between women and language." She helps her "primarily young, female, non-English majors" to "become feminists" as they examine connections between "contemporary theories of women and language and Chopin's novel—her feminist critique of male-centered language and her exploration of an alternative women's language."

Backgrounds

Emily Toth, drawing from work on her forthcoming Chopin biography, reexamines—with some surprising results—the answers to questions many students ask about Kate Chopin and her personal experience: How independent *was* she? Did she earn a living from her writing? What really went on in her marriage? And how did she know all that in 1899?

Nancy Walker guides students to approach the novel as "an account of the clash between the dominant southern culture in which Edna was raised and the New Orleans Creole subculture in which she finds herself after her marriage to Léonce." She concludes that Edna is "a woman who does not belong to her time" but says that "it is equally important to realize that she does not belong to her place."

Mary Papke looks with students at stories Chopin wrote before beginning

The Awakening, stories that reveal a "shift in focus from that on the limitations women confront in the public and private spheres to those limitations women discover in desire itself." She and her students "recapitulate Chopin's process of perception and reflection" and become as a result "active rather than passive readers."

Peggy Skaggs, concentrating on how the novel "illustrates virtually all America's major intellectual and literary trends of the nineteenth century" and focusing on regionalism, romanticism, realism, and naturalism, offers recent criticism to show students that Chopin, in creating *The Awakening*, "uses, transcends, and expands her received tradition."

Course Contexts

Barbara Ewell uses the novel as the "touchstone" of her "rather traditional" approach to a course on women in literature because students easily become involved with this text, which, she argues, offers them gifts of tolerance, empathy, confidence, and understanding. "Weak and confused as Edna may be," students discover, "her conflict with an uncomprehending society has" for them "a piercing and resonant reality."

Ann Morris and Margaret Dunn find their introductory course in literature works best if they begin by centering a three-week unit on the novel. Drawing on Chopin's "provocative subject matter and relatively simple symbolism" as well as on students' ability to empathize with an Edna who is "becoming herself," they devote one week to literary analysis, one to using critical materials, and one to research writing.

Thomas Bonner, Jr., explores questions about the placement of the novel in his American literature survey course. Should Chopin's classification as a local-color writer be a "continuing consideration"? "Should her fiction be studied in the wider context of southern literature? What part does Chopin fulfill in the mainstream realist tradition? What is the effect of her persistent use of romantic elements? And how does one address the feminist character of her works?"

Evelyn Sweet-Hurd describes possible topics the novel opens for students of various talents and backgrounds learning beginning research techniques. She considers time and place in the novel, along with language and literary criticism, and she concentrates on sociological and psychological questions.

Jo Ellen Jacobs, examining "love in the twentieth century" in a course on philosophical ideas in literature, reads the novel alongside Rollo May's *Love and Will*, urging students to look closely at Edna's development of what May calls a "mature will." "Why does Edna stop growing?" she asks her classes. "Where did she fail?" And "does Edna consciously choose suicide?"

Patterns That Yield Meaning

Barbara Solomon asks students to pay attention to Chopin's "use of major and minor characters as foils to Edna Pontellier"—to the "shadowy pair of lovers" early in the book, to the "provocative Mariequita" and the "sophisticated Mrs. Highcamp," and to Adèle Ratignolle and Mlle Reisz, who are foils not only for Edna but for each other.

Suzanne Jones discovered "that if students evaluate Edna's behavior against the background of the two settings" in the novel, the islands and the city, "they can most clearly see Chopin's ambivalence" at "every level" in the book—"characters, narration, and language." And, she adds, they can understand Chopin's "use of place to initiate conflict and reveal theme."

Joyce Dyer sets out to show students that "Kate Chopin is a psychological symbolist," that her symbols "elaborately and meticulously connect to tell the complete and complex story of Edna Pontellier." She concentrates on the sea, the Kentucky meadow, the moon, the gulf spirit, the oaks and violets, and on the ironic paired symbolism of the colors yellow and red and of Wagner's *Tristan and Isolde* and Frédéric Chopin's impromptu.

Nancy Rogers, teaching in West Germany but thinking of American students as well, guides classes to a study of "literary discourse from a linguistic orientation," exploring the novel's vocabulary, grammar, figures of speech, cohesion, narrative stance, and speech and thought presentation. Such analysis, she notes, tends to "bolster the claims" to Chopin's status as "a psychological realist rather than a regionalist."

Lawrence Thornton looks with students at "Chopin's major symbolism, the myth of Icarus," to establish "a broad context for a study of ambition and overreaching." Such an approach, he says—focusing on the "peculiar conversation" between Edna and Alcée Arobin in chapter 27—"reveals a protagonist considerably more interesting and sympathetic than she would be as a mere political victim."

Rosemary Franklin examines the Eros and Psyche myth with students because it "mediates the extremes of seeing Edna as either consummate hero or pathetic victim" while avoiding "the psychological approach that suggests Edna's conflict is narrowly pathological." And, she adds, "this is an opportunity to introduce Jung and archetypal criticism to undergraduates."

Elizabeth Rankin reminds students that "Robert Lebrun and Edna Pontellier are readers. It is one of the things they share with each other, one of the things they share with us as well." Like Robert, who in chapter 36 tells Edna the ending of a novel she is reading, Rankin intervenes in the reading process. She asks students to "stop halfway through the novel and predict where it is heading." She closes this volume with an approach to

The Awakening that teaches "a habit of reading, a self-conscious approach that can be applied to the reading of any novel, any story, any poem."

The parenthetical citations in the articles throughout this section refer to the chapter numbers of *The Awakening* rather than to the page numbers of any specific text of the novel. Because most chapters of *The Awakening* are quite short, teachers should have little difficulty locating citations.

B. K.

WOMEN'S EXPERIENCE

The Awakening as a Prototype of the Novel of Awakening

Susan J. Rosowski

I have taught *The Awakening* almost every year for over a decade now, in a variety of courses—Survey of Late American Literature, Introduction to the Novel, Women's Studies—and have found that whatever the course or level, students include two questions in their responses. First, what alternatives did Chopin provide for Edna Pontellier? and, second, what alternatives do other writers provide for other female characters? It is the second point that I wish to discuss in this paper, in which I describe teaching *The Awakening* as a prototype for what I have termed the "novel of awakening," a type of literature about women analogous to, yet different from, the bildungsroman.

With the opening books of the semester, students begin to identify ways in which patterns of male and female experience differ. In courses on late American literature, we begin with *Huckleberry Finn*, then James's *Daisy Miller* and *Portrait of a Lady*. The two set the stage for *The Awakening*—Twain's account of male growth through independent experience in the world, James's stories of female tragedy through independent experience. In classes on women's studies, we begin with *The Awakening*. Whether in American literature or women's studies classes, I ask students to identify and define the context provided by each writer (e.g., New Orleans Creole society), then the alternatives each provides for his or her character within that world. These are questions we continue to ask throughout the semester.

When we do turn to Chopin, we begin by discussing *The Awakening*—never a simple matter, for we immediately confront paradoxes. The book is about Edna Pontellier's growth, from being her husband's possession to acting independently, yet this growth involves regression. Edna releases her inner self, yet simultaneously she shrinks from the outside world. Students agree that changes in Edna are positive, but they recognize that those changes are ultimately destructive. Edna does, after all, die, and students agree also that Chopin provides remarkably few alternatives to her character.

As we broaden our discussion from Chopin's novel to other novels of development, I present background on the bildungsroman, or apprenticeship novel. Few of my students are familiar with either term, but with a relatively brief introduction they all recognize a familiar type. I begin with the most general definition, noting that in *A Handbook to Literature*, C. Hugh Holman and William Harmon cross list *bildungsroman* with *apprenticeship novel*, describing it as

> a novel that recounts the youth and young adulthood of a sensitive protagonist who is attempting to learn the nature of the world, discover its meaning and pattern, and acquire a philosophy of life and "the art of living." Goethe's *Wilhelm Meister* is the archetypal *apprenticeship novel*; noted examples in English are Samuel Butler's *The Way of All Flesh*, James Joyce's *A Portrait of the Artist as a Young Man*, Somerset Maugham's *Of Human Bondage*, and Thomas Wolfe's *Look Homeward, Angel.*

For those students wishing to read further, I describe *The Apprenticeship Novel* by Randolph P. Shaffner and *The Voyage In: Fictions of Female Development*, a collection of essays edited by Elizabeth Abel, Marianne Hirsch, and Elizabeth Langland.

When we compare *The Awakening* to the bildungsroman, students note that Chopin begins her novel with her character not as a child who will learn the ways of the world but as an adult who seems successfully placed in that world. Twenty-eight years old, married to a wealthy and attentive husband, the mother of two healthy children—from all appearances Edna Pontellier has everything to make a woman happy. Chopin then moves her character backward and inward, away from this public world and toward a private one. Unlike the bildungsroman hero's passage from youth to maturity, from dependency to independence, Edna Pontellier learns that her youthful experience did not equip her for life, her suicide serving as a powerful reminder that she has not acquired an "art of living."

As we extend our discussion to other stories of women, I have found it useful to begin with the fairy tale, which "depicts processes of development and maturation" (Luthi 139). When I ask my students to name fairy tales about female experience, they respond with "Sleeping Beauty," "Snow White," "The Little Mermaid," "Cinderella," "Rapunzel." I then ask for volunteers to summarize various tales (many of the students know only the Disney versions). After we have heard summaries of several, I ask what is it to be a woman, according to them? When the students respond (as they usually do) that these women are beautiful and passive, we discuss those qualities: when and under what conditions do they occur? Fairy tales tend to pass quickly over the childhood of would-be princesses; we learn that the girl is good and protected from worldly experience, sometimes by a loving home such as in "Sleeping Beauty" and sometimes by exile as in "Snow White" or "Cinderella." It is with adolescence, when girlish loveliness becomes threatening sexuality, that a spell is either cast or takes effect. "What is the effect of the prolonged sleep, or exile?" I ask. Students are usually surprised when they realize that, as presented in these tales, sleep (or exile) is positive, for it preserves the rightful princess from worldly knowledge (i.e., experience) until a prince awakens her, at which time she is rewarded with love, marriage, and a privileged life. By this point students are making their own extensions, noting, for example, that if the female character is not cast into a sleep, she is isolated, her beauty hidden in a tower (Rapunzel) or in a kitchen (Cinderella), with the common effect of being protected. Sleeping (or isolation) and awakening are critical stages of these characters' lives; they are worthy of love and happiness because they are pure; they are pure because they are inexperienced.

Students will usually point out that Chopin draws directly on fairy tale conventions of sleep, specifically on "Sleeping Beauty." During a day-long excursion to the Chênière, Edna and Robert play the parts of the tale: they leave the real world and enter one of fantasy, where Edna falls into a luxurious sleep, then awakens to ask, "How many years have I slept?" Then she remarks, "The whole island seems changed. A new race of beings must have sprung up, leaving only you and me as past relics," and Robert answers as the fairy-tale prince, "You have slept precisely one hundred years. I was left here to guard your slumbers . . ." (12). I sometimes refer students here to "Thanatos and Eros: Kate Chopin's *The Awakening*," in which Cynthia Griffin Wolff interprets the fairy-tale quality of this scene by psychological analysis, using both Laing and Freud as her sources.

We follow the same general procedure, though greatly abbreviated, in identifying patterns characteristic of fairy tales about male characters. Tales come less easily to mind, for "the principal characters [in fairy tales] are more often female than male," so that "we find ourselves nearly at a loss when called upon for the names of male protagonists" (Luthi 135). But students do identify, then summarize, a few—"The Dragon Slayer," "Jack and the Beanstalk," "Beauty and the Beast," this time focusing on the Beast. As we talk, someone usually notes that the pattern in these tales is similar to that of the bildungsroman, in which a character meets a series of tests, then takes his place in the world. When spells occur, they cast the male character not into sleep so much as into an alien form—a frog or a beast. As a result of this spell, the hero cannot win approval through his appearance, for it now evokes revulsion; therefore, he must succeed by his actions.

When we move from fairy tales to novels, I ask students what this move means, and we talk briefly about what we expect from each genre. "What would happen if we told the story of Sleeping Beauty as a novel?" I ask. And we discuss ways in which a novelist would place the fairy tale in the real world of historical time and geographical place. Sleeping Beauty and the Prince would be given individual names; setting would become circumstantial; time would be specific (I sometimes ask students to write the initial paragraph of a novel telling the story of Sleeping Beauty, and we compare "Once upon a time there were a king and a queen who were very unhappy that they did not have any children . . ." to the often wonderfully funny and usually quite specific openings they have written).

A brief discussion of fairy-tale patterns is especially useful as background to novels of awakening because often these novels are about fantasy at odds with reality. Fairy tales play a large role in shaping the private, romantic selves that will struggle against an adult society. The girl Jane Eyre hears from Bessie old fairy tales of love and adventure; the narrator in Cather's *My Mortal Enemy* dreams of a Sleeping Beauty's palace; Joan Foster in Atwood's *Lady Oracle* compares herself to the Little Mermaid.

Possibilities are myriad for discussing the pattern of awakening through literature, and each teacher will have her or his favorites. My own include a core of three novels—*Madame Bovary, The Awakening*, and *My Mortal Enemy*. Of the three, *Madame Bovary* provokes the most objective discussion, the least emotionally charged. Students immediately recognize how closely *Madame Bovary* resembles *The Awakening*, of course, and as we talk about those similarities ingredients of the novel of awakening appear. Flaubert introduces Emma Bovary not as a child but as a young woman, on the brink of entering adult life. Like the fairy-tale characters about whom she read, the girl Emma Rouault was protected from worldly experience. Isolated in a convent school (the prosaic form of a tower), Emma had lived a dual life, her outer asceticism strikingly unlike her passionate religious mysticism and romantic dreams. Again as if from a fairy tale, she expects Charles Bovary to be her prince, awakening her to everlasting happiness. In tracing Emma Bovary's descent to suicide, Flaubert presents what is, to my mind, the most pessimistic type of the novel of awakening. Emma Bovary's awakenings are to the inadequacies of the world when measured against her dreams: she comes to see that Charles Bovary is ordinary, that Rodolphe Boulanger tires of her, and that the clerk Leon is banal, but she remains blind to the insufficiency of her fantasies. While my students usually have mixed but basically sympathetic responses to Edna Pontellier, they generally judge Emma Bovary quite harshly: she is pathetically ignorant and wilfully selfish, they say. I ask why they respond differently to the two characters, and we discuss differences in narrative voice. Flaubert maintains ironic distance from his character, so that we more often observe than participate in Emma Bovary's life; Kate Chopin tells a similar story, but with a high degree of narrative sympathy.

As Willa Cather's version of a novel of awakening, *My Mortal Enemy* enables students to continue to explore ideas about female development. I introduce this novel by distributing copies of Cather's 1899 review of *The Awakening*, in which she criticizes a "feminine type"—women who are "the victims of the over-idealization of love."

> Edna Pontellier and Emma Bovary are studies in the same feminine type. . . .Both women belong to a class, not large, but forever clamoring in our ears, that demands more romance out of life than God put into it . . .[;] they are the victims of the over-idealization of love. . . . These people really expect the passion of love to fill and gratify every need of life, whereas nature only intended that it should meet one of many demands. They insist upon making it stand for all the emotional pleasures of life and art; expecting an individual and self-limited passion to yield infinite variety, pleasure, and distraction, and to contribute to their lives what the arts and the pleasurable exercise of the intellect gives to less limited and less intense idealists. So this passion, when set up against Shakespeare, Balzac, Wagner, Raphael, fails them. They have staked everything on one hand, and they lose. They have driven the blood until it will drive no further, they have placed their nerves up to the point where any relaxation short of absolute annihilation is impossible. . . . And in the end, the nerves get even. Nobody ever cheats them, really. Then the "awakening" comes. (698–99)

As if an extension of ideas in that review, *My Mortal Enemy* includes ingredients used by Flaubert and Chopin. Once again there is a story of a childhood protected from worldly experience. Myra Driscoll grew up in a small town (yet another prosaic version of the fairy-tale tower) amid wealth and privilege, then fell in love with the dashing but penniless Oswald Henshawe. Though they knew they would be disinherited, they eloped, one night fleeing the small town of Parthia. Cather's narrator, Nellie Birdseye, remembers that while growing up in Parthia, the Driscoll house seemed "under a spell, like the Sleeping Beauty's palace; it had been in a trance, or lain in its flowers like a beautiful corpse, ever since that winter night when Love went out of the gates and gave the dare to Fate" (17).

Two elements distinguish Cather's version of a novel of awakening. First, she uses Nellie Birdseye as a female narrator who, a generation younger than Myra Driscoll Henshawe, goes through her own awakenings. When she was young, Nellie was herself a romantic, fond of the legendary heroine and disappointed by the real Myra Driscoll, a rather plump middle-aged woman. Nellie encounters the Henshawes at two later times: she anticipates each meeting with romantic expectation; she is disillusioned when reality contradicts her expectation; finally, she reaches deepened understanding. Nellie matures from a romantic girl to a compassionate woman, capable of telling Myra Henshawe's story. The second element that distinguishes this novel of awakening is that Cather takes her major character, Myra Henshawe, from youth into old age, from a romantic figure of small-town legend to a complex individual.

Discussion about *My Mortal Enemy* is always lively, provocative, and intense, partially because attitudes change dramatically as students talk. Although initially students focus on the book's spare prose and grim theme (the aged Myra Henshawe tells Nellie that her and Oswald's youthful love has been the ruin of them both), they come to consider it an exceptionally positive novel of awakening. Students usually begin by saying they do not like Myra Henshawe, and when I ask why, they mention her cruelty to her husband, Oswald, "a sentimentalist" who is tender, patient, faithful, and forgiving. He is, in other words, what we expect of female characters. As we talk about Oswald's love, students recognize that he is devoted to his sentimental memory of Myra when she was a girl, not to the woman she has become. We talk at some length about his request that Nellie remember Myra not as she was in her final years but as she was when she was young, then his remark that he had felt as if he had been caring for the mother of the girl who ran away with him.

Students come to respect Myra Henshawe because she defies their expectations, because she challenges the romantic role the narrator (and the reader) put her in, and because she becomes more fully herself, a contradictory, complex person. Comparison with Edna Pontellier is useful, for students note that Myra Henshawe does mature and she does learn a philosophy of life, which she benefits from and passes along to Nellie Birdseye. Like Edna Pontellier, Myra Driscoll goes to the ocean to die, but Myra's is not a suicide, nor does she return to dreams of her childhood. Instead she turns to religion and art, both of which became important to her only as she matured. Finally, her death is not of desperation but of indomitable, independent will. She drags her ailing body from her bed, hires a cab to take her to a bluff overlooking the ocean and reminding her of Lear, and apparently lives to see the dawn: her body is found, rosary still in her hand. By awakening to possibilities of religion and art, Myra Henshawe provides an alternative to an "over-idealization of love"; by telling Myra Henshawe's story with compassion, Nellie Birdseye provides an alternative to romantic idealism (for a fuller discussion, see Rosowski, *Voyage*).

Once we have established a reference for discussing novels of awakening, we can look at other versions. *Jane Eyre, Pride and Prejudice, Emma, Middlemarch*—all present a female character's development through a series of awakenings to limitations. All learn that their inner, private values are incompatible with public ones; all measure their achievement by their capacities to realize restrictions; all receive reward through male characters (the women tame or circumscribe men in marriage; they bear men-children). Variations on this pattern are dramatic because they overturn a firmly established convention. Maggie Tulliver dies rather than sacrifice her independence (in this *The Mill on the Floss* resembles *The Awakening*); Isabel Archer marries, only to find herself deceived about Osmund's character.

Of these novels I find *Middlemarch* especially effective, because in it Eliot strongly presents and comments on gender conventions. In the end Dorothea Brooke marries Ladislaw, a man she admires and loves, then has a son who will inherit her father's estate. Her accommodation to the world is to withdraw from it; her resolution of conflict is to disappear. Eliot's final question to the reader poses the dilemma that runs through novels of awakening: "Many who knew her, thought it a pity that so substantive and rare a creature should have been absorbed into the life of another. But no one stated exactly what else that was in her power she ought rather to have done" (611). If we were to substitute drowning for absorbing a life into another's, we have the question Chopin implicitly evokes from readers of *The Awakening*.

What alternatives are there? my students inevitably ask, and when I turn the question back to them, they usually cannot recall any novel in which a female character follows the optimistic development of the bildungsroman hero, from apprentice to master, from ignorance to a philosophy of life and an art of living that are independent of a husband and children. That realization is troubling to students; in some classes I include books that provide examples of positive independent female growth, and in others I describe such books. Agnes Smedley's *Daughter of Earth* and Willa Cather's *Song of the Lark* are two of my favorites; some of the students may have read more recent examples (e.g., Erica Jong's *Fear of Flying* and *Fanny: Being the True History of the Adventures of Fanny Hackabout-Jones*).

But it is one thing to find literature about women analogous to the optimistic bildungsroman, another to distinguish the novel of awakening from the bildungsroman. At the end of those semesters in which literary patterns of female development have been of major interest, we summarize by again comparing the novel of awakening with the bildungsroman. As a starting place for discussion, I may list five presuppositions of the bildungsroman: "(1) the idea that living is an art which the apprentice may learn; (2) the belief that a young person can become adept in the art of living and become a master; (3) the key notion of choice; (4) the prerequisite of potential for development into a master; (5) an affirmative attitude toward life as a whole" (Shaffner 18).

With such a summary of bildungsroman characteristics before us, we can review prerequisites of the novel of awakening. What emerges are differences so profound that I question calling these novels bildungsroman at all: (1) the idea that living is suspended until adult years; (2) the belief that a young woman is incapable of becoming adept in the art of living and must be guided through it; (3) the assumption that a woman does not have choice (indeed, this assumption is so basic that choice is seldom central to novels of awakening; characters have choices made for them or assume responsibilities unknowingly, as Edna Pontellier assumed motherhood); (4) the prerequisite of potential for disillusionment (these characters are sensitive, vital, intelligent, perceptive, passionate; because they are capable of great aspiration, they are capable of intense disillusionment); (5) a negative or, at best, cautious attitude toward life as a whole.

In writing this essay, I have asked myself what has been the overall experience of teaching *The Awakening* as a prototype of the novel of awakening, and I realize that it has been that of a widening gyre. Students begin with Chopin's novel, then make connections to one other novel—then another—until they recognize that the pattern Chopin presented runs through literature about women. I believe that sense of discovery is extremely exciting and satisfying for them as students.

The *Awakening* in the Context of the Experience, Culture, and Values of Southern Women

Elizabeth Fox-Genovese

Kate Chopin, on her own accounting, had scant interest in "social problems." She did not, for example, last long as a member of St. Louis's Wednesday Club, in which worthy matrons met to promote their intellectual improvement and the welfare of their city's poor (Seyersted 65). Yet *The Awakening* has, at least in part, earned its new-found place in our canon since it purportedly addresses a social problem: the condition of women. The possible disjuncture between Chopin's intentions and the perspective of her modern readers, especially the female ones, challenges those of us who wish to teach the novel with some attention to historical context.

There seems little doubt, to take the obvious comparison, that we can legitimately teach Charlotte Gilman's "The Yellow Wallpaper"—whatever its intrinsic merits—as a tract against the constraints of the "patriarchal" institution of marriage. The legitimacy of so teaching *The Awakening* remains far more questionable. Yet most critics, however divergent their specific readings, implicitly treat *The Awakening* as a problem novel that cries out for a "solution." Chopin's distinctive style and structure—her mode of composition and her literary strategy—fashioned this destiny for her text. For the novel follows the pattern of her own short stories, visibly influenced by Maupassant, in suggesting that the ending reveals the meaning of the text. This strategy invites readers of *The Awakening* to look to Edna's suicide as the key to the preceding account of a brief period in her life. Edna's suicide, in sum, represents a complex—one is tempted to say overdetermined—judgment on the society and institutions that have forced Edna to commit the act, or perhaps a judgment on Edna herself.

Chopin's explicit discussion of women's sexuality establishes the visible point of conflict between her heroine and society, as it also establishes the point of conflict between Chopin and the dominant mores of her day. American culture in the late 1890s was not ready for an open assault on women's social identification with marriage, or even for an open defense of women's sexual and sensual individualism (Ziff). The social and personal questions apparently merge in Edna's "awakening" to sexuality, which Chopin identifies with her protagonist's "beginning to realize her position in the universe as a human being, and to recognize her relations as an individual to the world within and about her" (6). Yet Chopin's own diction makes the nice and necessary distinction that I find fruitful in teaching the novel in historical context. For Chopin's words differentiate between the realization of self as a human being (a private and psychological matter) and the recognition of one's relations as an individual to others (a public or social matter).

The Awakening shocked Chopin's contemporaries for the same reason that it has earned the admiration of recent generations: it candidly acknowledges women's sexual impulses. Modern readers, especially students, tend to view Edna's awakening to her sexuality as logically portending her struggle for liberation. Yet Chopin remains more ambiguous, thus inviting multiple, even contradictory, readings. Nonetheless, close attention to *The Awakening*'s historical context helps to clarify Chopin's probable views and, even more, to recapture the discourses and social expectations within which they unfolded.

It would be difficult to argue that Chopin intended *The Awakening* to be primarily a polemic against marriage as a social institution, or even primarily a polemic against the social limitations on women's relations as individuals to others. Yet Chopin does hint that late-nineteenth-century marriages cast women as the objects of others rather than as the free subjects of their own fates. Thus she introduces Edna through her husband's gaze and, in a frequently cited line, allows that he regarded her as a "valuable piece of personal property which has suffered some damage" (1). This view of marriage permits us to link *The Awakening* to the growing public complaints of some American women against the subordination of women to men within marriage. Yet Chopin, unlike an Elizabeth Cady Stanton or a Charlotte Perkins Gilman, does not let the question rest there. Having allowed for the social dimension, she rapidly reveals the multiple possibilities for happiness and shared understanding between husbands and wives, including Edna and Léonce. Since Chopin's Edna invites comparison with Ibsen's Nora, it is worth recalling Chopin's scornful dismissal of Ibsen's work as too deeply hostage to specific, transitory social conditions:

> Human impulses do not change and can not so long as men and women continue to stand in the relation to one another which they have occupied since our knowledge of their existence began. It is why Aeschylus is true, and Shakespeare is true to-day, and why Ibsen will not be true in some remote tomorrow, however forcible and representative he may be for the hour, because he takes for his themes social problems which by their very nature are mutable.   (qtd. in Seyersted 86–87)

In fact, Ibsen's depiction of the ways in which marriage imprisoned women and stunted their development more closely resembled the concerns of northern than of southern women. The differences are subtle, but worth attention. The driving force of the women's movement, narrowly understood as the movement to improve women's social position or rights, came out of the Northeast and its offshoots, the Old Northwest and the Western Reserve, where the movement had been closely and explicitly tied to the antislavery movement. In the 1850s, the gifted proslavery and antifeminist polemicist

Louisa S. McCord had mercilessly castigated the advocates of women's rights as would-be topplers of all social order worthy of the name. McCord never doubted women's capacities; she merely deplored the self-indulgent and irresponsible attempt to see those capacities as identical to men's or to extrapolate from them egalitarian social principles. In substance, she agreed with the radical northern analysis: the social position of women was inextricably linked to what she called "the social question." But whereas northern reformers saw the link as justification for change in both gender and social relations, she saw it as proof that women must accept the roles that their physical weakness and social arrangements had allotted to them (Fox-Genovese, *Within the Plantation Household*).

By the period of the Gilded Age, during which Chopin wrote, some southern women of her class were becoming committed to various kinds of social reform, including that of their own social and political status (Scott). Nonetheless, their efforts on behalf of women's rights, especially the right to suffrage, remained as firmly bound as ever to the social question—which, in the postreconstruction South, meant the race question (Kraditor). Although southern women differed in the conclusions they drew from the necessary connection between gender relations and race and class relations, they agreed—and how could they not?—on the force of the connection. Chopin appears to have avoided taking a stand on the relations between what she called women's "independence" and women's social and political rights, much less on the relations between women's independence and race and class relations in general. That silence provides an important caution against any simple social interpretation of *The Awakening*. Does Chopin, in other words, give any indication that she intends her novel as an intervention in the narrow institutional discussion of women's rights?

The legacy of antebellum slave society, and especially of the war that destroyed that society, weighed heavily on southern women of Chopin's generation (Carter). Few had not lost kin or suffered reversals of fortune. Most, like Grace King and Chopin herself, had fathers, uncles, or grandfathers who fought in the war, and they also had their own memories of confrontations with, or flights from, federal troops (Seyersted; Bush). The ensuing period of reconstruction left its special scars—personal, financial, and political. For Chopin, her years on her husband's plantations in Natchitoches Parish must have been like a return to the ancien régime, albeit a return sprinkled with bitter reminders of that régime's passing. Perhaps above all, for the women of Chopin's class, race, and generation, the late antebellum years harbored formative childhood memories. In their early teens during the collapse of southern slave society, they had been being reared to take their places as ladies in that society, following the tradition of the mothers, grandmothers, even great grandmothers who provided their most important models. For such women, the special legacy of slavery's passing lay in their having the responsibility as women to help to preserve the closest possible facsimile of antebellum class and race relations, especially if they or their families had suffered reversals of fortune.

Perhaps never more than during the postwar decades, white womanhood stood as the bulwark against social and racial chaos. The burden must have been heavy, as Ellen Glasgow, in the succeeding generation, would suggest. But for many southern women, committed as they were to the values of their class and race, it also had its compensations. In any event, it is difficult to find any systematic rebellion against women's prescribed role in the writings of the first postbellum generations of women writers. Not that those writings lack their share of strong, resourceful, and even, to use Chopin's word, independent women. They simply lack women who challenge the social order in the name of women's individual rights.

This argument may seem a strange one to advance as a possible guide to teaching *The Awakening* in historical context, but it does provide precisely such a context however one ultimately interprets Chopin's position as manifest in Edna. More, it provides a fruitful perspective from which to encourage students to articulate their own responses. In this respect, I have found it useful to encourage students to distinguish between gender and sexuality in assessing Chopin's notion of female independence. The distinction inevitably remains messy, but withal heuristically helpful. For gender can be presented as the social construction of sexuality, and sexuality itself as a dimension of women's private, biologically rooted identity. Gender roles, in this context, consist in what we might call society's views or expectations of women: daughter, wife, mother, nurturer, lady. Gender roles remain deeply hostage to considerations of class and race. Sexuality, in contrast, refers to women's nature or essence, to what women share across class and racial lines, to the eternal woman.

Complications in the application of this distinction arise because different cultures treat the relations between gender and sexuality differently. With respect to the examples at hand, northern middle-class culture tended to present gender and sexuality as isomorphic. For a northern woman to revolt against her sexual suppression was to call into question her gender role. For a northern woman to challenge the constraints on her gender was, in her community's view if not always in her own, implicitly to assert her sexuality. The egalitarian ideals of northern democracy—republicanism to be precise—imposed the association of gender and sexuality. The private feelings and behavior of middle-class women had implications for the behavior of all women, who, at least in ideology, were assumed to resemble them in both gender and sexual attributes.

Southern culture had traditionally viewed the question differently. To be sure, southern society placed as high a premium on female chastity (some might say a higher one) as did northern society—and for social and racial reasons. The sexuality of upper-class white women—like its reverse, their chastity—constituted the visible and sacred prize of upper-class white men, who were honor-bound to defend it. But this very claim also reveals the defense of white female sexuality to have been a class and racial, rather than an individual, matter (Hall).

Life in the postbellum South intensified the explicit identification of the tight relations between gender, class, and race relations (Williamson). Southern suffragists varied in degree, but not in substance, on their analysis of the necessary link between women's rights and the racial balance of their society: they concurred that the woman's vote should not be allowed to increase the black vote (Kraditor). Chopin did not participate in the heated discussions about women's rights, which she surely viewed as yet another side of the social question. But aspects of her work strongly suggest that she sought, as it were, to write around or above the issue. Neither *The Awakening* nor any of her other writings suggest that she secretly espoused woman suffrage or related causes. To the contrary, everything that she wrote, including *The Awakening*, indicates that she viewed women's independence as a personal more than a social matter. In one moving passage, she does imply that her own independence derived in no small measure from the deaths of her husband and her mother—that is, from her release from social constraints as embodied in those she loved (Seyersted and Toth 92–93). Passages in *The Awakening* even suggest that she recognized children as a possible fetter on women's self-determination, although she never otherwise hinted that she felt so about her own. But the constant, underlying current in her writings makes it clear that she took no inconsiderable pride in having attained a sophisticated and independent maturity on her own, within the limitations that her society imposed. In *The Awakening*, she carefully delineates both the possibility for women's happiness within marriage (Mme Ratignolle) and the possibility for their independence from it (Mlle Reisz).

Strange as it may seem to modern readers, there is reason to believe that Chopin intended her explorations of women's sexual self-awareness to pose less of a threat to the social order of her world than explorations of their social independence would have. In this respect, her attitudes represent a stark reversal of those of Gilman, as manifested in the two women's attitudes toward doctors. For Gilman, the doctor constituted a kind of political vanguard and buttress of the husband, understood as oppressor. For Chopin, he constituted a wise confidant who fully appreciated the complexities of woman's nature. Chopin's open discussion of women's sexuality proved, in the event, to shock her southern contemporaries as profoundly as her northern ones. The South, after all, remained too American. Even the veneer of

New Orleans local color—and all southerners accepted New Orleans as different—and of Chopin's self-conscious European style did not protect her. Chopin may not fully, or more to the point consciously, have known what she was risking, but she did know what she was attempting.

Chopin's sympathy for women's personal and sexual independence sank its roots in a tragic view of the human condition derived from a Catholic sensibility that persisted long after Chopin had abandoned regular Catholic practice. This view of human nature resulted in the notion that personal matters should be personal, should not challenge the social order (Fox-Genovese, "Kate Chopin's Awakening"). Chopin's preoccupation with European naturalism only reinforced her inherited sense of how original sin and established social relations pressed on the individual's internal and external possibilities for freedom (Walker). Edna ultimately fails in her bid for freedom because she lacked the personal strength to realize her nature within the possibilities afforded by her society, because she failed to recognize the difference between the contingent and the essential. Chopin gambled on presenting woman's nature as a universal problem. She set her sights on Aeschylus and Shakespeare, not on Ibsen. She may have thought that her attempt to treat sexuality independent of gender relations respected the social values of southern society, but she misjudged.

In *The Awakening*, Kate Chopin self-consciously sought to move beyond the specific southern identification of her local-color stories. She surely did not intend her novel as a specific reflection of the values of southern women, parochially defined. Yet today, the novel gains resonance if read and taught in historical context. As a novelist, Chopin navigated between specificity of detail and universality of theme. It is difficult not to wonder if she fully understood how firmly that strategy linked her to the emerging modern tradition of southern letters. No social or domestic novelist, she wrote of the female human condition as a full member of that distinctive culture which would also inform the work of William Alexander Percy and William Faulkner.

Childbirth and Motherhood in
The Awakening and in "Athénaïse"

Patricia Hopkins Lattin

As throughout *The Awakening* the ocean seems to cast a spell on Edna Pontellier, so does the sensuous novel itself seduce a reader, inviting the soul "to lose itself in mazes of inward contemplation" (6). The spell it casts results in good reading but somewhat problematic teaching. I have found that the novel works best in an undergraduate class if it is taken out of isolation and read in conjunction with at least one Chopin short story. My favorite choice is "Athénaïse," a story included in the Modern Library, Penguin, Signet, and Rinehart paperback editions of the novel. The title character provides a reference point for introducing Edna and for dealing with the important themes of childbirth and motherhood in the novel. In addition, analyzing the role of Gouvernail in the story and the novel enriches a significant scene in *The Awakening* and gives students a sample of the dense social reality of Chopin's complex fictional world, a world with numerous repeating characters and places.

I begin setting the stage for Edna by looking at Chopin's characterization of the headstrong Athénaïse, who as a hard-to-handle young girl ran away from the convent and whose rebellious streak continues when, after two months of marriage, she slips away from her husband's Cane River home. Students need to see from the beginning that Athénaïse is a tentative, incomplete model of an independent woman. Her entire "escape" to New Orleans is planned and arranged by her brother Montéclin, and in the city her neighbor Gouvernail replaces Montéclin, soothing her homesickness and watching after her; the narrator tells us that Athénaïse could not have made it through the month without Gouvernail. Even when she decides to return to her husband, Gouvernail takes her to the railway station, secures her seat, and loads her belongings onto the train. Nonetheless, the instructor should not trivialize the plight from which Athénaïse extricates herself. Answering the simple question Why does Athénaïse leave Cazeau? can take students into a discussion of nineteenth-century American attitudes toward sex and marriage and Athénaïse's apparent entry into marriage with no knowledge of sex. Sexual intimacy—"his ugly bare feet—washing them in my tub, befo' my very eyes, ugh!" (sec. 2)—has so shocked and repelled her that she wishes she were back in the convent. She is not even sure why she married: "She supposed it was customary for girls to marry when the right opportunity came" (sec. 2). Athénaïse's attitudes reflect a time when young women had few choices except marriage or the convent.

A good way to lead a class into the novel is to point out some similarities and contrasts between Athénaïse and Edna. Both women are married to basically decent men who are respected authority figures, Cazeau with his jangling spurs and Léonce with his cigars. In parallel scenes, Athénaïse and Edna act out their rebellion against their husbands: Athénaïse throws her household keys to the floor, and Edna flings her wedding ring onto the carpet and tries to crush it with her heel; both move out of their husbands' houses. The women have fathers who expect their husbands to keep them in line and who use strong language like "master hand," "a strong will that compels obedience," "coercion," and "the only way to manage a wife" ("Athénaïse," sec. 3; *Awakening* 24). Although both husbands initially protest their wives' behavior, they are wiser and more sensitive than their fathers-in-law and decide to let the women have their way. Athénaïse's comment that marriage is "a trap set for the feet of unwary and unsuspecting girls" (sec. 3) is echoed by Edna's statement that "a wedding is one of the most lamentable spectacles on earth" (22). Despite these similarities of circumstances and attitudes, however, the educated, sophisticated Edna is quite different from the simple, provincial Athénaïse. The independence Edna develops—by the time she moves out of her husband's house, she has enough money from her small inheritance, her race-track earnings, and the sale of her sketches to pay her own living expenses—contrasts with Athénaïse's pitifully ineffectual attempts to find employment and live alone in New Orleans. While Edna experiences a growing pleasure in solitude, a recurring sensation that forms a prominent pattern in the novel, Athénaïse constantly needs people. By looking at each woman's interactions with other characters, an instructor can lead students to discover numerous contrasts between Athénaïse and Edna.

The most significant contrast relates to childbirth and motherhood, a conventional, superficial theme in the story but an ambiguous, complex theme dominating the novel. Athénaïse's "awakening" comes in a flash as soon as she realizes she is pregnant, and it sends her rushing back to her husband's arms, where she responds to his passion for the first time. Pregnancy has liberated her physically and caused her to accept her sexuality. In this story Chopin implies a traditional attitude familiar even to today's students: that motherhood changes a girl to a woman and therefore makes her complete —in modern jargon, a "total woman." In *The Awakening* actual childbirth and motherhood define the limits of Edna's awakening, but the pattern is complex and includes no simple cause and effect. Already a mother when the novel begins, Edna, unlike Athénaïse, has gone through two pregnancies without sexual arousal. The narrator sums her up as "not a mother-woman" (4); an anomaly in her nineteenth-century Creole society, she can forget her children for hours at a time and frankly enjoys her solitude when they are gone. In the novel's presentation of motherhood, Edna appears in the middle, with a contrasting role model on each side. (See Fox-Genovese, "Kate

Chopin's Awakening," for a discussion of these role models.) Adèle Ratignolle, a charming, beautiful "sensuous Madonna" (5), has a child every two
years, wants her children constantly around her, and is chiefly defined by
them. Two births occur in the novel: Adèle's baby and a litter of ten pigs;
the parallel is obvious. And yet Adèle's gentle caressing of Edna's hand is
a stimulus in the early stage of Edna's physical awakening. Edna's other role
model, Mlle Reisz, is Adèle's complete opposite: unmarried and seemingly
sexless, homely and unpleasant, she openly dislikes children, an attitude
the narrator emphasizes, partially defining her by her childlessness. Her
fingers are "wiry" and touch Edna's hand "loosely without warmth" (21); the
music her fingers produce, however, stimulates Edna and plays a crucial
role in her physical awakening. During this awakening Edna moves back
and forth between the spheres of influence of these two women, between
the mother-woman's pole of conventional society and family and the childless
Mlle Reisz's pole of artisthood and personal freedom. An instructor will want
to trace this movement, analyzing the numerous occasions on which Edna
seeks the two women out; that both influence her physical awakening is one
of the novel's many complexities. Further complicating the pattern, on several occasions Edna, excited and aroused by events related to her awakening,
does not draw away from her children but, rather, turns to them hungrily,
apparently trying to incorporate them into the experience.

　　After looking at actual childbirth and motherhood in the novel, students
are ready to deal with childbirth at another level, as a metaphor for Edna's
awakening: Edna's "self" is reborn, through a rebirth that is harder even
than dying, since in the end she chooses death as a solution to the problems
threatening her newly reborn self. One of Chopin's favorite images, dawn,
frequently associated with Edna's awakening, suggests rebirth; so does Edna's learning to swim, a major physical event of her metamorphosis. The
narrator presents Edna as "daily casting aside that fictitious self which we
assume like a garment with which to appear before the world" (19), a romantic
image of rebirth—a molting, a shedding of an old skin for a new one. It is
important to analyze this rebirth and to establish that, even though the
narrator frequently undercuts the process, complicating our reading of her,
Edna truly changes. An outside observer, Dr. Mandelet, notices "a subtle
change which had transformed her from the listless woman he had known
into a being who, for the moment, seemed palpitant with the forces of life"
(23). His noticing "no repression in her glance or gesture" implies an earlier
repressed manner. She has changed from a physically unawakened woman
to an alive, sexual creature, reminding Dr. Mandelet of "some beautiful,
sleek animal waking up in the sun" (23). More important, this growing self
develops, at least in Edna's perception, a spiritual component that interacts
with and reflects the physical. The physical act of learning to swim makes

her feel "as if some power of significant import had been given her to control the working of her body and her soul" (10). After her first passionate sexual experience with Arobin, "[s]he felt as if a mist had been lifted from her eyes, enabling her to look upon and comprehend the significance of life" (28). Asserting the independence necessary to move from her husband's house into a smaller one makes her feel that she has risen on the spiritual scale (32). Stronger both physically and spiritually, this new, reborn self can say to Robert during a long-awaited, sexually charged meeting, "I give myself where I choose. If he [Léonce Pontellier] were to say, 'Here, Robert, take her and be happy; she is yours,' I should laugh at you both" (36).

With its parallel development of physical and spiritual halves, Edna's reborn self suggests the "self" that Whitman refers to when he asserts the equal importance of the soul and its physical manifestation, the body: one "must not be abased to the other" ("Song of Myself," sec. 5; it would be useful for students to read at least this section of the poem). Edna's self, however, runs into problems that halt its growth when childbirth and motherhood as biological realities clash with the metaphorical birth she is experiencing. Adèle's accouchement, which causes Edna to recall the births of her own children and to respond with "an inward agony" and "a flaming, outspoken revolt against the ways of Nature," leaves her "stunned and speechless with emotion." In an image vibrant with suggestions of the natural world and her sudden aversion to it, Edna sees Adèle's long braided hair "coiled like a golden serpent" on the pillow (37). The birth, followed closely by Adèle's haunting plea, "Think of the children," which could well have been a subtitle of the book, overwhelms Edna with the realization that has been nudging her consciousness throughout the novel: she cannot in her society discharge her responsibility toward her children and still live in complete freedom, experiencing self-actualization. Whitman's belief in the continuing expansion of the self, with the possibility of incorporating an endless series of polarities, would be foreign to Edna at this moment. Her self can no longer embrace her biological role and her connection to the natural world.

Edna's reborn self is in grave danger. It is resisting its physical component, and it cannot survive divided. As she thinks of her children as "antagonists" who have tried to drag her soul into "slavery" and as she devises "a way to elude them," she understands fully the meaning of her earlier statement to Adèle, "that she would give up the unessential, but she would never sacrifice herself for her children" (39). Mention of her "self" shows that she is considering this newborn entity as she plots her escape.

Does she save her newborn self when she takes her lonely swim of no return into the ocean? An instructor will want to explore this question, and even here images of birth must be dealt with. Before Edna steps into the ocean, she undresses and, naked in the open air for the first time ever, appears to experience another symbolic rebirth, a preparation for her plunge into the paradox of nature: "She felt like some newborn creature, opening its eyes in a familiar world that it had never known" (39). The suggestion of a new beginning hints that Edna's final act of escaping her children may be a triumph that keeps her reborn self intact. Balancing that reading, however, is the image of the disabled bird with the broken wing circling down to earth, clearly symbolizing a defeat. As she swims into deeper water, Edna is herself torn between the two possibilities of triumph and defeat, and the scrupulously objective narrator provides no solution to the ambiguity facing the reader.

As Adèle Ratignolle's reminding her of the children has pushed Edna toward her defiant act, so the words spoken by Adèle's foil, Mlle Reisz, echo in Edna's ears in the last minutes of her life, as she imagines how the old lady would sneer if she could see her now. A reader acquainted with Athénaïse will hear also superimposed onto the scene the echo of a third voice, that of Athénaïse at the end of her story, when she draws back from her husband's embrace to say, "Listen, Cazeau! How Juliette's baby is crying! Pauvre ti chou, I wonder w'at is the matter with it?" (sec. 11). One cannot but be jarred by the contrast between young Athénaïse's pleasure at her pregnancy and Edna's desperate attempt to save her "self" from her children. Nothing is dated about this contrast. Even today, with birth-control information freely available and with the concept of equal rights growing in the workplace and home, women in real life and in fiction still struggle to reconcile their self-actualization with the inescapable biological reality that the human race can be perpetuated only by childbirth.

Like her contemporaries Howells and Crane and like Faulkner a few decades later, Kate Chopin created many characters who appear in more than one work (see Lattin). This is an unfamiliar literary technique for most students, and they enjoy observing the sparks that jump back and forth and illuminate the scenes involving the repeating characters. An excellent example is provided by the urbane New Orleans journalist, Gouvernail, a major figure in "Athénaïse" and a very minor figure in *The Awakening*. He appears in three Chopin writings, each time in the presence of a beautiful woman experiencing an emotional awakening, and an instructor will want to refer briefly to "A Respectable Woman," even if students have not read it. In this story a happily married woman, Mrs. Baroda, becomes physically aroused and attracted to Gouvernail after he quotes lines from Whitman's "Song of Myself" that suggest companion lines containing vivid sexual imagery. The points to make here are that Gouvernail has special insights allowing him to understand a woman's emotional nature and that he uses literary allusion subtly, implying more than he says.

It is then important to analyze Gouvernail carefully as he interacts with Athénaïse. Although Athénaïse sees him as rather nondescript, his eyes have a "mild, penetrating quality," and his dealings with Athénaïse show how shrewdly he judges character. He guesses that she probably has no literary tastes and gives her a magazine to read; she in fact enjoys the pictures more than the story. He accurately sums her up: she is "self-willed, impulsive, innocent, ignorant, unsatisfied, dissatisfied" (8). Gouvernail also understands that he only serves as a substitute for Athénaïse's brother. More significant, Gouvernail's "mild, penetrating" eyes see beyond Athénaïse's immature behavior and recognize her potential for sexual arousal. He hopes he will be able to make love with her when she experiences her awakening, and he sensitively waits for that moment. Athénaïse's sudden arousal confirms that Gouvernail has understood her well, although he had no way of predicting the pregnancy and the form that her arousal would take.

During the analysis of Gouvernail's brief appearance in *The Awakening*, students should be encouraged to carry over their insights from "Athénaïse" so that the Gouvernail in the novel has all the traits of the character in the story. Listing the guests at Edna's birthday party the night she moves out of her husband's house, the narrator mentions Gouvernail, "of whom nothing special could be said, except that he was observant and seemed quiet and inoffensive" (30). The single word "observant" jumps out at the reader, warning that the same powers of perception that allowed Gouvernail to understand Athénaïse even better than she understood herself will be at work in *The Awakening*. Edna's birthday dinner scene is a masterfully crafted tableau, with sensual details of red, yellow, and gold: a yellow table cover, wax candles burning under yellow shades, yellow and red roses, Edna's satin gown with a golden shimmer, a sparkling, deep red cocktail. Likened to a queen as she sits in the midst of the fine crystal and gems, Edna is struck by "the old ennui," a "hopelessness," a "chill breath," as she longs acutely for the absent loved one, perhaps, but not necessarily, Robert. The reader should assume that Gouvernail's penetrating eyes are watching Edna closely and that he has noticed the familiarity between her and Arobin, who is seated beside her. He is also watching as Mrs. Highcamp, attracted to Robert's brother Victor, weaves a garland of yellow and red roses, places it on Victor's head, and then covers his body with her white silk scarf. Superficially observing the tableau, Gouvernail's dinner companion, Miss Mayblunt, exclaims, "Oh! to be able to paint in color rather than in words!" (30). At that point Gouvernail murmurs under his breath the only words he speaks in the novel: " 'There was a graven image of Desire / Painted with red blood on a ground of gold.' " Having already injected, through Gouvernail's presence, one of her own texts into this scene, Chopin now adds the text of another writer. Since we already know Gouvernail, we know that, when he quotes from Swinburne's "A Cameo" (see Koloski, "Swinburne Lines"), he is not simply referring to the attraction between Mrs. Highcamp and Victor and the brilliant colors surrounding it; he is reading the scene more deeply and is also referring to Edna as she is overcome by strong, despairing emotions. We know, too, that when this literate man quotes the first line of the poem, he is suggesting the whole poem: in addition to Desire, Swinburne's cameo portrays Pain and Pleasure, with Satiety clutching the wrist of Pleasure. More significant, watching the scene from behind a grate is Death. In uttering only one sentence, Gouvernail implies a commentary and a prophecy: Edna's desire is mixed with pleasure and pain, but death will soon rescue her from her despair and turmoil.

Reading "Athénaïse" and *The Awakening* together can enhance students' understanding of Edna and the theme of childbirth and motherhood in the novel. The combination also makes an important scene of the novel richer than it is when read in isolation, thereby providing a taste of the dense social reality of Chopin's fictional world. Since this will be many students' introduction to intertextuality, those students should also take away from the course some invaluable insights into how to read fiction.

The Awakening and the Woman Question

Dale Marie Bauer and Andrew M. Lakritz

At the heart of Mikhail Bakhtin's dialogic model of discourse is the notion that people engage in various social and cultural dialogues—both authoritative and internally persuasive ones. According to Bakhtin's theory, texts as well can be dialogic. To our students, we suggest that Kate Chopin calls into question the ideologies and assumptions about women's place articulated by leading thinkers of her time. In this way, students may be asked to regard the novel not as a mere cautionary or inspirational tale but, rather, as a complex social document engaged with its history—at times contentious, at times acquiescent. If a novel is a kind of dialogue, as Bakhtin argues, then *The Awakening* calls on readers to take part in the conversation Chopin orchestrates, compelling them to distinguish between competing versions of the real and ultimately to choose a language with which to engage in that dialogue.

Without overtly stating her position, Chopin makes counterclaims about women throughout *The Awakening* and has produced a novel that was scandalous in what it suggests about its heroine's sexuality. In "Discourse in the Novel," Bakhtin suggests that the novel in general undermines the absolutism—scientific, moral, psychological, or religious—of any one language, undermines the normative structure language affords and through which we understand experience. In fact, Bakhtin argues that the novel presents the images of many "social languages,"

> all of which are equally capable of being "languages of truth," but, since such is the case, all . . . are equally relative, reified and limited, as they are merely the languages of social groups, professions and other cross-sections of everyday life. The novel begins by presuming a verbal and semantic decentering of the ideological world. . . . (367)

Chopin's novel in particular demonstrates the lack of "truth" in any of the ideological positions on women she orchestrates as "voices" in the novel. Not only do all these languages fail to describe women's place or to appropriate Edna into their schemes, but Edna also fails to use the languages as her own. These languages, then, illustrate the struggle over her signification and over her right to speak within the social realm.

Reading the novel as if it were engaged with other voices current in Chopin's time allows us to introduce two issues simultaneously. First, it leads students into the strange world of the past, underscoring the differences between their assumptions and those of the historical figures in the debate. Second, it forces students to look carefully and sharply at the text itself in order to distinguish among similar, but competing, versions of prose discourse (Bakhtin 348). For instance, Chopin calls on a capitalist simile to describe Léonce Pontellier's attitude toward his wife: he looks at Edna "as one looks at a valuable piece of personal property which has suffered some damage" (1)—as "human furniture," in Henry James's memorable phrase from *The Golden Bowl* (541). We place this simile next to a passage from William James's *The Principles of Psychology* to establish relations of similarity, dissimilarity, influence, and rejection, the classroom being the site in which we trace out what these two writers have to say to one another: *"In its widest possible sense,* however, *a man's Self is the sum total of all that he CAN call his,* not only his body and his psychic powers, but his clothes and his house, his wife and children, his ancestors and friends, his reputation and works, his lands and horses, and yacht and bank-account" (291). We call on the students in this discussion to draw the lines of convergence and divergence between these two texts and to establish the probable contexts that illuminate their textual relations. We build the course on a series of such readings or interreadings in order to develop or extend the students' historical sense.

Another example we use comes from Thorstein Veblen's *Theory of the Leisure Class,* an evolutionist reading of history and gender: "In the last analysis, according to her own sense of what is good and beautiful, the woman's life is, and in theory must be, an expression of the man's life at the second remove" (356). And Veblen suggests this is so as a matter of "divine right of prescription" (355). Veblen writes that "any action on the part of a woman which traverses an injunction of the accepted schedule of proprieties is felt to reflect immediately upon the honour of the man whose woman she is" (354). Veblen's irony notwithstanding, such statements and arguments reveal the precise nature of Edna Pontellier's transgression, helping students who might otherwise misunderstand her peculiar torment with the "accepted schedule of proprieties."

James and Veblen offer two sorts of authoritative discourses about the self and women's place, both discourses that objectify women as appurtenances to the male self. We also discuss how medicine has essentialized women. Medicine is a discipline with claims on the definition of human culture, claims that are ostensibly intrinsic, biological, and, therefore, essential. Ward Hutchinson is typical in his argument to the American Academy of Medicine (1895) that prostitutes nearly always begin as women who work outside the home. He claims in "The Economics of Prostitution," an essay published in the *American Medical-Surgical Bulletin,* that

> the woman who works outside of the home or school pays a fearful penalty, either physical, mental, or moral, and often all three. She commits a biologic crime against herself and against the community,

and woman labor ought to be forbidden for the same reason that child
labor is. Any nation that works its women is damned, and belongs at
heart to the Huron-Iroquois confederacy.   (qtd. in Ziff 280)

James's, Hutchinson's, and Veblen's are equally pointed arguments for the
continued subservience of women to men; theirs is a claim for the scientific
or biological justification of women's social limitation. For women to surpass
their limits, they must confront the institution of science itself and, ultimately, what Hutchinson, Veblen, and James called human or sexual nature.
Given these attempts to define women by what society of the time knew as
"science," we focus class discussion on the reaction against these definitions
by Chopin, by Charlotte Perkins Gilman in "The Yellow Wallpaper," or by
Edith Wharton in *The House of Mirth*.

After these introductory comments about the cultural background on which
Chopin draws, we ask our students to consider Dr. Mandelet's claims about
"woman" as a "peculiar and delicate organism" in general and about Edna
in particular (22). We ask whether Dr. Mandelet's claims for "women" are
consistent with the "science" of women at the turn of the century. He has
defined woman as a peculiar specimen, an "organism" that exceeds the ability
of conventional science to understand it, an organism that demands "inspiration" in order that men "cope with [its] idiosyncrasies." All the terms the
doctor uses to describe Edna are calculated not so much to attend to Edna's
peculiarities as to pacify the husband: "moody," "whimsical," "sensitive,"
"peculiar." It appears curiously appropriate that the doctor should represent
himself as knowing precisely how much conventional science does not know
about cases like Edna's. Nevertheless, what is clear is that science maintains
its central assumption that problems of Edna's sort result from the "peculiar"
internal organization of the body, the female body. The body is defined by
those with an authoritative voice, a univocal utterance of what they consider
to be the "truth" of human nature. That Léonce Pontellier consults Dr.
Mandelet suggests the trouble Edna's culture has separating its social problems from bodily illnesses. The class learns, then, about the disposition and
claims of science as well as about the nature of literature.

The novel is, fortunately, a sufficiently plastic medium that often this
polyvocality takes place in the narrative itself. We cite Bakhtin, who defines
the novel as an orchestration of various voices through a narrative designed
to reveal or clarify tensions (263). This definition opens up other possibilities
for seeing in the text the workings of social and historical dramas. For
instance, the class may be led to enumerate and discuss how Edna differs
from her Creole counterparts. This discussion may focus on religious assumptions (chastity and its *naturalness*), on cultural differences (Edna's silence in the presence of sexual discourse), or on gender and difference

(Adèle's admonishing of Edna to keep her desires under self-surveillance).

By questioning the ideological and social validity of these discourses, we can take a closer look at how Chopin decenters the social languages of the Creoles, as well as the doctor's pseudoscientific authority. The "scandal" of Chopin's novel lies not so much in its sexual explicitness as in Edna's subversion of authoritative discourse. For instance, just after Chopin describes Mr. Pontellier as looking over Edna as if she were some valuable piece of property, the narrator herself looks at Edna, seeing in her something quite different. Where Mr. Pontellier sees only a surface—Edna's sunburnt skin—the narrator suggests an internal landscape quite beyond the sort of reduction Léonce expounds:

> Mrs. Pontellier's eyes were quick and bright; they were a yellowish brown, about the color of her hair. She had a way of turning them swiftly upon an object and holding them there as if lost in some inward maze of contemplation or thought.
>
> Her eyebrows were a shade darker than her hair. They were thick and almost horizontal, emphasizing the depth of her eyes. She was rather handsome than beautiful. Her face was captivating by reason of a certain frankness of expression and a contradictory subtle play of features. Her manner was engaging.   (2)

The narrator sees no more than a third-person narrator might be expected to see: she describes Edna's character through the facial landscape. In this context, however, such a description has political meaning underscored by what Chopin does not claim: to know what Edna is thinking, what Edna is. She says only that her appearance looked "as if" Edna were a deep thinker. In other words, Chopin resists essentializing Edna, which is precisely the method of the science of James, Hutchinson, and Veblen. Their science attempts to uncover the totality of what some category of life or nature is by making a social condition or fact dependent on some larger, deeper somatic fact. And even when the narrator seems to know more about Edna's thoughts and feelings than another person can properly claim to know, still the narrator resists the scientific claim for mastery or truth: she calls Edna's anguish, for instance, "an indescribable oppression," something "unfamiliar" in origin, like a shadow or mist (3).

These few traits may be enough to suggest the nature of Edna's difficulties in the novel—and the difficulties students may have in distinguishing the various ideological voices in the book. For example, her difficulties clarify the degree to which a given trait—chastity, for instance—can appear to be "inborn and unmistakable" (4) to someone who looks at that trait from the outside as Edna does. In other words, chastity—a deeply cultural and social trait—seems to Edna to be genetic, a part of woman's "nature," and not an acquisition of culture or of language. And because it is an internal element of the Creole culture, it remains unsaid. What makes Chopin's novel radical is that it *says* it; Chopin articulates the values of the culture and, in that very articulation, calls them into question. Because she speaks the unspeakable—the values of the Creole culture—she opens up the issue of chastity, among other values that we have proposed, as a topic of discourse. In the very act of suggesting that Creole chastity is natural, Chopin undercuts that suggestion, that certitude. Furthermore, she demonstrates how Edna has internalized this ideology of the body and must stand in opposition to herself in order to escape its tyranny. The Creole freedom of expression regarding sexual matters indicates only that such expression is all the more proscribed, all the more given over to a predictability and familiarity that contain it and prevent it from seriously disrupting the social order. In a sense, we replicate through class discussion Edna's articulations about her culture.

Edna, however, is never in solitude but must come to realize herself as a social being, thoroughly steeped in the Protestant and Creole ideologies of her time. Her language is interanimated with the ideologies of the cultures she inherits that proscribe her place. Edna's alienation from the Creole culture makes possible her inner speech, an inner discourse that is always disruptive of any social order because it denies the right of the community to have knowledge of it. Moreover, it denies the right of the community to control, to discipline it. This interanimation—the effect of other languages on the self—is the ground on which we build our discussion of Edna's social awakening. In addition, it becomes a useful metaphor for the dialogic operation of narrative itself. Edna's alienation is necessary to her awakening because it forces her to confront the values of her culture and to articulate her own. She needs to find her own stance, without allowing her voice to be silenced by the voices (those that we present in class as making their own cultural and normative claims on Edna) that try to drown her out—Léonce's, Robert's, Alcée's, even Adèle's. Only by articulating her own stance, by bringing into the open what is her own ambivalence toward her culture, can she overcome both her self-imposed isolation and the repressive demands made on her by society. Edna's gradual awareness of her voice, her burgeoning consciousness, is crucial to her resistance. We argue, then, that Edna awakens to her cultural alienation rather than to sexual passion.

Our reading of the novel harmonizes with our classroom practice. To see Edna awakening and clarifying her ambiguous relation to her past—that which has imposed various proscriptions and demands on her life—and to her current circumstances is to see the self in relation to its history. Getting students to discuss the turn-of-the-century debate surrounding women's place opens the way toward illuminating which ideas have survived, which have wholly died out, and which are in the process of emerging into being in our time. To see Edna as a participant in a larger conversation enables us to elicit student participation in that discussion, perhaps allowing students to achieve a self-awareness of history. We compel students to engage their history in ways they had not done before.

In addition, our approach to Chopin's novel lets us revise the treatment of historical figures like William James, Veblen, Hutchinson, Gilman, and Chopin herself. We treat the ideologies of, for example, James and Veblen neither as self-evident historical truths, relative to their time and circumstance, nor as unaccountable falsehoods. Rather, we present James and Veblen as two thinkers who have had enormous impact on our history. Their attitudes live on and color the way we understand family, business, and the workplace, even after women have entered into dialogue with those attitudes. Kate Chopin has special meaning for us and for our students, given this dialogue, but not because the desire for domination and pecuniary advantage have themselves come under control. Women now have to face the same choices—the "necessity of *having to choose a language*," as Bakhtin puts it (295)—that made men their own putative masters outside as well as inside the family.

Women's Language in *The Awakening*

E. Laurie George

"I shall use the word 'feminist,' " writes Elaine Marks in a review of contemporary literary theory by French feminists, "to refer to women who are exploring the connection between women and language" (833). Marks's definition provides my rationale for focusing on language in *The Awakening* when I teach it to my Introduction to Women and Literature students. Primarily young female non-English majors, these students become feminists while they explore connections between feminist theory and its practice, between contemporary theories of women and language and Chopin's novel—her feminist critique of male-centered language and her exploration of an alternative women's language.

To keep my objectives from overwhelming students in the five class sessions I devote to teaching *The Awakening*, I follow Marks's approach and summarize the findings of review essays and research articles concerning gender politics and language. Most of the studies are anthologized and thus easily available for student reference. Using my summaries, which, unlike those in Marks's essay, reflect the research of both American and French "feminists" (in Marks's sense of the term) as well as that of some male linguists, the class checks the viability of individual theories by testing them on the various speech patterns Chopin writes into the novel. In this way, students learn by the end of the fifth class enough about feminist and linguistic theory to make political sense of characters' verbal and nonverbal language and to determine if the differences are stereotypes or "genderlects," Wayne Dickerson's term for languages peculiar to each sex (qtd. in Kramer, "Women's Speech" 44).

Along with Ann Rosalind Jones's "Writing the Body: Toward an Understanding of *l'Ecriture Féminine*," Marks's review essay provides an excellent critical text to use when introducing Chopin's feminist critique of patriarchal language. Students wholly uneducated in literary theory can understand Marks's discussion of French feminists who, despite their differences, condemn this kind of discourse since it objectifies and silences the female, leaving her "present but invisible" and able to speak only by imitating the voice and values of males (836). So, too, can students comprehend Jones's definition of phallogocentrism, the male's "appropriation of the world," his need to dominate it by a symbolic discourse that "reduces it to his terms" (362).

With these concepts clarified, students readily detect the male characters' phallogocentric language. They see how Léonce Pontellier objectifies his wife, equating her with the many material possessions that he, with his primarily financial values, worships. They also see how his insisting that Edna respect and conduct herself according to his values, as Adèle Ratignolle centers her life on her husband, steadily alienates her from him, leaving the Pontelliers by the novel's midsection without "anything to say to each other" (23). Moreover, students realize that the other two men who are important to Edna's sexual and spiritual awakening, Alcée Arobin and Robert Lebrun, eventually prove themselves as phallogocentric as Léonce: Alcée, who would sexually enslave Edna, implores her not to "bother" thinking about her character since he can "tell her . . . what manner of woman" she is (27); and Robert, who tells Edna his dream of Léonce's setting her free so that he might claim her himself, abandons her when she chides him for his presumptions. In short, students have little trouble recognizing the basic parts all three men play in forcing Edna to her marginal and finally suicidal position at the novel's end.

Another helpful review essay is Francine Wattman Frank's "Women's Language in America," which surveys the work primarily of American feminists and male linguists and discusses the sociopolitical implications of research conducted on male and female intonation patterns. The work of Cheris Kramer (now Kramarae) concerning stereotypical perceptions of male and female speech reveals that male speech is regarded most commonly as "authoritarian," "blunt," and "forceful" (qtd. in Frank 54), indicating that a phallocratic society values male speech more highly than the stereotypically polite, gentle speech of the female. This kind of speech, Sally McConnell-Ginet makes clear, sounds "relatively unstable and full of affect" to the ear of the conventional, androcentric male (Frank 52). Ruth M. Brend hypothesizes that American men develop narrower intonational ranges than females and that they avoid using the higher pitches associated with women, corroborating the stereotype of women's intonations as "questioning," "polite," and "exclamatory" (Frank 52). And Robin Tolmach Lakoff has found that the American male tends to use more declarative and less subdued intonation than the female (Frank 52), providing still more evidence that gender intonations and their hierarchical values are perpetuated by a culture that devalues women.

Using these hypotheses students analyze intonational features of the novel's male characters, both major and minor, and see that Léonce's intonation, of course, is the most stereotypically male. They draw the connection between his irritation at the birds' high-pitched, fluty voices in the novel's first scene and his shrinking from the "high voice" of Mme Lebrun, whom Léonce terms noisy when she delivers domestic orders in a "monotonous, insistent" but nevertheless authoritative way. He demands that Edna defer to his wishes until she, finally becoming conscious of his strategies, breaks from her conventionally feminine speech habits to rebut his imperatives with commands of her own. Then not even her father (whom students rightly perceive as no less stereotypical than Léonce because of the Colonel's "ponderous oaths" against Edna [24]) can persuade Léonce to use "authority and coercion" to discipline an errant daughter now lacking all conventional "womanly considerations" (24). Students also scrutinize Arobin and Dr. Mandelet: the first, because his sexual entreaties are more often than not commands; the second, because he refers to woman as a "very peculiar and delicate organism" and because he addresses Edna as his subordinate, as "my dear child" (22, 38). Moreover, once Robert consciously decides to join Léonce in the money-making business, he unconsciously adopts that man's phallocratic values. His voice, which had once sounded to Edna "not pretentious" but rather "musical and true" (14), is transformed into a "high voice . . . with a lofty air, which reminded Edna of some gentleman on the stage" (15). Even M. Ratignolle, who is perhaps the most attractive of the male characters, has a way of speaking that gives "an exaggerated importance to every syllable he uttered" (18).

Frank's summaries of research concerning male vocabularies, topics of conversation, and conversational behavior, supplemented with discussions of other research, provide students with additional methods of analyzing the speech of the novel's male characters. A study done by Goldine C. Gleser, Louis A. Gottschalk, and John Watkins indicates that whereas women use more words "implying feeling, emotion, or motivation and [make] more reference to self," men use more words "implying time, space, quantity, and destructive action" (Frank 56). In like manner, Lakoff finds that women's technical vocabularies focus on fashion, cooking and decorating, whereas male terminology centers on sports, autos, or business (Lakoff 141). Léonce's vocabulary corroborates these theories. Léonce is most often planning activities for his business partners and himself, economic dealings that take him away from Grand Isle first to New Orleans, then to New York, where he plans his great venture to Europe. Even though the vocabulary of male characters does not always fit this mold, students can usually explain why these men sometimes use conventionally female vocabulary. For example, the class notices that Robert speaks often of himself when vacationing at Grand Isle. Yet they also understand the reason for his indulging in this so-called feminine habit: as Chopin explains, "he was very young, and did not know any better" (2). Once Robert decides to leave Edna for his foreign business venture—that is, once he decides to play the part of the conventional male—he either talks of possible fortunes to be made in faraway Mexico or he does not talk at all. So, too, does Alcée Arobin sound more conventionally feminine than masculine because he talks almost exclusively of his desire for Edna. Yet that talk of love, the class soon realizes, is likewise the talk of subversion, since Arobin's livelihood, his business in life, is to seduce well-to-do wives into his harem.

Researchers have also identified gender distinctions in conversational topics and behaviors. According to Frank, studies dating back to the 1920s "corroborate the stereotype that men talk to each other about money and business, sports, amusements, and other men, while women prefer such topics as men, clothing, decoration, and other women." Of all these studies, one by M. H. Landis and H. E. Burtt and another by Carney Landis suggest that women "adjust their conversational topics to the interests of male companions," while a third by Don H. Zimmerman and Candace West finds that men frequently interrupt the female discussant if they are in any way dissatisfied with the topic of conversation (Frank 57). Testing these hypotheses, students again find Léonce the easiest to classify. His early conversations with Edna, which might as well be termed lectures, concern finances. The class also sees that Victor Lebrun most often rules the topic of conversation at the Grand Isle dinner table, just as they detect his later attempts to rule it at Edna's dinner table back in New Orleans. He does not realize that she has shed her conventional female manner until she shuts him up by flattening her hand over his mouth.

Finally, Nancy M. Henley's "Power, Sex, and Nonverbal Communication" and Jack W. Sattel's "Men, Inexpressiveness, and Power" prove valuable theoretical sources for information about the differences in gender demeanor and their sociopolitical implications. Males, Henley explains, enjoy a freedom of demeanor and personal space. Their freedom to touch, stare, point, and withhold self-disclosure is culturally sanctioned. But such freedoms are denied the female, who is at once more confined and exposed and who is socialized to adopt the submissive gestures of lowering her eyes, smiling, tolerating another's touch, and, though hesitating, disclosing information about herself. In other words, she is denied the privilege of keeping silent about her thoughts and feelings, a privilege, Sattel maintains, that men use to gain personal power.

Students have little trouble linking these theories with the behavior of the three major male characters. Even in the novel's opening scene, Léonce stares in disgust at his sunburnt wife as he would at one of his valuable domestic decorations grown tarnished. When he tires of her company, he leaves for Klein's, then New Orleans, his travels in the course of the novel becoming increasingly more distant. Robert, too, has freedom of movement, and after he decides to leave Grand Isle for Mexico, his behavior helps to confirm Sattel's theory: Robert refuses to disclose his motives to Edna, though the two have by that time become intimate friends. Thereafter, he adopts his silent behavior whenever he chances to meet her, in an effort to keep her from reestablishing their intimacy. His motive is the opposite of Arobin's, though the latter also controls his intimacy with Edna by at first touching and then caressing her despite her weakening reprovals.

When related to the behavior of the novel's female characters, these same theoretical summaries introduce nicely the second of Chopin's feminist concerns, her exploration of an alternative women's language. Students conclude that the female characters generally fit the stereotyped, acculturated mold described in the summaries, the "mother-women" being the easiest to type (4). Mme Ratignolle, for example, almost always behaves in the conventional female manner. Her intonation is polite and exclamatory; her words are charged with emotion, particularly when she speaks of her pregnancy; her topics of conversation are domestic; and her conversational demeanor toward men is highly deferential: "Madame coquetted with him [Edna's father] in the most captivating and naive manner, with eyes, gestures, and a profusion of compliments till the Colonel's old head felt thirty years younger on his padded shoulders" (23). Mrs. Highcamp provides another good example. Although more worldly than Adèle, the aging socialite nevertheless conforms well to the submissive female role: "Mr. Highcamp was a plain, baldheaded man, who talked only under compulsion. He was unresponsive. Mrs. Highcamp was full of delicate courtesy and consideration toward her husband. She addressed most of her conversation to him at table" (25). Both women, obviously, are content to perform the role of conversational "shitworker" that Pamela M. Fishman finds delegated to the female sex (99).

Students also note that before Edna defies convention, her speech patterns basically fit the same mold. Although never as coquettish as either Adèle Ratignolle or Mrs. Highcamp, Edna at first behaves in a polite, uncertain, and hesitant manner, reflecting the common feminine standard that Cheris Kramer, in "Excessive Loquacity: Women's Speech as Represented in American Etiquette Books," finds in the etiquette books of Chopin's lifetime. More specifically, as Paula A. Treichler notes, Edna's perceptions in the first part of the novel "are hedged in modals and conditional structures, negatives, and relative clauses" (243); and whenever Edna is in the company of men, her language is characterized by "abstract nouns, stiff formal phrases," and "a sense of abstract passivity" (247).

Yet in the novel's second half, students find, Edna's speech and demeanor in mixed company reveal that she has adopted certain masculine traits to gain power denied her. They agree with Treichler's observation that Edna increasingly resists physical confinement, that even though she does not travel as far as either Léonce or Robert, her "movement through space in the novel—swimming, walking—is important because she is the only female character capable of it: capable of change, capable of learning a new language" (254). Certainly, the class concludes, Edna's travel habits align her more with the males than with the females in the novel, for she exchanges domestic for artistic concerns, eventually seeking to market her painting to gain financial independence. Students use as their best evidence Edna's learning to speak with authority to one, then to another, and finally to all the novel's male characters.

At this point, I ask the class to analyze the behavior of female characters when males are absent from the conversation. Specifically, I ask students to focus on two apparently unrelated dialogues occurring in separate halves of the novel, one between Edna and Adèle when alone on the beach at Grand Isle and the other between Edna and Mlle Reisz when alone in the artist's studio apartment in New Orleans. In neither scene can students categorize Edna's behavior as entirely masculine or feminine. But they are even more puzzled to discover that in neither scene can they stereotype Adèle as feminine or Mlle Reisz as masculine. Instead, they find that during the earlier conversation Adèle is for once preoccupied not with domestic concerns but, rather, with Edna's existential struggles; she even ventures to rebuke Robert in a most masculine manner when he interrupts them. So, too, does the class realize that Mlle Reisz relinquishes her normally dominating manner when alone with Edna, preferring instead to listen to the younger woman's romantic problems and to advise her about her artistic aspirations.

The class begins to make sense of this oddly unclassifiable behavior after I have related it to two of Adrienne Rich's feminist essays. About the first, "Women and Honor: Some Notes on Lying," I point out her argument that women need to break silences and to stop telling lies so as to establish honest dialogue among themselves. About the second, "It Is the Lesbian in Us . . . ," I emphasize her implication that such intercourse creates a "primary intensity between women" that she terms "lesbian" (200). With Rich's views in mind, students reread the two scenes, now focusing on Edna's susceptibility to the "candor" of Adèle's "whole existence," a candor that forges "the subtle bond which we call sympathy, which we might as well call love" (7). The class also notes that Mlle Reisz, whose equally candid but cryptic speech is described by Arobin as "demented" but by Edna as "wonderfully sane" (27), plays for Edna on the afternoon of their private visit a musical composition "so insistent, plaintive, and soft with entreaty" that Edna's habitual reserve dissolves into uncontrollable sobbing (21). The intensity of these conversations, students eventually determine, causes the women to relinquish their social role-playing to engage in intimate, honest, and meaningful conversation.

Yet the class also concludes that Chopin must have believed this kind of communion between women short-lived. For evidence, students point to Mlle Reisz's silence—a result of her disappearing from the novel—when Edna seeks her out in the final episodes, and to Adèle's final pledge of allegiance to institutionalized motherhood, her postnatal plea to Edna to think not of herself but only of her children. So, too, do students agree with Treichler's conclusion that "by the time the doctor offers meaningful conversation—to 'talk of things you have never dreamt about before' [38] —it is a language Edna no longer speaks" (252).

Though the novel as a whole supports this pessimistic end to our class discussion, it also encourages a more optimistic one when I ask students to reconsider Mandelet's parting comment to Edna and to consider it as it relates not to her speech but to Chopin's. That is, I ask the class to regard the novel as Chopin's attempt to "talk of things" in ways never dreamt of before, as her means of engaging the reader "in meaningful conversation." Guiding the students toward this point of view, I can finally return to Marks's review-essay of French feminist criticism to discuss it in more detail, the students now being better able to think theoretically. I aim to connect certain of these French theories about women's language with Chopin's use of language, her overall style. I therefore ask the class to consider if the description of the sonorous, murmuring voice of the sea that soothes Edna's nerves like a lullaby is perhaps Chopin's way of writing experimentally, of developing an alternative female discourse. I ask them to consider whether this language at all reflects the one Julia Kristeva terms "le semiotique," the preverbal language based on rhythm, intuition, and melody, and how this melody might relate to the highly evocative music that Mlle Reisz produces in Edna's presence (Marks 837). I ask them to consider how the silent communion between Edna and Adèle, the one woman relishing the other's physical expression of affection, relates to somatic theories concerning the female's ability to communicate better with her body than with articulate speech (Marks 840). And, finally, I ask them how Chopin's diffuse and erotic style pertains to Luce Irigaray's and Hélène Cixous's theories of a female poetic discourse (Marks 840–42).

Students' answers to my questions are often hesistant, uncertain, fragmented—delivered in the stereotypically feminine manner. This being an introductory course, I expect such replies and am not disappointed by them. Yet I also expect that at least some of these students, having had their curiosity piqued, will enroll in other courses featuring Chopin that are structured essentially like this one but that are fleshed out with in-depth theoretical reading and discussion. In those upper-division surveys and seminars, I expect, these students will learn to speak more fluently and confidently about a most provocative and contemporaneous text for literary study.

BACKGROUNDS

A New Biographical Approach
Emily Toth

> If it were possible for my husband and my mother to
> come back to earth, I feel that I would unhesitatingly
> give up every thing that has come into my life since
> they left it and join my existence again with theirs. To
> do that, I would have to forget the past ten years of
> my growth—my real growth.
> Kate Chopin's diary, 22 May 1894
> (Seyersted and Toth 92)

Kate Chopin never expected us to read her diary—nor, most likely, did she expect us to read *The Awakening*. But my students are always intrigued by Kate Chopin. They want to know about her life and "real growth": How independent *was* she? Did she earn a living from her writing? (No; she lived on real estate investments.) What really went on in her marriage? And how did she know all that in 1899?

Literary critics have long presented Kate Chopin as a detached, objective observer who rarely wrote from personal experience—but as I show in my biography (forthcoming), she drew on real life for most of her inspiration. In short stories, Chopin used the names of real people and revealed their secrets with only the thinnest of disguises. She also was not above using fiction for satire and revenge. Even the plot of *The Awakening* is not a total invention; according to Chopin's brother-in-law Phanor Breazeale, with whom she enjoyed playing cards and arguing religion, *The Awakening* was inspired by the true story of a New Orleans woman, well-known to French Quarter residents (Waters; Rankin 92).[1]

But *The Awakening* also has its roots in Kate Chopin's own life, especially her pursuit of solitude, independence, and an identity apart from her children—and apart from the men who always admired her. Like Edna Pontellier, Kate Chopin knew "the outward existence which conforms, the inward life which questions" (7). From an early age, she developed both "a keen sense of humor," in her daughter's words, and "a rather sad nature," because of her many early losses. (Rankin 35; Seyersted 48).

Kate O'Flaherty, born in St. Louis in 1850, was the third of five children, but her sisters died as babies and her brothers died in their twenties—so that Kate was the only one to live past the age of twenty-five (M. Wilson, "Kate Chopin's Family"; interview).[2] But Kate had also been sent from the family nest much earlier than the others: she was barely five and a half when her parents enrolled her in boarding school, at the Sacred Heart Academy in St. Louis. Then, just two months after Kate began school in 1855, her father was one of the civic leaders riding the first train over the newly built Gasconade River bridge. The bridge collapsed, Thomas O'Flaherty was killed, and for the next two years Kate lived at home with her mother, grandmother, and great grandmother—all of them widows. (Nearly forty years later, Kate Chopin created a railroad accident in "The Story of an Hour," in which a woman newly widowed revels in her independence and freedom.)

Kate's great grandmother Victoria Verdon Charleville took charge of Kate's education, emphasizing French, music, clear thinking, and scandalous gossip about St. Louis women of the past. Charleville's own mother had obtained the first legal separation in colonial St. Louis—after which she'd raised five children while running a highly profitable shipping business on the Mississippi. But Mme Charleville's daughter, Kate's grandmother, had married a man whose every financial venture turned to dross, and when he disappeared, he left his wife with no money and eight children (Rankin 35–36; Mills 51, 56–57; Seyersted 13–21; M. Wilson, "Kate Chopin's Family," "Woman's Lib").

And so the eldest child, Eliza, barely sixteen, did the one thing she could do to save her family: she married. Eliza brought to her marriage the Charleville name and social standing, and her husband, Thomas O'Flaherty, a thirty-nine-year-old Irish immigrant, brought money, financial acumen, and a son from his first marriage. No "excessive and fictitious warmth colored her affection," Kate Chopin writes of Edna and Léonce Pontellier in *The Awakening* (7)—and it is unlikely that the O'Flahertys had any particular community of interests. Once Thomas died, Eliza—like her mother and grandmother—did not remarry.

Kate O'Flaherty attended school irregularly and lived in a house full of people. Besides her mother, grandmother, great grandmother, and brothers, there were aunts and uncles and cousins and servants and boarders. But there were no married couples in the house until Kate was sixteen, after the Civil War (1850 and 1860 censuses, St. Louis city directories). Kate O'Flaherty grew up surrounded by single and very independent women, both at home and at the Sacred Heart Academy, where the sisters were famous for their intellectual rigor.

Then, at the academy, Kate found a soulmate: Kitty Garesché, a classmate who also loved climbing trees, sharing candy, and laughing and weeping over popular novels—but their idyllic friendship was shattered by war (Seyersted and Toth 104; Rankin 37). The O'Flahertys and Gareschés were slaveholders and rebel supporters in a Union city, and when both girls were thirteen, Kitty's family was banished from St. Louis. The Gareschés spent the next four years in South Carolina (Holland 169). Kitty did return and their friendship resumed until she entered a convent, but Kate seems never to have been as close to another girl—a fact reflected in Edna Pontellier's girlhood memories. All Edna's friends had been "of one type—the self-contained," and her "most intimate friend at school had been one of rather exceptional intellectual gifts" with whom Edna "sometimes held religious and political controversies" (7).

Kitty was exiled in 1863, the same year Kate's great grandmother and mentor, Mme Charleville, died, three weeks after Christmas. Less than a month later, Kate's half-brother, George, a rebel soldier, died of typhoid on Mardi Gras Day. Their father had been killed on All Saints' Day, eight years earlier, and Kate grew more than a little skeptical about the consolations of religion: even the Presbyterian Edna, in *The Awakening*, finds church suffocating and races outside for air and freedom (8).

Most college students reading *The Awakening* have questioned their own religious upbringings; most also understand the social pressures that make young women deny their intellectual achievements. Although Kate Chopin claimed, much later, to have been "undistinguished" at the Sacred Heart Academy after the war, in fact she was an honor student. She was elected to the elite Children of Mary Society, she won medals, and she delivered a commencement address, an original composition called "National Peculiarities" (Schuyler 116; "St. Louis Convents").

Kate O'Flaherty was also a youthful cynic, and today's students enjoy her musings. Fawned over as a society belle, admired for her cleverness and musical talent, Kate wrote what she really thought in her diary: "I dance with people I despise; amuse myself with men whose only talent is in their feet." She wrote advice about how to flirt (just keep asking, "What do *you* think?" and you'll be praised everywhere for your intelligence), and she was desperate to spend more time with "my dear reading and writing that I love so well" (Seyersted and Toth 62, 63, 60).

Then, in 1870, she married "the right man." Oscar Chopin was twenty-five, handsome, from a wealthy cotton-growing family in Louisiana. (The name is pronounced "show-pan," like the composer's.) Both French Catholic by ancestry, Kate and Oscar spoke French and evidently had that kinship of tastes and values Edna hopes for but never finds (Carnahan; Seyersted and Toth 67; Rankin 58, 81, 82, 89; Seyersted 31, 38, 39; Waters). Kate used their European honeymoon to emancipate herself: she smoked cigarettes publicly, walked about alone, and drank beer; she learned to row and got herself a sunburn (probably, like Edna, she threw off the hats and gloves and veils that separated women from sensual experiences). Kate and Oscar also skipped mass—and that seems to have become a habit by the time they settled in New Orleans (Seyersted and Toth 75, 78, 81, 82, 85).

During the New Orleans years, 1870–79, Kate Chopin was abruptly separated from her community of women. She took long walks and streetcar rides alone, exploring the city and enjoying her own company. ("I always feel sorry for women who don't like to walk; they miss so much—so many rare little glimpses of life; and we women learn so little of life on the whole," Edna says in ch. 36). Still, Kate Chopin was also constantly pregnant—and therefore not to be seen in public. Forced to stay indoors except for Grand Isle vacations, Kate became a talented mimic, a keen observer, and even more of a social critic (Rankin 82).

By the time she was twenty-eight, Kate Chopin had given birth to five sons, with her mother by her side. (After the first birth, in 1871, Oscar departed on a summer-long European trip.) Still, Oscar was evidently a loving, jolly father but a failure as a breadwinner. After several disastrous seasons, he closed up shop as a cotton factor, and the Chopins moved to his old home in Cloutierville, Natchitoches Parish, northwest Louisiana. (The names are pronounced "Cloochy-ville" and "NACK-it-tush"; Louisiana has "parishes" instead of counties.)

For the first time Kate would be living in a small town—and when she arrived, she was pregnant with her last child, the daughter they named Lélia, born 31 December 1879 (Rankin 89–90; Seyersted 38). In Cloutierville—a tiny French village that became the site of many of her short stories—Kate Chopin shocked the longtime residents. She would lift her skirts too high, deliberately revealing her ankles, when she crossed the town's one street; she smoked Cuban cigarettes and wore fancy riding habits from New Orleans, and many local people tut-tutted. But after Lélia's birth, Kate was finally freed from constant pregnancy and able to listen much more to her own needs (Rankin 103; Carnahan).

After Oscar Chopin died suddenly of "swamp fever" in December 1882,

Kate ran his general store and plantation for more than a year. An attractive local planter, a married man, pursued her, and Kate was more than a little responsive—but she made a choice: in 1884 she sold her furniture and returned to St. Louis to live with her mother. (That choice is echoed in *The Awakening*, when Edna leaves a man—Robert—to be with a woman: the "mother-woman" Adèle, who is about to give birth [Carnahan; DeLouche; Hernandez].) But when Eliza O'Flaherty died the following year, leaving Kate with a modest income and sole responsibility for six children, Kate turned to writing. Her first published story, "Wiser Than a God" (1889), tells the story of a woman who becomes a great artistic success, but only after her mother's death.

By almost any standards, Kate Chopin was an immediate literary success. Within four years she was appearing in the most prestigious national magazines. Her first short story collection, *Bayou Folk*—mostly local-color stories of Cloutierville-area people—gained nationwide acclaim; her second, *A Night in Acadie*, was well-received. She was also one of the most popular and sought-after writers in St. Louis's literary colony. She held salons at her home, with visiting writers; she was friendly with journalists, poets, and editors of both sexes. She had numerous admirers and suitors, including an editor at the St. Louis *Post-Dispatch*, which published her son Oscar's sketch of his mother's study (Waters; "St. Louis Woman").

In the 1890s Kate Chopin also retained her ties with Louisiana friends and relatives, although some bristled when they recognized her characters. In her first novel, *At Fault* (1890), and in several short stories, she portrayed the Cloutierville priest Father Jean Marie Beaulieu ("Père Antoine") as obtuse and ineffectual—but in "Dr. Chevalier's Lie" (1893) she published a sympathetic portrait of her New Orleans obstetrician and anticipated the character of Dr. Mandelet. For several rakish characters, she drew on the Louisiana planter who had pursued her, and she named one story for his wife.

During her prime, Kate Chopin also wrote "The Storm" (1898), about a young Louisiana mother and a planter—both married to others—who take refuge in her house during a thunderstorm. The storm outside inspires a different sensual storm inside, which is described with a startling explicitness for the 1890s: "When he touched her breasts they gave themselves up in quivering ecstasy, inviting his lips . . ." (*Works* 2: 595). The enthusiasm in the story—and its lack of moral condemnation—suggests a personal experience, which may be why Kate Chopin never attempted to publish "The Storm."

Then, in *The Awakening*, Chopin reconsidered her years in New Orleans, the years of pregnancy and motherhood. The action takes place over nine months, the space of Adèle's pregnancy; *The Awakening*'s image of womanly beauty is a radiantly pregnant woman—perhaps the only one described in novels of the 1890s. Though Adèle, the traditional woman, prefers to give birth in pain, Edna (like her creator) took chloroform during her deliveries—and *The Awakening* is Edna's protest against physical and spiritual confinement and pain. Most of Edna's awakenings take place in the unconfined outdoors, in the sensual tropical paradise of Grand Isle (Toth, *Kate Chopin*, "Timely"; Seyersted and Toth 93).

The Awakening, of course, generated a storm of hostile criticism, but there is no documentary evidence that the book was actually banned or withdrawn from St. Louis library shelves. The story that it was kept from the public stems mainly from Kate Chopin's own ironic statement: "The libraries! Oh, no, they don't keep it" (*Works* 2: 722).[3] Nor was Kate Chopin totally ostracized in St. Louis: women wrote her warm letters full of praise for *The Awakening* (Seyersted and Toth 133–34, 137–39). They also invited her to give a reading at the Wednesday Club, the most prestigious intellectual women's club in St. Louis. Of the two women who reviewed *The Awakening*—Willa Cather in Pittsburgh and Frances Porcher in St. Louis —both had questions about the theme, but both warmly praised the book's artistry (Culley, *Awakening* 145–46, 153–55).

It was the male critics, editors, and gatekeepers in St. Louis and around the nation who condemned *The Awakening* and cut short Kate Chopin's writing career. She was stung by the negative reviews—some of them from men she knew well—and afterward wrote only a few more short stories. At the turn of the century, she was in failing health (her symptoms suggest diabetes); many of her close friends were dying; and her son Jean's young wife died in childbirth, along with Kate's first grandchild. Though Chopin rallied with enthusiasm for the St. Louis World's Fair in 1904, the August heat brought on a cerebral hemorrhage, and she died on 22 August. She was buried in St. Louis's Calvary Cemetery (sec. 17, lot 47) and virtually forgotten for half a century, until Per Seyersted rediscovered her in the 1960s and American feminists embraced her.[4]

My students like to know that Kate Chopin did not walk into the sea and that long after her death, she has been resurrected for us. They are also fascinated by the unconventional streak that seems to run through her entire life—including her refusal to remarry: obviously she preferred her freedom, her writing, and her solitude. Like Edna, she was "the regal woman, the one who rules, who looks on, who stands alone" (30). She was her own woman.

NOTES

[1] My Chopin biography, which will be published by Atheneum, will treat the real-life parallels in much greater detail. "Miss McEnders," for instance, is about a

recognizable St. Louis philanthropist whose money was obtained in questionable ways—which explains why Chopin published the story under the pseudonym "La Tour."

[2] The 1850 census lists "Cath. 7/12" among the O'Flahertys, meaning that "Cath." was seven months old as of the census date, June 1850—but Kate Chopin's tombstone and other biographies give her birthday as 8 February 1851. The definitive evidence, however, comes from Jean Bardot, who has recovered the baptismal record at the St. Louis Cathedral, showing that Kate O'Flaherty was born 8 February 1850. Kate's sisters Jane and Marie Therese died in infancy; her brother Tom was killed in a buggy accident at age twenty-five (US Census, 1850; Bardot 18; M. Wilson, "Kate Chopin's Family," interview).

[3] Librarians Erik Stocker of the St. Louis Public Library and Robert Behra and John Neal Hoover of the St. Louis Mercantile Library can find no evidence that the book was ever banned or withdrawn.

[4] For more than half a century, Kate Chopin's writings were virtually unknown outside Louisiana—except to Fred Lewis Pattee, who frequently anthologized the short story "Désirée's Baby." The Lesche Club, a drama club at the Louisiana Normal School in Natchitoches, used to write and perform plays based on Kate Chopin stories—and when the Normal School became Northwestern State University, it retained a dormitory called Kate Chopin Hall (but that dormitory was torn down in the 1970s). Three Kate Chopin homes still survive today: 1413–15 Louisiana Avenue in New Orleans, a house now belonging to a women's historical association; the Bayou Folk Museum and Kate Chopin Home in Cloutierville, open to the public; and 4232 McPherson Avenue in St. Louis, now a private home with city landmark status.

The Historical and Cultural Setting

Nancy Walker

One dimension of Kate Chopin's *The Awakening* likely to be overlooked in the classroom is the richness of the historical and cultural background against which the novel takes place. New Orleans Creole culture in the late nineteenth century constituted a world unto itself—a set of traditions, mores, and customs unlike any other in America. Indeed, Chopin's descriptions of this culture serve as more than mere backdrop; the contrast between Edna's upbringing in Kentucky and the Creole society of Léonce Pontellier creates a subtle but persistent thread in the novel, one that helps to explain Edna's restlessness and alienation from the society around her. Approaching the novel as—at least in part—an account of the clash between the dominant southern culture in which Edna was raised and the New Orleans Creole subculture in which she finds herself after her marriage allows students not only to better understand a part of American cultural history but also to see Edna as a woman influenced by her past as well as by the events and surroundings of her present.

As Per Seyersted's biography and the letters and diary entries in the *Kate Chopin Miscellany* make clear, *The Awakening* is far from autobiographical. Kate Chopin and Edna Pontellier were the products of very different backgrounds, and that difference influenced their individual responses to the mores and values of New Orleans Creole culture toward the end of the nineteenth century. Whereas Edna has come to her marriage directly from the stern Protestantism of her father's home, Chopin grew up immersed in the cosmopolitan life of the Creoles in both St. Louis and New Orleans. Chopin's maternal grandfather, Wilson Faris, was a Kentuckian, a circumstance that, though it may well have contributed to Chopin's understanding of southern life east of the Mississippi River, had little effect on the atmosphere in which she was raised. In addition, Chopin had traveled extensively before she settled in New Orleans, and her perspective on cultural variety was far wider than that of Edna. On her way to New York to embark on a several-month honeymoon tour of Europe, Chopin commented favorably on Cincinnati and its beer gardens but was not at all pleased by Philadelphia, which she described as a "gloomy puritanical looking city" (Seyersted and Toth 68). The breadth of Chopin's experience with travel and reading— especially by the time she wrote *The Awakening* in her mid-forties—distinguishes her from the unworldly Edna and provides her with a far greater sense of cultural relativism.

The setting of the novel derives from Chopin's residence in New Orleans from 1870 to 1879 as well as from earlier visits there with her family. Born in St. Louis to an Irish-Catholic father and a French-Creole mother, Kate O'Flaherty married Oscar Chopin, a Creole from Natchitoches, Louisiana, and the couple settled in New Orleans, where Oscar became a cotton merchant. The Chopins lived in what was known as the "American" part of the city, an area now known as the Garden District, across Canal Street from the French Quarter. Constantinople Street and Louisiana Avenue, where the Chopins had successive residences, formed part of a burgeoning suburb outside what most long-time residents considered "real" New Orleans: the Vieux Carré. In fact, Per Seyersted, Chopin's biographer, mentions that Oscar Chopin's father, who had come to Louisiana from France and had clung to his French heritage, disliked the fact that the couple chose to live in the American section of the city (37). Nevertheless, Kate Chopin explored New Orleans with a freedom unusual for women in the 1870s and became well acquainted with the colorful mixture of cultures and the bustle of trade in this port city.

Between 1860 and 1880, the population of New Orleans grew from 168,675 to 216,090 (nearly half of the residents were black), and the city was at that time "the only metropolis in the South" (Ezell 232). Founded in 1718, it was also one of the oldest cities in the southern part of the country. Age and size had their negative effects on life in New Orleans in the 1870s. Because the city lacked an adequate system of sanitation and stood below sea level, its narrow streets were filled with human and animal wastes and garbage; and epidemics of yellow fever, smallpox, and cholera were common, largely due to the miasmal swamps immediately adjacent to the city. The yellow fever epidemic of 1878, for example, claimed the lives of more than four thousand New Orleans residents. In an attempt to escape this threat, the wives and children of many Creole families, including those of Oscar Chopin, spent their summers on Grand Isle, which, because it is an island in the Gulf of Mexico about fifty miles south of New Orleans, enjoys gulf breezes that virtually remove the fever-carrying mosquitoes.

It is in this languid, semitropical setting that Chopin places the beginning and the ending of *The Awakening*. Because Grand Isle's summer population was almost entirely Creole, Edna is first shown here immersed in a culture with which she feels at odds and yet to which she is strongly attracted. Unlike Kate Chopin, who grew up speaking French and who managed to charm her Gallic father-in-law, despite his displeasure with her half-Irish heritage, Edna was born to a Kentucky Presbyterian family with values far removed from those of the warm, easygoing Creoles. Early in *The Awakening*, Edna recalls a day in her childhood when she felt a pleasant sense of escape from the rigidity of her home, and she says to Mme Ratignolle, "Likely as not, it was Sunday, . . . and I was running away from prayers, from the Presbyterian service, read in a spirit of gloom by my father that chills me yet to think of" (7). Although Edna's family subsequently moved to Mississippi, her severe Calvinistic Protestant background underwent no apparent change, and she is again reminded of it in the novel when her father comes to New Orleans to visit. She is relieved when he finally leaves, taking with him "his padded shoulders, his Bible reading, his 'toddies' and ponderous oaths" (24).

Differences in values and behavior between the Catholic French Creoles of New Orleans and the Kentucky Presbyterians during the years before and after the Civil War could hardly have been more striking. Religious and political forces combined in the early years of the nineteenth century to alter southern Protestantism in ways that created a gulf between it and both Catholicism and northern Protestantism. As Ezell points out in *The South since 1865*, the "Great Revival" of 1800 strengthened evangelical Protestantism among the middle and lower classes of the South. Although this revival spirit initially fostered democratic and even liberal social attitudes, beginning in the 1830s northern criticism of the South—especially of the system of slavery—caused an increasing conservatism among southern Protestants that eventually led to the splitting of most denominations into northern and southern branches. "A great resurgence of religious orthodoxy began to regiment thought to protect Southern vested interests. . . . Liberalism brought threats to the *status quo*; therefore, Southern reaction was conservative in religion as well as in politics" (341). Edna's Kentucky Presbyterian father, who had been a colonel in the Confederate army, is a member of the generation of southerners who were most directly affected by this intense conservative trend in both religious and social attitudes.

The Catholic church, in contrast, was largely unaffected by the wave of southern conservatism in the middle years of the nineteenth century, and the Creoles of southern Louisiana, although many of them owned slaves, preserved through the century virtually the same traditions and social attitudes that they had developed during the years since their settlement of the area in the early eighteenth century. New Orleans, during the period of Chopin's residence there, was dominated by Creole culture, and the Creoles, who had developed a highly sophisticated society, were notably hostile toward the backwoods "Americans" who poured into this major port city with boatloads of timber, furs, and tobacco. To the refined Creole, these hunters and farmers seemed crude, dirty, and socially backward, and although they came down the Mississippi from a variety of states, Kentuckians must have seemed particularly offensive, because the Creoles called all these outsiders "Kaintocks" (Chase 80).

From its street names and architecture to its Mardi Gras celebrations, New Orleans, under the influence of the Creoles, more nearly resembled a southern European than an American city. Edward King, a contemporary observer writing in *Scribner's Monthly* in 1873, stresses the European atmosphere of French New Orleans:

> Step off from Canal Street, that avenue of compromises which separates the French and the American cities, some bright February morning, and you are at once in a foreign atmosphere. Three paces from the corner have enchanted you; the surroundings of a Southern-American commonwealth have vanished; this might be Toulouse, or Bordeaux, or Marseilles. (10)

Long before the advent of jazz, music was an important part of the city's cultural life, and the French Opera House was the first in the country to stage productions of Wagner (Seyersted 42). Unconstrained by the Puritanism of their Protestant neighbors, for whom life was serious business, the Creoles played as hard as they worked. Indeed, to those from other parts of the country, Creole life seemed almost sinfully sensuous. Seyersted quotes Lafcadio Hearn, the author, who moved to New Orleans in 1877, as saying, "work . . . in this voluptuous climate . . . is impossible" (41). What appeared to some to be a hedonistic way of life, coupled with the Creole institution of concubinage with quadroon and octoroon women, gave New Orleans a reputation as a sinful city. As Clement Eaton notes in *A History of the Old South*, "Americans who came down the Mississippi were shocked at the Creole Sundays, when the Sabbath day was devoted to pleasure and commerce. Furthermore, these Latins were passionately fond of gambling, lotteries, and dancing" (183). Even those Americans living as neighbors to the French Creoles were vexed at their self-sufficiency, their lack of interest in political affairs. As Edward King describes the situation, "they seem as remote from New York and Washington as if limitless oceans rolled between" (12).

In keeping with this atmosphere of social freedom, women in Creole culture, as is evident in *The Awakening*, were far less affected by the Victorian strictures that dictated the behavior of middle-class women in other parts of the country. Although they tacitly supported a sexual double standard by their acceptance of their husbands' part-Negro mistresses and were legally as powerless as other women, Creole women participated fully in the sensuous atmosphere that surrounded them: drinking wine, enjoying music and literature, wearing bright colors, and entertaining lavishly. Well-educated, especially in the arts, these women were acquainted with literary trends, and many were accomplished musicians and painters. Although Creole culture was patriarchal in the extreme, women enjoyed life in ways that those subjected to Edna's father's "gloom" could not.

Teaching *The Awakening* with an awareness of the religious and social differences in Kate Chopin's cultural milieu enriches students' reading of the novel. It also removes Chopin from the narrow designation of "regionalist" or "local colorist" to which she has often been confined and demonstrates her understanding of the larger cultural patterns and problems of the late nineteenth century. Certainly Edna Pontellier's brave if doomed attempts at self-definition remain the central issue of the novel, but complicating those attempts are the romanticism that results from her rebellion against her rigid Presbyterian background and her inability to adjust that romanticism to the reality of her present environment.

Early in the novel, Chopin makes clear Edna's distance from the mores of the Creoles summering at Grand Isle: "Mrs. Pontellier, though she had married a Creole, was not thoroughly at home in the society of Creoles; never before had she been thrown so intimately among them. . . . A characteristic which distinguished [the Creoles] and which impressed Mrs. Pontellier most forcibly was their entire absence of prudery" (4). Edna is shocked by Mme Ratignolle's detailed recounting of her childbirth experiences, and she reads "in secret and solitude" an unnamed novel that the others read and discuss openly (4). The gossipy, confidence-sharing ways of the Creoles does not merge easily with Edna's Presbyterian reserve—"Mrs. Pontellier was not a woman given to confidences" (7)—yet she is seduced by the easy relations of this culture: "That summer at Grand Isle she began to loosen a little the mantle of reserve that had always enveloped her" (7). Significantly, Chopin places the Pontelliers' New Orleans residence not in the Garden District, the "American" part of the city, but on Esplanade Street (actually, Avenue), at the edge of the French Quarter. Chopin had been familiar with this neighborhood since before her marriage, since it was noted for its grassy promenades where the part-black mistresses of white gentlemen strolled, often with their illegitimate offspring, just minutes from their homes on streets with such names as "Desire" and "Good Children." Edna is thus immersed physically in the Creole world, both on Grand Isle and in New Orleans.

Edna's early desire to escape the grimness of her Kentucky home has led to her marriage to Léonce. Beneath her reserve lies a strain of romanticism and rebelliousness that early in her life manifested itself in imagined attachments to a series of unavailable men: the "dignified and sad-eyed cavalry officer," the young man in Mississippi who was engaged to someone else, and finally the "great tragedian" whose picture she kept on her desk. Chopin makes it clear that Edna's marriage is not the result of any such grand passion: "Her marriage to Léonce Pontellier was purely an accident" (7). One of her motives for marrying him, in fact, is her desire to flout the wishes of her father, who violently opposes her marrying a Catholic. Even after her marriage, her stern father attempts to dictate her values and her behavior.

Though proud of her artistic talent, he takes credit for it, "convinced as he was that he had bequeathed to all of his daughters the germs of a masterful capability" (23). The Colonel disagrees with Léonce's rather liberal treatment of Edna's "moods":

> "You are too lenient, too lenient by far, Léonce," asserted the Colonel. "Authority, coercion are what is needed. Put your foot down good and hard; the only way to manage a wife. Take my word for it."
> The Colonel was perhaps unaware that he had coerced his own wife into her grave. (24)

Caught between the Puritanical sternness of her father's world and the relaxed familiarity of Creole culture, Edna can belong fully to neither. Mme Ratignolle recognizes Edna's position as an outsider early in the novel when she exhorts Robert Lebrun to stop flirting with her: "She is not one of us; she is not like us. She might make the unfortunate blunder of taking you seriously" (8). Edna does, of course, take Robert seriously, just as he takes seriously her status as a possession of her husband, even though she tries to counteract this assumption toward the end of the novel: "I give myself when I choose. If he [Léonce] were to say, 'Here, Robert, take her and be happy; she is yours,' I should laugh at you both" (36). Robert cannot understand this freedom, and so he does the "honorable" thing by leaving. And having effectively left her husband, Edna can imagine no future; therefore, she swims into the Gulf of Mexico.

Readers of *The Awakening* have tended, correctly, to see Edna as a "misfit" in several ways. She is not a "mother-woman" like Mme Ratignolle, nor is she a self-fulfilled artist like Mlle Reisz. She tries to be an artist—with Mlle Reisz's encouragement—but tragically, considering the milieu, fails for lack of sufficient talent and commitment. She feels unconnected to her marriage and wants independence, but divorce is not an option and she does not have the means to be financially independent. In these respects she is a woman who does not belong to her time, but it is equally important to realize that she does not belong to her place.

Chopin's Stories of Awakening

Mary E. Papke

Having taught *The Awakening* in various literature classes over the last six years, I have seen a clear pattern emerge in my students' responses. Invariably, their first reading of the novel is an almost purely emotional experience. They sympathize or identify with Edna; they vicariously enjoy her rejection of social conventions and expectations. At the same time, however, most students are deeply disturbed by Edna's seeming helplessness or passivity, her dependence on others for a new, self-fulfilling life. In particular, I have found that discussion of the novel's end usually flounders. Few students can immediately grasp the complexities of Edna's suicide, and many feel that in that singular act Chopin robs both her heroine and her readers of a satisfactory conclusion. In other words, despite our careful analysis of Edna's romantic self-delusion and her inability to express or experience her new self in the social world of the novel, my students would succumb to their own desire for a romantic ending—Edna effecting a miraculous change in Robert or Léonce and living happily ever after, or Edna somehow achieving self-sufficiency somewhere sometime.

Through experimentation I found one way to circumvent such a return to romanticism: I learned that teaching *The Awakening* in all its complexity is made easier if one also studies several stories Chopin wrote before her work on the novel. These stories introduce in embryonic form the elements that make the novel the masterpiece we deem it to be and also make clear Chopin's shift from a focus on the limitations women confront in the public and private spheres to a focus on the limitations women discover in desire itself. More important, these stories teach students how to read Chopin; their careful delineation of self-delusion and thwarted self-desire shows us precisely how and why we must critique our too often unreflective, romantic response to Chopin's work, how and why we must become active rather than passive readers who feel but do not turn to account the experience presented in these texts.

Teachers often introduce Chopin through three of her earliest stories that, as Per Seyersted points out, set up Chopin's triad of female possibilities (103–08). "A No-Account Creole," first written as "Euphrasie" in 1888 and rewritten in 1891, reveals a woman complacent within the traditional patriarchy. "Wiser Than a God" (1889) draws the world of the woman as artist. "A Point at Issue!" (1889) examines the woman as divided self desirous of both self-fulfillment and union with another. This triad is later seen in *The Awakening*'s Adèle Ratignolle, Mlle Reisz, and Edna Pontellier. A second common approach is to teach the stories of awakening to social injustices, works such as "Ma'ame Pélagie" (1892) and "Désirée's Baby" (1892), in which Chopin takes up the true woman paradigm, sets it in the historical contexts of an antebellum and a postbellum South, and subtly exposes the power and the base of womanhood ideology, particularly in its relation to racial ideology. While these stories all offer important background to *The Awakening*, yet another set of stories comes closer to the novel's concerns. These stories offer concentrated descriptions of moments that shatter social complacency, the quickening of consciousness that leads to self-desire and self-recognition and, in Chopin's world, consequent despair and alienation. Most of the works I discuss below are available in the Signet edition of *The Awakening*, edited by Barbara H. Solomon; "Her Letters" and "An Egyptian Cigarette," rarely anthologized, are in *The Complete Works of Kate Chopin*, which can be placed on library reserve.

"The Story of an Hour" (1894) is undoubtedly Chopin's most well known and intense reading of the awakening to self-desire. It details a very ordinary reality and conscientiously analyzes that moment in a woman's life when the boundaries of the accepted everyday world are suddenly shattered and the process of self-consciousness begins. Louise Mallard, dutiful wife and true woman, is gently told that her husband has been killed in a train accident. Her response is atypical, however, and that is the subject of the story: what Louise thinks and feels as she finds herself thrust into solitude and self-contemplation for the first time. It is in the mid-section of the story, set in Louise's room, that Louise and Chopin's reader explore and come to understand reaction and potential action, social self—Mrs. Mallard—and private, female self—Louise.

Louise sits before an open window at first thinking nothing but merely letting impressions of the outer and inner worlds wash over her. She is physically and spiritually depleted but is still sensuously receptive. She sees the "new spring life" in budding trees, smells rain, hears human and animal song as well as a man "crying his wares." She is like both a tired child dreaming a sad dream and a young woman self-restrained but with hidden strengths. She is yet Mrs. Mallard.

As she sits in a "suspension of intelligent thought," she feels something unnameable coming to her through her senses. It is frightening because it is not of her true womanhood world; it reaches to her from the larger world outside and would "possess her." The unnameable is, of course, her self-consciousness that is embraced once she names her experience as emancipation and not destitution: "She said it over and over under her breath: 'free, free, free!' . . . Her pulses beat fast, and the coursing blood warmed and relaxed every inch of her body." It is at this point that she begins to think, the point at which she is reborn through and in her body, an experience analogous to Edna's in the novel.

Louise then immediately recognizes her two selves and comprehends how each will coexist, the old finally giving way to the one new self. Mrs. Mallard will grieve for her husband, who had loved her, but Louise will eventually revel in the "monstrous joy" of self-fulfillment, beyond ideological strictures and the repressive effects of love:

> she would live for herself. There would be no powerful will bending hers in that blind persistence with which men and women believe they have a right to impose a private will upon a fellow-creature. . . . What could love, the unsolved mystery, count for in face of this possession of self-assertion which she suddenly recognized as the strongest impulse of her being!

Louise embraces this new consciousness, her sense of personal and spiritual freedom in a new world. She then leaves her room and descends again into her past world. Though she carries herself "like a goddess of Victory" and has overcome the constraints of her past self, she is not armed for the lethal intrusion of the past world through her front door. Brently Mallard unlocks his door and enters unharmed. His return from the dead kills Louise, and Chopin's conclusion is the critical and caustic remark that all believed "she had died of heart disease—of joy that kills."

Usually my students are initially overwhelmed by the pathos of the story, a natural response since they come to consciousness of the text just as Louise awakens to self-consciousness. Chopin offers us only that one point of identification—Louise, whose powers of reflection have been repressed, suddenly shocked into being, and then brutally cut off. Similarly, students enter the text with little foregrounding, are shocked by the early "climax" of Mallard's death, share Louise's awakening to new possibilities, and then are cut off by the bitter irony of her death. I focus discussion on this process of limitation and denial and ask my students to explore their relation to the text, both how we are trapped by it and what we are asked to deny at the end. We talk about how it is beyond irony to be left at the conclusion with the knowledge that only Louise and we the readers perceived the earlier "death" of Mrs. Mallard and true womanhood and that what murdered her was, indeed, a monstrous joy—the birth of individual self—and the erasure of that joy when her husband and, necessarily, her old self returned. As class discussion can then bring out, far from being a melodramatic or pathetic ending, the conclusion both informs and warns: should a woman see the real world and her individual self within it only to be denied the right to live out that vision, then in her way lies non-sense, self-division, and dissolution. Chopin's earlier stories examined the destruction of women who lived within traditional society; this piece offers no escape for those who live outside that world but only so in a private world in themselves. Either way, we conclude, Chopin seems to be saying there lies self-oblivion if only the individual changes and not the world.

Usually at this stage in our study, several students point out what seems to them an important extenuating circumstance in Louise's story: Louise was alone and had no other acceptable world—as ideology had pictured the world of mothers and children—in which to fulfill herself. They then want to know Chopin's attitude toward motherhood, whether she thought Louise or any other woman could find self-fulfillment through her children. I offer that in such works as "Regret" (1894) and "Athénaïse" (1895), Chopin depicts the female desire for children as well as the supposed power and strength granted to mothers. Athénaïse, for example, is transformed by her pregnancy, which is described as her sensuous awakening and her self-contained experience. I also point out, however, that Chopin moves quickly from that line of argument and later focuses on motherhood as yet another form of ideological entrapment that some women accept, along with the loss of self, and some do not. "A Pair of Silk Stockings" (1896), which we then read, shows the dark side of motherhood and builds on the major elements from "The Story of an Hour," with only a few shifts in class and setting.

In this work, a genteel but poor woman, seemingly without support and alone except for her children, experiences an awakening of sensuous self. Mrs. Sommers is a woman born to a better class than the one she married into, but she is also a true woman who neither shirks sacrifice for her family nor thinks of anything beyond her immediate life as mother and martyr: "She had no time—no second of time to devote to the past. The needs of the present absorbed her every faculty. A vision of the future like some dim, gaunt monster sometimes appalled her, but luckily to-morrow never comes." As in "The Story of an Hour," the unexpected occurs: Mrs. Sommers comes into a veritable fortune, fifteen dollars, which she at first plans to spend on her children. Like Louise Mallard, she is physically and spiritually exhausted when she arrives at the moment of contemplation and action; one begins to see clearly Chopin's definition of the usual effect of womanhood ideology: self-depletion. Again just like Louise, she experiences a sensuous moment —here the particularly female response to a specifically feminine luxury, silk stockings, which reawakens her female self, an experience that simultaneously embraces her and engulfs her in monstrous joy from which there is no desire for escape.

After she buys and puts on the stockings, she too comes to a suspension of intellectual thought before the rebirth of her self: "She was not going through any acute mental process or reasoning with herself, nor was she striving to explain to her satisfaction the motive of her action. She was not thinking at all." She feels, she is sensuously alive, she begins to be her old self made new by her greater enjoyment of self-fulfillment. Of course, to-morrow does come for her just as Brently Mallard returned to Louise. While the realization of her momentary freedom—the pleasure of spending money on herself—and her permanent obligation—her duty to her children—does not kill Mrs. Sommers, she is thrown into a despair from which there is no rescue. For Chopin, as readers will see here and in her novel, there is never an easy resolution to woman's quest for self and fulfillment of desire.

These stories, as I have suggested, inform us of how Chopin exposes character and of how we must come to terms with Chopin's critique of self-desire lest we pass hasty judgment and fall prey to melodramatic responses. I use the next two stories to focus discussion further on the negativity of unreflective passion as well as on Chopin's increasingly complex use of symbols for limitation and despair born out of denied desire. Even as she celebrates the senses as the breaking ground for consciousness, Chopin also portrays the purely sexual as another trap into which both men and woman fall, a theme central to Maupassant's "mad" stories that Chopin translated and greatly admired. Desire becomes obsessive passion in these works, and passion proves as much an entrapment, a form of madness, as is ideologically conventional love.

"Her Letters" (1894) is important both because it examines male and female responses to passion and because it contains what will become the central image and act of *The Awakening*. In this short story, a woman "pained and savage" with passion goes to destroy her lover's letters. It is a leaden day of "no gleam, no rift, no promise," when she can no longer think but only feel and act as a wounded animal would: "With her sharp white teeth she tore the far corner from the letter, where the name was written; she bit the torn scrap and tasted it between her lips and upon her tongue like some god-given morsel." Unable to give up the letters, she entrusts them to her husband's care: he will destroy them without reading them.

A year later she has died, and on another leaden day of "no gleam, no promise," her husband finds the letters, suffers a conflict of will about reading them, and finally throws them unopened into a river. His initial discovery illuminates for us the relationship and rift between husband and wife, a point brought home by the bleak refrain, and his later journey to water clarifies the emptiness of ordinary life and the despair that goes hand in hand with willful nonconsciousness. He realizes that he will never know her true self and that he is forever alienated from her: "The darkness where he stood was impenetrable . . . leaving him alone in a black, boundless universe." His passion for the now forever unattainable union and his "man-instinct of possession" lead him to see her as his only salvation: to know "the secret of her existence" will be to know his own self and the meaning of his existence. As we discuss in class, this desire is the romantic dream of much of Chopin's early work become nightmare, madness, and self-destruction instead of self-fulfillment.

It is now that we can see how Chopin empowers her water symbol, as she will in *The Awakening*, here making it the unnatural subject of a madman's obsessive passion to know and to be known by another. The husband returns to the river and the darkness, emasculated by his inability to know, savage in his need for consummation. He believes he hears the call of the water: "It babbled, and he listened to it, and it told him nothing, but it promised all. He could hear it promising him with caressing voice, peace and sweet repose. He could hear the sweep, the song of the water inviting him." He answers by drowning himself, "to join her and her secret thought in the immeasurable rest." Both now "rest" in the same final state but not, as the romantic madman would have it, together; instead, they are forever alienated in death—the ultimate dissolution—as they were in life. We see here that passion makes no new worlds, that the dark side of desire illuminates only the funereal breach of self-faith and the impenetrable state of demented nonconsciousness that passion gives birth to and nurtures. For Chopin, passion alone is eventual self-death and not the way toward self-fulfillment.

Finally, I ask my students to read "An Egyptian Cigarette" (1897), Chopin's concentrated primal version of *The Awakening*, a dream within a tale in which the dreamer escapes the nightmare. In this work, Chopin creates a highly unconventional woman and situation that allow a nontragic if perplexing ending. That the female character who dreams is similar to the female writer who creates is obvious; indeed, that the fictional woman maintains a firm grasp of her self-possession despite her visions must have been a desire and dream of her creator as well.

In "An Egyptian Cigarette," a cosmopolitan woman is given a box of cigarettes that contain some sort of hallucinogenic drug. She smokes one and immediately experiences a distorted and perverse vision of passion and despair. In the dream, a woman driven wild with longing lies in a desert abandoned by her lover. She dreams of following him to entrap him once more with her love. Ensnared by her obsession, she lies dying in the heat and thinks only of reaching the river. She considers the irony of her life and its end: "I laughed at the oracles and scoffed at the stars when they told that after the rapture of life I would open my arms inviting death, and the waters would envelop me." Like Edna at the end of *The Awakening*, she reviews her life, how she lived outside religion and society for the sake of her love and how she is now abandoned by all. While she is physically tormented by sun and sand, she experiences a momentary shift in consciousness: "It seems to me that I have lain here for days in the sand, feeding upon despair. Despair is bitter and it nourishes resolve." Above her, as will be above Edna, she hears "the wings of a bird flapping, . . . flying low, in circles." She too reaches water and goes into it; like Edna she suffers a moment of fear at its embrace; like Edna she moves toward resolution and into "the sweet rapture of rest," her senses alive and fulfilled at last.

The dreamer awakens at this point, disoriented and distressed after having thus "tasted the depths of human despair." She contemplates the other dreams waiting for her in the remaining cigarettes: "what might I not find in their mystic fumes? Perhaps a vision of celestial peace; a dream of hopes fulfilled; a taste of rapture, such as had not entered into my mind to conceive." But she is not, finally, a seer. She destroys the cigarettes and is only "a little the worse for a dream. . . ." Chopin, however, did not deny her visions or forget those that had come before. She was moved to final exploration of woman's complicity in her self-oppression and her ability to overcome self-repression. A few months after writing this story, Chopin began *The Awakening*.

Students as well can be moved, through a process of emotional experience and intellectual comprehension, toward active and critical reading. The stories that I teach introduce them to the themes of mind split from body; dual and conflicting selves; the entrapment of wifehood, motherhood, and sex; the pull of desire and the pain of passion that will all become central issues in *The Awakening*. Through the creation of these works, Chopin had informed herself of subjects crucial to women and, at times, men. She taught herself to perceive and to portray precisely the fissures in the social fabric of her world; she then proceeded in her novel to tear apart that neat cover cloth. In turn, the stories teach us how to read Chopin's work so that we will be able to do justice to her masterpiece. In my class, we recapitulate Chopin's process of perception and reflection, then tear into the novel without floundering.

The Awakening's Relationship with American Regionalism, Romanticism, Realism, and Naturalism

Peggy Skaggs

In teaching literature, I try on the one hand to teach literary backgrounds and contexts to illuminate individual works of literature and on the other hand to teach individual works to promote an understanding of the literary tradition. Kate Chopin's *The Awakening* seems almost made-to-order for both purposes, since in the small compass of one short but fine work it illustrates virtually all the major American intellectual and literary trends of the nineteenth century. Recent criticism assists these efforts to bring together the two purposes. Numerous articles discuss the influence of other writers on Chopin, and critics have now documented in the novel elements of the important "isms" of American literary tradition—regionalism, romanticism, realism, and naturalism.

First, students need to view *The Awakening* at least partially from the perspective of Chopin's earlier work, which was often in the regional genre. During the last decade of the nineteenth century, when Chopin wrote most of her stories, the local-color story and the regional novel were still in demand. Perhaps for that reason Chopin set many stories in rural Louisiana among the black, French-Creole, and Acadian people there. Some are about young Acadian girls, like Martinette in "A Gentleman of Bayou Têche," and others are about Louisiana blacks, like Aunt Peggy in "Old Aunt Peggy." But still others—including "Athénaïse," "A Vocation and a Voice," and "The Story of an Hour"—treat some of the deepest, most universal aspects of human experience.

Students readily recognize the regionalism in *The Awakening*, since the novel depends on the language, culture, and traditions of the French-Creole people of New Orleans not only for atmosphere but also for central themes and important motivations of characters. But *The Awakening* goes well beyond regionalism. Edna's situation was familiar to women all over the United States, not only to Kentucky-reared Presbyterians who had married Louisiana-French Catholics. The novel portrays a common dilemma, not a narrowly limited one.

To arrive at a more comprehensive understanding of the novel, students may explore its romantic elements, including some that align it with regionalism but others that link it with universal human experiences. Certainly, the exotic regional settings establish a romantic mood. Edna Pontellier spends a languorous summer at a resort among a group of French-Creole people, whose manners, customs, and ways of viewing life differ charmingly from those of the typical student. A colorful parrot is the first speaker in the novel;

and he speaks, not in English as do most of Chopin's readers, but in French. A pair of lovers is always within view, and soft breezes off the Gulf of Mexico caress the characters. Even the music coming from the main building at the resort is an aria from a romantic opera. A young, unattached, charming gentleman pays constant attention to Edna, whose husband's wealth makes it unnecessary for her to bother with mundane chores. Almost half the novel is set here on Grand Isle, and even when the action moves into the city, where most of the characters make their homes, that city is not some degraded urban slum but, rather, the romantic part of New Orleans, with its quaint foreign architecture, customs, and traditions.

Not only is the atmosphere romantic, but so is the plot, with its action arising out of Edna's rebellion against Léonce and her wifely duties, gaining momentum through her affair with Alcée Arobin, and depending throughout on her feelings for Robert Lebrun. And if Edna takes her own life because she is disappointed in love (as a cursory reading leads many students to believe), then the plot ends romantically, as she strips away her clothes (the trappings of society) and plunges into the gulf to become one with the elements, while a crippled bird circles above.

More important evidence of romanticism in *The Awakening* includes the focus on Edna's emotional life, on her essential solitude as she searches unsuccessfully for her ideal love, on her inner being as she attempts to understand herself and her life. In this novel reality is found inside the person more than in that opulent world through which she moves. Through observing such romantic elements, students come to understand better both literary romanticism and this novel.

To further enhance my students' understanding, I share with them the insights of critics who have discussed the novel's romantic themes. For example, Warner Berthoff calls *The Awakening* "a New Orleans version of the familiar transcendentalist fable of the soul's emergence, or 'lapse,' into life" (89). Joan Zlotnick notes that Edna, like other Chopin heroines, is engaged in a "desperate quest for freedom" (3). Elmo Howell observes that "the end of [Chopin's] writing is to dramatize [the] conflict of body and soul" ("Kate Chopin and the Pull of Faith" 108), certainly a romantic theme. Donald A. Ringe finds in *The Awakening* the transcendental concept of the soul's emergence into a new life, thus linking Chopin with Emerson and Whitman ("Romantic Imagery"). Other critics who have noted Whitman's influence include Elizabeth B. House, Lewis Leary ("Kate Chopin and Walt Whitman"), and Gregory L. Candela. And Ottavio Mark Casale discusses the influence of two other romantic writers, comparing Edna to Hawthorne's Hester Prynne and to Melville's "composite figure of Ahab-Bulkington-Ishmail."

But in finding that Edna shares much not only with Hawthorne's romantic

Hester Prynne but also with Henry James's realistic Isabel Archer, Lewis Leary relates Chopin to both pre–Civil War romanticism and the postwar antiromanticism of American realism (Introduction). Indeed, Edna's dilemma seems to result from her unwillingness to confine her existence to playing out the romantic ideal of woman as wife-mother. Edna, in her "desperate quest for freedom," certainly is pursuing a romantic ideal—but, significantly, it is an ideal reserved for men. In the 1890s, for a wife and mother to engage in such a quest suggests the sort of rebellion against romantic ideals that played a prominent role in the development of realism in late nineteenth-century America. In a genuinely romantic novel, Adèle Ratignolle, that perfect "mother-woman" who "was the embodiment of every womanly grace and charm" (4), would not have been the satirically described foil of the central character; she would have been the heroine. Thus, Edna might be viewed as an unromantic woman living at odds with the romantic French-Creole world in which her marriage has placed her. Yet Lisa Gerrard believes that Edna's problems stem from a conflict between her own incurable romanticism and an unromantic world.

Although many readers believe that Edna romantically "awakens" to her personhood and the unlimited possibilities of individuality, Susan J. Rosowski finds a common theme of a realistic "awakening to limitations" in *Madame Bovary*, *Middlemarch*, and *The Awakening* ("Novel" 313). And Otis B. Wheeler declares that, in spite of the Whitmanesque imagery, Edna's story rejects the "romantic dream of the unlimited outward expansion of the self" (128) in favor of a more realistic view of circumscribed possibilities for the individual.

Lewis P. Simpson has written an analysis of Chopin's place in American literature that can contribute significantly to students' understanding of the tradition of American literature, the works of other important American writers, and *The Awakening* in particular (Foreword). Simpson does find romantic elements in the novel, noting parallels between Chopin and Harriet Beecher Stowe. But he points to an essential difference between the two, saying that Chopin (unlike Stowe) "explicitly grasped the nature and consequences of the worship of home and fireside." For students who have studied Stowe, this distinction can be helpful since it suggests both an important element in nineteenth-century American realism and a central truth in *The Awakening* that students sometimes overlook. Simpson aligns Chopin with several giants of American literature—Poe, Melville, Hawthorne, Emerson, Thoreau, and Whitman—in their consciousness "of the vacuous condition following upon the loss of a transcendent meaning for human existence." His essay thus enables students who may be distracted by the novel's surface romanticism to grasp its realistic portrayal of human experience.

By sharing Simpson's insights with my students, I can also direct their attention to several points that Chopin has developed with a subtlety that delights the sophisticated reader but that may mislead less experienced ones. Simpson identifies Chopin as the first American writer to focus on the "sexual identity of the family and the individual in Southern settings" and the first except for Dreiser and Whitman in their different ways to focus on the "vexing and often agonizing relationship between sexual and social identity in American society." Edna, like Huck Finn, is a "self-creating character, one who . . . has a life larger than the confines of the story." According to Simpson, both Twain in *The Mysterious Stranger* and Chopin in *The Awakening* were trying to bring under the control of art their despair over the destruction of the moral interpretation of the world. Except through the persona of Huck Finn, Twain was unable to achieve the detachment of the modern literary artist, but Chopin did achieve such a perspective in her novel, thereby contributing significantly to late nineteenth-century American realism.

During the 1890s, naturalism became an important literary mode in America. The tendency toward naturalism is clear enough in *The Awakening* to enable students to grasp its basic deterministic philosophy, as Edna finds that her life must be lived within socioeconomic and biological boundaries as unyielding as the walls around any penitentiary.

Edna's first act of rebellion—and the beginning of the end of her relationship with Léonce—is her refusal to hold her usual reception day for people important to Léonce's business. Her friendships are expected to contribute to her husband's success. In fact, the romantically charming Creole society dictates that its women find all their satisfactions through wifehood and motherhood. It produces ideal mother-women like Adèle Ratignolle but forbids women to develop any other talents or interests. Although Mlle Reisz creates beautiful music on the piano, everyone despises her. The neighborhood grocer declares that he is thankful she has left the neighborhood; although Reisz is the only genuine musician the Ratignolles know, they never invite her to their musical soirees; even Edna often finds Reisz offensive. No one in the entire novel ever addresses the pianist by her first name, if indeed she even has one. And as soon as Edna begins trying to develop her own ability to paint, Léonce accuses her of neglecting her family. Procreation should be enough creativity to satisfy any woman. Edna's social life and personal development are thus circumscribed by socioeconomic forces as powerful as those that control the life of Dreiser's Sister Carrie, for example, or of any other naturalistic protagonist.

Biology has also helped to determine Edna's destiny. When nature made her female, it established the rhythm of her life, a subtle but important point that Chopin makes by structuring the novel around Adèle's pregnancy.

And the inescapable pain of Adèle's childbirth as well as Edna's overwhelming love for Raoul and Etienne result at least in part from the women's biological nature. Motherhood enchains women in *The Awakening* through a combination of pain and love. Although Edna's sons play only minor roles in the novel, they nevertheless control her destiny and lead her to suicide. Many students dismiss Edna's declaration that she is taking her life because of her love for Raoul and Etienne, because they feel that she has exhibited little warmth toward the boys throughout the story. But such judgmental attitudes tend to fade when students understand Edna's social milieu and the naturalism in the novel.

Among the critics who have enlarged my awareness of naturalism in the novel and to whom I often refer students who wish to write on this topic are Emily Toth, Per Seyersted, Barbara Culver Van Sittert, and Harry Scott Butler. Toth compares and contrasts *The Awakening* and *Sister Carrie* ("Timely and Timeless"). Seyersted believes that Chopin concentrates on biological aspects of woman's situation, whereas Dreiser, Norris, Garland, and Crane all concentrate on socioeconomic forces. Van Sittert observes both kinds of determinism at work in Chopin's novel. And Butler notes Chopin's ambivalence in viewing human sexuality at times as a naturalist but at other times as a romantic-transcendentalist. This ambivalence, Butler believes, reflects Chopin's responsiveness to nineteenth-century intellectual currents.

What Butler says about Chopin's treatment of human sexuality may be expanded to apply to other aspects of *The Awakening*. This novel can be viewed as both a product and a climax of nineteenth-century American literary tendencies. Regionalism and romanticism predominated in the earlier nineteenth century—and in the setting and plot of *The Awakening*. Romanticism yielded after the Civil War to an antiromantic impulse that resulted in the psychological and social realism of James, Howells, and Twain; similarly, the romantic setting and plot of *The Awakening* become antiromantic as they stifle Edna and prevent her expansion as a person. Before the turn of the century, naturalism was emerging with its focus on biological and socioeconomic determinism; and Edna's tragedy is that she yearns to live fully, to fly high above tradition and all limitations to her personhood —yet finds her flight blocked at every turn by biological and social limitations.

Jerome Klinkowitz in *The Practice of Fiction in America* reconciles the various perspectives on Chopin's place in the tradition, saying:

> Chopin's development as a writer . . . reflects in microcosm the larger movement in American literature from romanticism and local color to realism and naturalism. . . . Chopin's stories and novels reflect . . . clearly the general trend in American literature of that era. Her theme

is a romantic imaginative awakening; the catalyst for it is drawn from the materials of local color; and her method of following the action is naturalistic. (39–40)

The different critical views of Chopin's fiction may not be as contradictory as they seem, and teachers can use them all in helping students to appreciate America's literary history and to understand that a genuine artist like Kate Chopin transcends and expands her received tradition in creating a fine novel like *The Awakening*.

COURSE CONTEXTS

The *Awakening* in a Course on Women in Literature

Barbara C. Ewell

The Awakening may be the quintessential text for a course in women's studies. Greeted with polite dismay at its publication in 1899, revived and hailed as a lost classic sixty years later on the crest of the most recent women's movement, the novel offers a paradigmatic tale of a woman's abortive struggle toward selfhood in an oppressive, uncomprehending society. Who could ask for a more rousing exemplar of the fate of women who seek personal integrity in a world that reduces womanhood to role-playing? Or, for that matter, of the fate of women writers who dare to reveal the "life behind the mask" of conventional propriety? The stories of Edna and her author are the real stuff of consciousness-raising. And consequently, often without trying, sometimes even actively resisting, I have found *The Awakening* emerging as a touchstone if not the resonant centerpiece of my course on women in literature.

The centrality of *The Awakening* has been consistent over ten years of teaching the course, primarily in the South: to young sophisticates of a women's college, to the more provincial young people of a rural state university, or, most recently, to the professional adult students of a liberal arts college in a major city. Variations of student responses do occur, of course, but a common identification with the southern landscapes hardly accounts for students' consistent and riveted fascination with Chopin's novel.

These southern, and thus relatively conservative, contexts have also shaped my own rather traditional approach to the course itself. Women in Literature, as I teach it, is an intensive study of novels, short stories, poems, and occasionally plays by women. Partly in deference to student interest and, until recently, to the dearth of handy texts, the bias has been toward nineteenth- and twentieth-century British and American writers. Of late, *The Norton Anthology of Literature by Women* and my own expanded reading have encouraged the inclusion of many earlier and more international works, though I persist in avoiding translations. My usual practice is to assign one or two nineteenth-century novels—Austen's *Pride and Prejudice*, a Brontë novel (*Jane Eyre* or *Villette* work well), a selection from Wollstonecraft; then Chopin's *The Awakening*, often preceded by regional short stories by Jewett, Chopin, and Freeman; sometimes Wharton's *The House of Mirth*, Woolf's *Room of One's Own* and *To the Lighthouse* or *Orlando*, Hurston's *Their Eyes Were Watching God*, Plath's *The Bell Jar* (less and less), a Lessing novel (*The Golden Notebook* or *Memoirs of a Survivor*); sometimes Welty's *Delta Wedding* or Rhys's *Wide Sargasso Sea* (excellent with *Jane Eyre*), Angelou's *I Know Why the Caged Bird Sings*, Morrison's *Sula* or *The Bluest Eye*; and from time to time, Atwood's *Surfacing*, Ellen Douglas's *A Lifetime Burning*, Brown's *Rubyfruit Jungle*, Jong's *Fear of Flying*, Rebecca Hill's *Blue Rise*, or some other contemporary work that has piqued my—or other reviewers'—interest. In addition to the six to eight novels finally chosen, we often read selections from a short-fiction or drama anthology and always spend several weeks with an anthology of poetry.

My aims in this course are perhaps apparent from the reading list—to expose students to some of the great British and American works by women that focus on female concerns: marrying, dealing with social roles, discovering sexuality, developing selfhood. I emphasize the "other" perspective that women have on their lives, the way stereotypes disintegrate when one sees this other point of view, and the peculiar constraints women must face and resolve. These thematic approaches seem appropriate in a course frequently elected by non–literature majors, but the texts themselves are studied principally as aesthetic rather than cultural documents.

The susceptibility of *The Awakening* to the approaches of women's studies is clear even in the biographical introduction with which I try to begin any new text. These life sketches, which are pointedly not going to be "on the test," encourage students to appreciate not only the very human creators of these wonderful textures and narratives but also—I hope—the pleasures of knowing some things solely for their own sake. Chopin's biography, which I know better than most other biographies of women writers, is an especially good instance of a writer whose life and fiction interact in oblique, but perhaps typically female, ways. The fairly conventional patterns of her youth in St. Louis and adulthood in New Orleans and in the Cane River country, for example, are broken by her widowhood in midlife and the writing career that followed. Chopin's fictional exploitation of these settings is fairly obvious, but students are also always intrigued by the contradictions of her apparently happy marriage to Oscar and Edna's less fortunate relationship with Léonce, factors that underline the inventive dimensions of art. The scandalized reaction to *The Awakening* is also instructive, focusing for students the differing historical realities of the novel and preparing them better for the social inhibitions that later limit Edna's alternatives. Finally, Chopin's response to the rejection of her work and the oblivion of the novel after her death are poignant examples of the power of the critical industry to suppress or neglect whatever voices that unsettle its complacent self-conceptions. That particular lesson usually has considerable impact.

Having thus established some biographical context for the novel, I generally turn to the students to discover what their initial impressions of and reactions to the novel have been. I am rarely disappointed. *The Awakening* has always seemed to me easy to teach precisely because it does elicit such various—often passionate—responses. It is difficult, I think, not to read Edna's story without some response: outrage, disgust, pity, wonder, terror. All these good old Aristotelian cathartic emotions are particularly elicited by the ending: why did Edna kill herself? what does it mean that she did? More often than not in this initial discussion, students bring up most of what I consider the significant elements of an interpretation—Edna's relations with others, men and women; her role as mother and wife; her notions of self and sexuality; the role of setting—and thus set the stage for my eventual comments. But the students' engagement is itself a liberating classroom experience. Many who had never ventured any opinion suddenly become vociferous defenders—or protesters—of Edna's fate. And frequently, their involvement with this text frees them to express themselves on other texts as well. Of course, that kind of engagement is central to a women's studies class, which, in the best traditions of liberal education, proposes to examine the moral and personal relevance of historical texts.

The pertinence of Edna's dilemma—how to be an individual in a society that insists she play specific roles—is certainly a key to its fascination since it uniquely engages both younger students (who are much involved in articulating their selves) and older students (who are well aware of the compromising forces of social reality). But in presenting the terms of that dilemma, Chopin exposes a number of specifically female concerns, issues that are inevitably the focus of women's studies: the nature of female sexuality, the conventional opposition of romance and passion, the moral isolation of women in patriarchal systems, the role of female friendship, the importance of the body and the physical world to self-realization, the ambivalence toward children and childbearing. One good approach to many of these matters—which also helps to define Edna's dilemma and thus to interpret the novel's disturbing ending—is a close scrutiny of chapter 6, the first and most deliberate of Chopin's editorial intrusions. Not only does the chapter articulate the nature of Mrs. Pontellier's crisis—"to realize her position in the universe as a human being, and to recognize her relations as an individual to the world within and about her"—but it also epitomizes the features of that crisis. The "two contradictory impulses," for example, that Edna obeys in first refusing and then following Robert to the beach underline the spontaneity of her awakening; a corresponding ambivalence is reflected in the image of the "certain light" that both shows the way and then forbids it. Edna's irrational and moody behavior is thus shown to be a function of deep and deeply uncomprehended recognitions about her "position in the universe as a human being." While these observations help to explain Edna's erratic and impulsive, almost involuntary quest, Chopin also insists on the unsettling uniqueness of Edna's awareness—"a ponderous weight of wisdom to descend upon the soul of a young woman of twenty-eight." This characteristically wry irony is immediately followed by the narrator's sympathetic regard for anyone expecting to survive such interior chaos. Edna's moral isolation as a woman—not to mention as a Protestant and a Kentuckian in this Catholic Creole society—is thus made a prominent and ominous element of her self-awakening. The sensuality that for women is often a path to awareness is also beautifully evoked here, coupled with its major symbol, the sea. A lyric refrain personifies the sea as lover, whose initial invitation to solitude and reflection conceals depths that Edna has only begun to plumb. A comparison of the initial version with the altered repetition in the final pages offers a dramatic instance of the subtleties of Chopin's style even as it underlines the real possibilities of choice that do remain for Edna, if only for the short space of the novel.

Although all these seminal elements can be made the focus of critical discussion, the sensuality of the passage seems to me particularly useful in launching an examination of the overall role of setting—especially of the sea. The alternation between Grand Isle and New Orleans clarifies the conflicts Edna experiences between the sensuous and physical realities that awaken her self and the strict social conventions that have previously defined her. A good place to focus on the specific role of the sea is Edna's learning to swim. Paula A. Treichler has a fine analysis of the ambiguity of the language in this passage and its relevance to female perceptions of power, but most students quickly grasp there the metaphoric power of Edna's struggles with the sea and the prescient vision of death her conquest of its forces eventually yields. The ensuing battle of wills on the gallery with Léonce and his efforts to enforce his sexual desires on her only emphasize Chopin's narrative skills and her ability to mingle event and symbol provocatively.

But it is Edna's own character that most clearly embodies the complexity of women's choices in a world defined by male concerns. The ambivalence, for example, highlighted in chapter 6 recurs both in decisions Edna makes later and in the figure that she poses to the reader. Exploiting that duality in classroom discussions is a good way, I find, to dramatize the difficulty of "objective" judgments or even of moral absolutes. Such an approach calls into question not only the conventional structures of Edna's society but our complicity with them—challenges to our assumptions about reality, which are obviously basic to Chopin's intent in this novel as well as central to the perspectives of women's studies. It is useful at this point, then, to pose to students two possible views of Edna: is she a hopeless, irresponsible romantic, revenging herself on the universe, or a purposeful individual, seeking selfhood, but lacking any real alternatives? Although such formulations oversimplify the matter, they do provide a basis for discussion and a means of understanding both Edna's personal dilemma and ours in attempting to comprehend its significance. The evidence for either perspective is persuasive; witness the available criticism of the novel. Edna's natural sensuality, for example, her "sensuous susceptibility to beauty," is everywhere: from her admiration of Adèle to her awareness of her body, especially at Chênière Caminada, to her recurrent eating and sleeping and dreaming in the novel. While this affinity for the physical implies very female concerns, if not some substantiality in her self-awakening, evidence for her romanticism is also powerful: her adolescent fantasies about unattainable men, her prosaic and thus "real" marriage to Léonce, and her general equation of "life's delirium" with the desirable and the ephemeral and of reality with the mechanical and endless. At the same time, Edna declares her need for self-determination and quite consistently abandons Léonce's house and money in her effort to cast "aside that fictitious self which we assume like a garment with which to appear before the world" (19). In contrast, she does not think very much or very clearly about her predicament; Adèle calls her an unthinking child, and even en route to her suicide she appears to have no definite insight or plan.

But the central ambivalence in Edna and the critical issue for nineteenth-century women focuses on her understanding of love and passion. The crucial passage here is another (though less intrusive than the first) editorial chapter, chapter 28, recounting Edna's response to Arobin's passionate embraces. Like most nineteenth-century women, for whom sexual passion was deemed at least unladylike if not downright vitiating, Edna had learned as a child to confuse sexual passion with romance. In Arobin's purely physical attractions, the separateness of these experiences is revealed. The mist is "lifted from her eyes, enabling her to look upon and comprehend the significance of life, that monster made up of beauty and brutality." As Edna's illusions about sexual passion begin to fall away, she understands more clearly what she wants, not from Arobin, but from Robert—a romantic, physical relationship, the consummation of body and soul, self and other. Her romantic, adolescent dreams of fulfillment—"life's delirium"—now disclose their physical component, sexual desire. But what Edna has yet to understand is that physical passion, real contact with real people, has concrete consequences. The complications of that insight are the crux, not only of Edna's dilemma, but, as Chopin saw, of the contemporary woman, attempting to forge a realistic, implicitly modern perspective on the dissolving paradigms of Victorian culture. This crisis of sexual identity, posed so prominently and disturbingly in the life of a woman, is a central issue of the age, forming a primary if often unacknowledged undercurrent of realist fiction in Chopin's time. But Chopin's explicitly feminine perspective challenges those paradigms more profoundly and thus more threateningly than any vision before that of the modernists themselves.

This female perspective is similarly apparent in Chopin's treatment of Edna's women friends. Adèle Ratignolle and Mlle Reisz are Edna's primary confidantes and models; she admires and loves them both and values their counsel. At the same time, Chopin exposes their insufficiency as models and embodies in them aspects of Edna's basic conflict between her romantic desires and her longing for self-sufficiency. Adèle's romantic beauty, her absorption in the role of "mother-woman" are attractively conventional, but Edna cannot sacrifice "the essential" for the sake of such blissful immersion in others' needs. Similarly, Mlle Reisz possesses the courageous soul of independence—the essential self Edna cherishes—but Edna cannot bear the pianist's lonely solitude or the lack of romance in her life. Chopin creates in these two women rich models of the limited alternatives late nineteenth-century America offered women. The different responses they elicit from that society (as well as from Edna)—its benevolent protectiveness toward Adèle or its condescending tolerance of Mlle Reisz—are instructive. A significant insight of women's studies has been the power of roles—of social structures—to determine personal choices, complicating the search for self (a sympathetic quest, particularly for adolescents), especially a search as undirected and unhappy as Edna's.

But it is Edna's final awakening that centers this novel in a course about women. For the real complication of sexual identity and selfhood for women remains the responsibility for children. Edna's climactic recognition begins with her unexpected meeting with Robert at Catiche's garden café and their return to the "pigeon house" where they finally confess their love (36). But Edna's response to Robert's "mad" dreams of divorce is a dramatic measure of how far even an errant soul like Edna's can go toward insight and freedom. No one can any longer set her free, she explains to a stunned Robert: "I give myself where I choose." But Chopin brilliantly interrupts any reply

Robert might offer with a knock on the door and Adèle's request for her friend's presence at her imminent labor and delivery. Not only does Edna's departure reveal the priority of her friendship with Adèle over her tryst with Robert, but that seemingly chance intrusion on their imminent sexual encounter is also a summons to recognition. Precisely as Edna is about to realize "life's delirium"—the merging of passion and romance with Robert —its results, especially before effective and widespread birth control, are vividly recalled to her: children. That relation of passion and children, which for women remains the chief issue of sexuality, is more fully expounded in Edna's conversation with Dr. Mandelet, who understands "intuitively" the sources of Edna's dismay (38). Romance is an illusion, and, deliberately confused with passion for young Victorian girls, it becomes "a decoy to secure mothers for the race"; but the children that result from that illusory confusion are real responsibilities, whose rights even Edna cannot ignore or "trample on." To awaken thus, as she must, to these bitter facts of life is to incur responsibility for one's choices, even ignorant choices; it is to recognize one's position in the universe as a responsible individual and to relinquish the romantic dream of union with others—the very dream that had led to that self-recognition—at the very moment when selfhood had made communion really possible. And though Edna tries to defer this unpleasant recognition, Robert's pusillanimous note—"I love you. Good-by—because I love you" (38)—which confirms his own inability to deal with real consequences, leaves her no choice.

But Edna's return to Grand Isle is as ambivalent as her spiritual path. I find it a lively exercise to review with students her final deliberations, especially her focus on her children, whom she will not allow "to drag her into the soul's slavery" but who are still the only ones that "matter" (39). The wonderfully complex tone of that final passage, with its insistence on Edna's despair and its symbolic bird with a broken wing, coupled with the deeply attractive imagery of birth and the sensuous pleasure of the sea, only heightens the ambivalence of Edna's plight. But it also provides excellent material for either side of the debate that, we hope, is now raging in the classroom about whether Edna's deed is justifiable or even defensible. Appropriately, too, children become the key element in such a discussion— as children have always been in the seemingly endless—if not timeless— debate about the nature and place of women in human being.

If the classes on *The Awakening* have gone well, many inhibitions are dissipating both in the classroom and in the informal journals that I have found a vital writing component of a women and literature course. When students have to articulate their thoughts and feelings about texts and discussions—even, perhaps especially, negative ones—classroom participation is dramatically improved, in both quality and quantity. Moreover, rewarding students for at least trying to see the moral and political as well as intellectual pertinence of these texts to their lives reinforces the sense of literary engagement that I want to encourage. Indeed, the many unresolvable and emotionally confusing issues raised in such a class almost require this expressive outlet. But the other well-known function of journal writing is its usefulness in generating formal papers. While I generally do not assign research papers in this course, I do ask for at least two short essays. And *The Awakening*, which evokes such strong responses, also provides very manageable material for analysis, especially for a first paper, when student insecurities loom large. Assignments on the role of setting, the use of female models or foils, image patterns (birds, the sea, eating and sleeping), and the function of minor characters have all proved fairly successful. Broader topics are also possible, such as the conflicts of women and society, the ambivalences of childbearing, the portrayal of men, the alienation of the outsider, female friendships, the value of suicide, or the nature of freedom or of female sexuality.

Though, as I have tried to suggest, *The Awakening* broaches many issues central to the perspectives of women's studies, the crucial value of the novel in a classroom remains for me its ability to generate excitement and real involvement with a text. Throughout my years of teaching the novel, those responses have varied, but they remain intense. Younger, less sophisticated students, for example, who still believe the world is their liberated oyster, seem more intransigent toward Edna's suicide (why didn't she just move away? elope with Robert? get a job?) and less forgiving of her abandonment of her children, who, for these students, are still part of a misty, happy future. To such students, Chopin can teach tolerance and empathy. Many black women, especially older ones, who have a long heritage of overcoming vastly greater obstacles than Edna's, are frankly disgusted with her cowardice (white ladies just don't know what real trouble is!). Chopin's gift to them can be renewed confidence in their own powers and traditions. Edna's problems perhaps find greatest understanding among other older, middle-class women, who have known the bittersweet burdens of children and who recognize the silent, choking restrictions of bourgeois respectability. But most students, while they may not agree with Edna or may even find her weak and foolish, as perhaps Chopin's ironic distances suggest she is, rarely fail to see the poignance of her dilemma. They recognize, as Chopin obviously intended us to, that weak and confused as Edna may be, her conflict with an uncomprehending society has a piercing and resonant reality. And while even Chopin withholds her judgment on its outcome, none of us is rendered exempt from evaluating its causes or its complex components of sex, freedom, and the demands of society and selfhood. Such engagement, of course, is the manifest goal of women's studies and, indeed, of all effective learning and teaching.

The Awakening in an
Introductory Literature Course

Ann R. Morris and Margaret M. Dunn

Probably no other course in literature attempts to do as much as an introductory course for first-year students. Ideally it should introduce literary terminology, give some historical perspective, present the three major genres, teach analysis, and offer instruction in research writing. Inevitably, however, some compromise must be reached between the ideal and the possible, and the literary research paper is thus often eliminated as an assignment or given little class time and relegated to a "due date" on a syllabus. Yet the assignment is more valuable to students than any other, forcing them to analyze a literary work, survey critical materials, and hone the term-paper skills that they will need throughout their college careers. Addressing this dilemma, we based our solution on *The Awakening*—a novel that. as the focus of an introductory unit, permits us to teach both in-depth analysis and the mechanics of literary research writing without taking too much time or sacrificing other necessary aspects of an introductory course in literature.

The Introductory Unit

We base an early three-week research-paper unit on the novel (usually beginning with the third week in a thirteen-week semester), using as our text the Norton Critical Edition, edited by Margaret Culley. During the first week, students read and discuss the novel and write a short paper (approximately 500 words) on an aspect of the book that particularly interests them. This paper and the critical materials in the Norton text that they read and discuss during the second week help them decide on a focus for the short research paper (4 to 6 pages) that they write during the third week. For this paper they need use only three or more sources in the Norton. In a short period of time this "casebook" approach permits classroom concentration in three areas: analysis of a longer fiction, an introduction to critical materials, and instruction in the mechanics of research writing.

The First Week: Analysis

Before the first week of this unit, students are given a list of literary terms and definitions along with several study questions on *The Awakening*. The literary terms include *symbol, allusion, point of view, irony,* and the like. Many students already have at least some familiarity with these terms, but the list helps students to apply them when reading the novel. The study questions prompt students to make connections. For example, we might ask whether it is incongruous that, considering the novel's title, Edna seems to spend a great deal of time sleeping. Or we might ask what would be gained or lost if Edna herself told the story. We talk just a few minutes about the terms and questions, and then the students begin their reading.

Because of its manageable length, many students finish reading the novel before classroom instruction begins; most students, even slow readers, can finish it by the middle of the first week. Immediately, then, students can be led into a discussion using basic literary terminology from the list distributed to them. They quickly see that setting is more than just a vaguely defined background for the story. The students usually enjoy the exotic flavor of the old New Orleans locale, but they recognize that Edna's Presbyterian background alienates her from upper-class Creoles, who are frank about pregnancy and casual about flirtations. Since the novel contains no hysterical outbursts, no steamily explicit trysts, no violent personal encounters, the plot seems to students very simple and straightforward at first, and the tone understated, even placid. To stimulate discussion about this, we show the film of *The Awakening* from Children's Television International. Short enough (15 min.) to permit both viewing and discussion during one class period, the film includes, along with shots of Edna learning to swim and walking to her death in the sea, brief episodes with major characters. For example, Edna quarrels with Léonce, discusses with Adèle the vast differences between them, and talks with Robert on the beach shortly before he leaves her. Though not overplayed, these encounters emphasize the conflicts in Edna's life. Warming to the idea that such conflicts indeed exist in abundance, few students remain unmoved by the smouldering intensity of emotions that play beneath well-bred surfaces. Whether or not they condone Edna's actions, or Léonce's, or Arobin's, students begin to question the social and psychological factors that make the characters what they are.

The symbolism in the novel is particularly rewarding to teach. From the opening image of a caged parrot speaking of departure in a language "which nobody understood" (1) to the closing image of "a bird with a broken wing . . . circling disabled down" to its watery grave (39), the symbolism of caged and free-flying birds provokes discussion and aids understanding. The symbolic contrasts of waking and sleeping, city mansion and coastal cottage, and the ebb and flow of the sea are equally provocative; students themselves point out the significance of Edna's "dual life—that outward existence which conforms, the inward life which questions" (6). Because they can grasp these symbolic concepts easily, students question others that are less accessible: the inseparable young lovers often juxtaposed with the woman in black who is "telling her beads" (1–7), Edna's longing for the "sad-eyed" cavalry officer

(7, 39), and the description of Edna as "Venus rising from the foam" (39). Instead of being overwhelmed by complexity, the students are intrigued by their developing insights.

At the end of this first week, students turn in a short paper on some aspect of the novel that interests them, such as local color, symbolism, Adèle Ratignolle and Mlle Reisz as character foils, the status of women in Creole society, the credibility of Edna's reactions to her situation, the appropriateness of the title. This paper helps them define a focus and synthesize what they have learned in class discussions.

The Second Week: Using Critical Materials

The critical material that follows the novel in the Norton text is assigned for the second week. It is short enough that students have no difficulty finishing it early in the week or before. Classroom discussions are seldom subdued. The "Contexts" section (115–40) prompts formerly recalcitrant students to sympathize with Edna's predicament. Culley's, Tillett's, and Gilman's articles, especially, provoke outrage over the situation of women at that time. For many students, Dorothy Dix's statement that "no amount of gilding ever made a cage attractive to the poor wretch within" encapsulates the theme of the novel (132). Equally provocative are the contemporary reviews of the novel (145–59). Students are quick to note that given the historical context, the novel's early reception ("sick," "morbid," "mad," "sex fiction," "gilded dirt," "vulgar") is not surprising. More important, these materials bring a dawning awareness of the revolutionary aspect of art and often arouse a desire to study literary history.

The material in "Essays in Criticism" (160–228) offers further perspectives both on the novel itself and on just exactly what it is that one does when writing about literature: Pollard questions the story's credibility (160–62); Rankin ties Chopin's life to her art (163–65); Eble analyzes Chopin's style (165–70); others discuss the novel's Creole aspects, its theme, realism, local color, the ending, "the woman question," its imagery and symbolism, the love-death dichotomy. Unlike the background information that came before, these essays demonstrate various ways of approaching a literary work. Students see that a plot synopsis is not critical writing, that these essays include only that material from the novel that is relevant to a central idea. In addition, the essays expose students to new concepts that they might miss if they were doing their own library research. For example, although many students have studied at least some Freud, few have encountered psychoanalytic criticism, as in Cynthia Griffin Wolff's "Thanatos and Eros" (206–18). Most are intrigued by Wolff's application of Freudian theory to the novel and, in the subsequent essay, by Suzanne Wolkenfeld's analogy of Edna's story to that of the well-known fairy tale "The Sleeping Beauty." Others are more interested in judging Edna's actions, particularly her suicide, which they often see as a defeat or a "cop-out" rather than an act of triumph or self-affirmation. The critical essays by Wolkenfeld and Margaret Culley show them that other readers have also questioned Edna's final act and even whether or not Chopin approves of her heroine.

By now the students feel informed enough to agree or disagree with various critical essays in the text, and they revise the first week's paper in the light of their own developing thoughts. A few find that they must rewrite almost totally, and most see the need for significant revision. This process helps them decide finally on their approaches to the novel, and at the end of this second week they turn in a brief outline of their research papers with a bibliography listing the in-text sources that they will cite.

The Third Week: Research Writing

Students are given a handout containing one model paragraph about the novel and three ten-line quotations from in-text essays or reviews, chosen for possible inclusion in the model paragraph. Their instructions are to rewrite the model paragraph as follows: (1) include one indented quotation and two short quotations, introducing and integrating them effectively and using the ellipsis at least once; (2) include parenthetical author or page citations for each quotation; (3) list the three sources in correct bibliographic form on a short "Works Cited" page. The smooth introduction and integration of sources is invariably a new and troublesome technique. For practical examples, students are directed to observe the way in which authors of the in-text critical essays cite their sources. In class, the students evaluate one another's techniques when we use an opaque projector to show their re-written model paragraphs on a screen. Very quickly, most students learn to use sophisticated research writing techniques correctly. The opaque projector also permits in-class perusal of students' drafts. Because students are familiar with the material, they can comment on the coherence and effectiveness of one another's writing—in effect using peer tutoring in an open forum.

At the end of this third week, they turn in their short research papers. Because analysis of the literary work has been taught rather than assumed and because emphasis has been on the process and techniques of research writing rather than on length, the quality of student papers is generally good. Later in the semester we assign a longer library research paper that students write independently; thus this short paper is excellent preparation. Even without such a subsequent assignment, however, this exercise in supervised research writing is of proven worth to students. Because they have had to call on their powers of analysis and synthesis throughout the process, they are now prepared to approach other literary works in the same way.

Why Chopin's Novel and Not Another?

Critical editions of other novels are easily available for use in an introductory unit of this sort, but we have not found one that works as well as *The Awakening*. Longer novels are difficult to treat comprehensively, and works of comparable length are fewer than one might suppose. *Heart of Darkness*, *The Turn of the Screw*, and *The Red Badge of Courage* come to mind, but none of these offers quite the same combination of provocative subject matter and relatively simple symbolism as *The Awakening* does. In addition, students usually find it easy to empathize with Edna, who in "becoming herself" is "daily casting aside that fictitious self which we assume like a garment . . . before the world" (19). Becoming oneself is a problem that students themselves face—unlike the problem of absolute evil faced by Conrad's Kurtz and James's governess or that of war's absurdity faced by Crane's Henry Fleming. Of course, the question inevitably arises whether male students enjoy spending extra time on a work with whose protagonist they may find it difficult to identify. Our answer is a question in return: Does anyone ever ask whether female students find it difficult to identify with Holden Caulfield or Stephen Daedalus?

The Awakening in an
American Literature Survey Course

Thomas Bonner, Jr.

The survey course in American literature has changed dramatically over the years. Syllabi of these courses from the beginning years through the present offer as perceptive an account of the developments in American literature as some of the most authoritative published studies, for every time the course is taught, questions of inclusion, exclusion, emphasis, and deemphasis occur.

Much has happened since Sidney Smith in the January 1820 *Edinburgh Review* asked rhetorically, "In the four quarters of the globe, who reads an American book?" The acceptance and growth of American literature as an academic discipline and a literary tradition began slowly and experienced a number of fits and rushes. Before 1850, Amherst College and Middlebury College were the only institutions offering courses in American literature. John Seely Hart's *Manual* became the first college textbook for this subject in 1873. John Macy's *Spirit of American Literature* in 1908 called for less emphasis on the traditional New England poets and more on writers from other regions of the country. As a result of this effort and others, Mark Twain's works entered the canon. By 1920 the Modern Language Association approved the establishment of the American literature group. The New Criticism of the 1930s, under the leadership of Cleanth Brooks, shifted attention from extratextual aspects like authorial biography and historical context to the text itself. Anthologies of American literature began to reflect the effects of these changes in subsequent decades (Leary, *American Literature* 3–10).

By the 1980s vast social changes spurred scholars like Paul Lauter to begin a project called Reconstructing American Literature, a systematic process of locating, drawing attention to, and publishing literary works by women and minority ethnic authors, many of whom had been previously overlooked for nonliterary reasons. American literature is, as Lewis Leary has observed, a living literature (*American Literature* vii), with new authors being published, some books being elevated to high critical status, others being lowered from that status, and still others being rediscovered. Kate Chopin's status in American letters is still developing, although her reputation has far exceeded her original designation as an obscure local colorist. Hardly an anthology of American literature in print today fails to include her work, and she ranks among the most frequently taught authors in American literature courses at colleges and universities.

If Chopin's position in American literature remains unclear, then there are questions about her placement in a survey course of that literature. Even though her works have been perceived as having value beyond local color, should that original classification be a continuing consideration? Should her fiction be studied in the wider context of southern literature? What part does she fulfill in the mainstream realist tradition? What is the effect of her persistent use of romantic elements? And how does one address the feminist character of her works? The short stories in anthologies frequently settle some of the questions. For example, "Désirée's Baby" is nearly always included in a local-color and southern context. "The Storm" borders on mainstream realism. And "Wiser than a God," "A Pair of Silk Stockings," and "The Story of an Hour" reflect feminist themes. Unlike these stories (whose placement in an anthology often determines approach), *The Awakening* suggests significantly wider possibilities for teaching approaches in a survey course, whether it is taught as a separate volume or as a work included in its entirety in an anthology.

The Awakening provocatively offers answers to all the questions posed about Chopin's place in the American literary tradition. The criticism provides ample evidence of the diversity of the novel. As a local-color novel its settings are essential to development in structure and theme. As a southern novel, it offers a contrast in addressing the myth of the chaste heroine. As a novel of realism, *The Awakening* is linked closely with *Madame Bovary* in its treatment of adultery. As a romantic novel, it presents a theme of self-discovery using thoroughly consistent patterns of imagery. And as a feminist novel, it emphasizes the particular nature and situation of the heroine with respect to her gender.

The versatility of the novel in a survey course is quickly apparent. Most surveys taught in a two-semester sequence use the Civil War as an approximate dividing point. The emphasis on fiction falls on the symbolic romance in the first course and on realism at the start of the second course. In the latter *The Awakening* effectively demonstrates the changing approaches to fiction and illustrates the tension between the symbolic romance and the novel of realism, especially for students who might not have taken the first sequence.

A good way to introduce students to the novel as a romantic-realistic work is to read from appropriate passages as a prelude to discussion. Edna Pontellier's going to the gulf beach with Robert Lebrun offers an extended text with a romantic orientation (6). Here begins the pattern of light and water imagery that permeates the narrative, and here too is the growing emphasis on the heroine's self-knowledge. In contrast, the sexual realism for which the novel achieved notoriety can be found in several passages, especially the closing paragraph of chapter 27 when Arobin and Edna embrace to kiss and the last two sentences of chapter 31 when Edna becomes "supple to his gentle, seductive entreaties."

In exploring the romantic elements, one might examine the role of vulnerability in a character like Hester Prynne from *The Scarlet Letter*, a celebrated symbolic romance, and in Edna, whose weaknesses are catalysts in her beginning to know herself. The journey motif, used frequently by both Hawthorne and Melville, fulfills a similar function here when Edna goes by boat from Grand Isle to Chênière Caminada (12) and when she takes her walks on the island (1, 7, 10, 16) and in New Orleans (18, 20, 36). Conventional romantic images occur throughout: birds (esp. 27, 39); eyes (14); music, including the "Ah, si tu savais" refrain (9, 14); art (5, 18); night (17); visions of the past (7); and sleeping and waking (13). Chopin also develops the tension between the macro and the micro; students have often been intrigued by the ambivalence of Edna's search for large and open spaces in natural environments (Grand Isle and a suburban garden) and small closed spaces in architectural ones (Mlle Reisz's rooms and the "pigeon house").

Nearly as intense in *The Awakening* is the mimetic impulse, the recording of the experiences of life in a specific time and place. The most immediate way to grasp this element may be to consider the character Edna, since a hallmark of both English and American novels of realism is a well-developed and memorable character portrayed in the round. Since one meets Edna in medias res, her past comes to the reader as she begins to experience and address the conflicts vexing her from summer through winter to early spring. It has sometimes been helpful to pose questions about her life to the students: What do we know about her youth in Kentucky and Mississippi? Was religious faith important in those years and how does it affect her in her maturity? What is her father's nature and how does Edna respond to him? Does the absence of her mother make a difference in her life? What does her relationship with her sister reveal about Edna? How does her marriage occur and what effect do the circumstances have on her attitude toward her husband, Léonce? toward her children? Does age have a role in Edna's situation? The discussion inspired by these queries nearly always leads the students to see Edna's universality and to appreciate Chopin's ability to create a character rooted in the real world.

In considering similar questions about Léonce, Adèle Ratignolle, Mlle Reisz, and Dr. Mandelet, the reader-students continue to rely on Chopin's creative strength in character development as they come to know the characters and their middle-class society. Invariably the minor supporting characters also come into the discussion. As this tapestry of bourgeois life is woven, the relation of place and time to the characters is an important area of inquiry: Are they motivated by their ethnic and geographical environments? Are there communal expectations regarding behavior and achievement? If so, how do these affect their personal growth? How does the past—history, if you will—influence their lives? As students gain a more complete view of the characters and their milieu, they also form a portrait of the community.

Chopin's presentation of marriage and the ritual of courtship not only provides a way to consider *The Awakening* from the perspective of turn-of-the-century realism but also easily engages the serious attention of students. The passage describing Edna's view of her marriage to Léonce (7) illustrates the tension between the ideal and the real that still surrounds this formal establishment of a human relationship. The courtship motif as observed in the lovers occurs throughout the first Grand Isle section of the narrative (7, 8, 12, 15). Edna and Robert are treated almost like icons. This romantic technique stands in high relief to Chopin's direct handling of marriage and presents an opportunity to study her coordination of contrasting approaches.

The most celebrated element of realism in *The Awakening* is Chopin's depiction of sexuality. Edna's having an affair with Arobin without the justification of love does not shock readers today, but it certainly startled those of earlier eras—a fact acknowledged by the critical reception of the novel from its publication through the 1930s. Students are so used to detailed descriptions and depictions of sexual matters and scenes that they often fail to grasp how daring Chopin's prose was considered at the time. Edna's refusal to go to bed with her husband (11) is similarly overlooked and the drama of the moment lost. A comparison of Edna's sexuality with that of the heroines of Crane's *Maggie*, Garland's *Rose of Dutcher's Coolly*, Norris's *McTeague*, and Dreiser's *Sister Carrie* makes Chopin's achievement in sexual realism apparent; Per Seyersted in his biography of Chopin comments that "Maggie, Rose, Trina, and Carrie . . . are all rather sexless compared to Edna" (190–91). Assignments of papers on sexuality in *The Awakening* and one or several of these other novels have brought good results. At a time when a highly refined moral view was the standard in popular and serious fiction, Chopin's detached perspective and nonjudgmental tone in sexual matters made the novel nearly unique.

Although most teachers tend to place *The Awakening* within the major romantic and realistic traditions, it would certainly be appropriate to recognize the novel's local-color elements. John R. May's essay "Local Color in *The Awakening*" shows the pertinence of this tradition to broader readings. Students are sometimes suspicious of the value of local color and tend to view it as provincial and negligible. It helps to remind them that local color is not just a southern literary eccentricity: Victor Hugo in his preface to *Cromwell* emphasized its importance to his use of realism in writing. Gustave Flaubert stressed the importance of observation, documentation, and dialect. Italian literature uses the term *verismo* to describe a work emphasizing provincial life and dialect. The midwesterner Hamlin Garland coined the term *veritism* to indicate the centrality of local color in realism. That Chopin's work from the earliest reviews has been allied with local color argues for at least a minimal discussion of her part in that tradition.

The most sustained sequences of local color occur in the first sixteen chapters of *The Awakening* and trail off in the middle and closing sections. Several questions emerge from these opening chapters to aid in initiating a discussion: What is a Creole? What is the difference between a Creole and an Acadian (Cajun)? How is life as depicted in New Orleans different from that in other cities? And how does Chopin's intense focus on a specific location affect the universality of the narrative? A problem of local color is that it often fails to lead beyond itself; however, Chopin skillfully composes *The Awakening* so that local-color elements possess a critical duality of function. A good example occurs in her treatment of southern and Creole women (4, 7), which gives rise to the feminist themes. Edna states, "I would give up the unessential; I would give my money, I would give my life for my children; but I wouldn't give myself" (16). When she observes Adèle Ratignolle's fastidious attention to her husband's every word, "Edna felt depressed. . . . The little glimpse of domestic harmony which had been offered her, gave her no regret, no longing. It was not a condition of life which fitted her, and she could see in it but an appalling and hopeless ennui" (18). Passages emphasizing the self, personal choice, and assertiveness increase in number with the widening range of Edna's experiences.

These comments and thoughts on a woman's condition complement the work of other nineteenth-century writers pursuing similar themes like Rebecca Harding Davis's *Life in the Iron Mills* (1861) and Charlotte Perkins Gilman's "The Yellow Wallpaper" (1892). For class comparisons both of these works are available in anthologies. Since women's writings during this period are still being discovered, the assignment of research projects that compare *The Awakening* and similar sources (published and unpublished) gives students the excitement of being "on the cutting edge" of an academic discipline and involves them with a pressing social issue.

The Awakening works well in an American literature survey course less for its capacity to define distinctive periods than for its textual power to pose questions about those periods and their relations. Like classical Greek literature, which is deeply rooted in time and place, it easily transcends those composing elements and appeals in form and content to contemporary students and readers.

The Awakening in a
Research and Composition Course
Evelyn Sweet-Hurd

The catalog may state "Research and Composition," but many students (and more than a few instructors) may read "Fear and Trembling 102." Teaching research techniques presents a variety of challenges: instructors may see the school library as too small, students may see the library as too large, and all those involved spend weeks searching for an appropriate topic. When a research class—or an individual student—uses a fine novel as a beginning point, the task can become much more rewarding for both the writer and the reader of the essay. When a novel is assigned to an entire class, the research process can be enhanced by class discussions and lectures. Professors who have used E. L. Doctorow's *Ragtime*, for example, have discovered the ease with which a research and composition course may flow when it focuses on an interesting novel. Kate Chopin's *The Awakening* is another excellent novel that lends itself to student research.

Students, of course, vary in their talents and backgrounds, and school libraries may be huge boons or rather small frustrations. *The Awakening* will work for a research class of various talents, and it may be used for extensive library research or for what I would call "internal" research, which involves a careful reading of the text or a careful study of two related texts.

Students unfamiliar with the time and place of Chopin's work may enjoy some historical or sociological research. For example, in chapter 1, Chopin introduces summer life on Grand Isle. Students in search of a research topic might ask, Where is Grand Isle? What was it like in the 1890s? Chopin mentions the quadroon nurse: What were race relations like in that time and place? A student researcher could study the role of the quadroons or compare Chopin's quadroon nurse with other literary quadroons. How does Chopin's depiction differ from that of, say, Faulkner (in "That Evening Sun," perhaps, or, for the better students, *Absalom, Absalom!*)?

Students may want to explore the sociological ramifications of marriage and family life of the 1890s. Chapter 4 contains Chopin's famous description of the "mother-women," and chapter 7 offers some of Edna's views on marriage and motherhood. Student researchers could find studies of marriage and motherhood in the South in the 1890s to determine whether Chopin's portrait of Mme Ratignolle is a prototype for the then accepted norm. Another possibility would be an examination of key decades in American women's studies to ascertain similarities and differences in attitudes toward marriage and motherhood. Along similar lines would be an investigation of the Creoles (see chapter 4, among others) historically and socially or, more basic, perhaps, a study of New Orleans society in the last decade of the nineteenth century. Such explorations could be as interesting as the available library materials would allow—from newspaper dailies and magazines of that locale and time to sociology and history journals. Instructors may need to remind their students about the wealth of resources available through interlibrary loan.

The character of Mlle Reisz offers another possibility for sociological study. Beginning with chapters 9 and 21, students may explore the roles of the artist in American society of the 1890s or, more particularly, the difficult world of the woman artist of that decade. Researchers may investigate some of the American women who were artists then and ascertain whether their lives in some ways paralleled the life of Chopin's Reisz. The women intellectuals of that period were also causing some concern and consternation; using Dr. Mandelet's comments in chapter 22 as a starting point, students could look into the "woman question" and the intellectual societies that sprang up in that time.

Psychology intrigues many readers, and the opportunities for psychological research abound in *The Awakening*. Students could use only the text to "research" such matters as the character of Léonce. Is he the "best husband in the world" (3)? Do we as readers believe that "his wife . . . was the sole object of his existence" (3)? An interesting study might result from a comparison of Léonce, who looks at his wife "as one looks at a valuable piece of personal property" (1), and Robert Browning's famous Duke of Ferrara in "My Last Duchess." Another interesting comparison would be that of Léonce with the husband in Charlotte Perkins Gilman's short story "The Yellow Wallpaper." (Other intriguing parallels between Gilman's story and *The Awakening* could be followed up as well; for example, a student may investigate the attitudes of society toward the creative woman as depicted in the two works.)

Other internal kinds of researching may include comparative character studies of Edna, Mme Ratignolle, and Mlle Reisz. Edgar Roberts's chapter 10, on writing character studies, helps students get started on such a project. Or students could trace the role of the sea in the novel, the depictions of the children, or, most obvious, the controversy of the ending: Is Edna noble and victorious in her suicide, or weak and defeated? What evidence throughout the text leads to that answer?

Students with serious interests in psychology may want to explore the symbolism of the sea in the novel as it may connect with Freudian or Jungian theories or study the "birthing" motif from a Freudian perspective (the novel begins with Mme Ratignolle pregnant and concludes with that birth, parallel to Edna's own "birthing" of self). Or students may want to read Eric Berne's *Games People Play* and then try to interpret some of the games between Edna and Léonce (esp. in ch. 9, the "I'm not coming to bed, one more cigar" scene), or the game Edna plays in seeking an "opinion" regarding her art (see ch. 18).

Other psychological studies might include an examination of Edna's infatuations (15, 16, among others) and research into the subject of infatuations. The topic that usually draws attention from students is, of course, Edna's suicide. Students intent on that topic might benefit from researching a particular aspect, such as women and suicide in the late nineteenth century in the United States or the incidence of suicide among artists (although the writer would have to establish textually that Edna fits the label *artist*, or perhaps the paper could study would-be artists). More promising might be a paper on female sexuality in the latter nineteenth century, using chapters 27, 28, and 35 as starting points.

A totally different approach would be to use the novel as a beginning of a study of language. A short paper that requires careful examination of only the novel and the *Oxford English Dictionary* would discuss usage unusual to today's readers, such as the meaning of *crash* in "two huge hair pillows covered with crash" or of *draperies* in "the women at once rose and began to shake out their draperies" (7). Or students might consider the characters' use of French, to try to determine what it reveals about their social standing or personality traits. Another linguistic path would be for students to follow Chopin's diction in her depictions of characters: is there any bias? Close attention to diction also affects the reading of Edna's drowning.

Another avenue for research would be the study of Chopin criticism. What was the reception of the novel in its own time? When was there a renewed interest in it? How was Chopin regarded in comparison with other women writers of the day? Instructors should note that the Norton Critical Edition offers a good bit of this information; with that as their text students could use a casebook approach if extensive library research is not available or desired.

I have always preferred to have students discover their own research topics while reading a given novel. This ideal, however, sometimes fails since most students are reading the novel for the first time and many, in a panic to "get a topic," latch onto the first idea that crosses their minds. Because of the usual time constraints, students often do better jobs of reading and researching when they have been offered research topics at the beginning of their study. I have found that some of the ideas I present here can make "Fear and Trembling" into a satisfactory research and writing course for students and teachers of Chopin's fine novel.

The *Awakening* in a Course on Philosophical Ideas in Literature

Jo Ellen Jacobs

Most college-age students are concerned about love and, if they are sensitive, often aware of the difficulties of love in the twentieth century. They may view the causes of these problems naively ("men are too unliberated," "women are too liberated," "sex is too casual," "people get too hung up over sex"), but at least they are interested in the subject. I use this interest to draw them into an exploration of existentialism and twentieth-century literature —in particular, how self-consciousness relates to love and will. The course I teach, entitled Philosophical Ideas in Literature: Love in the Twentieth Century, is suited for advanced English and philosophy majors. During the first class period I warn the literature majors that I will be plundering the works of literature for ideas and hence will not be discussing such traditional topics as narrative, character, or plot. I believe that recognizing the philosophical ideas behind a character's choices gives English majors and philosophy majors an appreciation for each other's disciplines and a new way of looking at literature.

The course begins with four weeks of background reading, which include one literary critic (Colin Wilson), one psychologist (Rollo May), and two philosophers (Plato and Sartre). These works are followed by Dostoyevsky's *Notes from Underground*, Chopin's *The Awakening*, Eliot's "Love Song of J. Alfred Prufrock," Tolstoy's "Kreutzer Sonata," and Rilke's *Notebooks of Malte Laurids Brigge*. I give students all the conceptual background first for two reasons. One is that the concepts overlap in the novels. Second, this arrangement encourages students to compare the novels with one another (using the concepts from the background material), which I find preferable to pairing a novel and a philosophical text.

Using the ideas of Rollo May's *Love and Will* I sketch an interpretation of *The Awakening* that demonstrates the way philosophical ideas serve as a springboard for thinking about fiction. Since I also teach *The Awakening* from the points of view of Plato, Sartre, and Wilson, the interpretation given below is only one approach to the philosophical issues in this novel.

May claims that the twentieth century is an "age of disordered will" (27), whose coming was anticipated by many nineteenth-century artists. A vast number of people today are incapable of mature will or love. The source of the problem, May argues, is general apathy. Bombarded almost hourly with catastrophes, either public or personal, people defend themselves by developing a feelinglessness that, when extreme, is "schizoid."

A person can escape this condition, May suggests, by moving through three stages while developing a mature will. The first step beyond apathy is to allow oneself to wish. "Wish occurs at the level of *awareness* . . . the experiencing of infantile wishes, bodily needs and desires, sexuality and hunger" (262). In becoming open to the surrounding environment—both internally (experiencing sexual arousal or hunger, e.g.) and externally (enjoying the sensation of spring air on the skin or appreciating the color of the ocean)—a person begins the process of renewal, of feeling. Clearly associated with the body, wish also involves fantasy and memory (211). One must allow oneself to dream.

The next level requires that a person learn to will. *"Will is the capacity to organize one's self* so that movement in a certain direction or toward a certain goal may take place. *Wish is the imaginative playing with the possibility* of some act or state occurring" (218). A person's situation in the world can no longer be solipsistic. When one wills, one responds to the world, one realizes one's place in the world (233). Instead of merely delighting in the sensual experience of the environment, as happens at the wish level, one begins to sense the possibility of "relatedness" with other persons, of being able to "do something about these wishes" (266). Will aims at the future: "Both meanings—simple future, something will happen; and personal resolve, [one] will make it happen—are present in varying degrees in each statement of intentionality" (243). This stage requires self-consciousness—the very element that is missing from the wish stage. Furthermore, "this is the dimension on which human creativity emerges. The human being does not stop with the naive delight, but he paints a picture, or he writes a poem, which he hopes will communicate something of this experience to his fellowmen" (267).

The most mature form of intentionality is decision. This level requires courage. The self-consciousness of will must become action. A person must actively accept responsibility, must become "responsive to and responsible for the significant other-persons who are important to one's self in the realizing of the long-term goals" (267).

It is here the subject of love comes in. In chapter 11, "The Relation of Love and Will," May discusses two types of immature love. Will can block love, as when the "dried-up Victorian man" insists that "it's Saturday night, time to have sex." But, just as certainly, love that does not incorporate will is insipid. May offers the example of "hippie" love. This type of love—perhaps infatuation is more accurate—is spontaneous and honest; however, it fails to discriminate (278). Based on wish without will, it is dissatisfying because it is unenduring. At the level of wish one can be open to sexual excitement, but in order to love one must self-consciously commit oneself at the level of will. For lack of self-consciousness, or lack of courage, some people cannot love, cannot get beyond the wish level.

Chopin's work makes May's ideas more understandable, and May's ideas open a new way to see Chopin's work. Edna Pontellier shares a feelinglessness with her twentieth-century sisters and brothers. She refuses to enter into the life that has been assigned her, but she begins to feel and to wish. This gradual change is her awakening. Swimming, eating, and lying in a strange bed all take on a new meaning. She begins "seeing with different eyes" (15). "There were days when she was very happy without knowing why . . . when her whole being seemed to be one with the sunlight, the color, the odors, the luxuriant warmth of some perfect Southern day. . . . And she found it good to dream and to be alone and unmolested" (19). With the self-absorption characteristic of wish, she begins to remember her childhood and dream of her adolescent crushes (7). And she experiences "the first-felt throbbings of desire" (10), recognizing "anew the symptoms of infatuation which she felt incipiently as a child" (15). Chopin makes the reader recognize what a positive step Edna has taken in beginning to wish, in beginning to feel.

But Edna fails to realize her wishes through a mature creative act of will. Chopin describes her as "blindly following whatever impulse moved her, as if she had placed herself in alien hands for direction, and freed her soul of responsibility"; she "felt as if she were being borne away from some anchorage which had held her fast, whose chains had been loosening—had snapped . . . leaving her free to drift whithersoever she chose to set her sails" (12). If only she could choose a course, but "the future was a mystery which she never attempted to penetrate" (15). "She began to do as she liked and to feel as she liked . . . lending herself to any passing caprice" (19). "She wanted something to happen—something, anything; she did not know what" (25). Yet she cannot will any future.

This lack of will demonstrates itself in her attitude toward her children. "She was fond of her children in an uneven, impulsive way," and when they are gone, "their absence was a sort of relief, though she did not admit this, even to herself. It seemed to free her of a responsibility which she had blindly assumed and for which Fate had not fitted her" (7).

Nor can she will to paint. The starts and stops of her painting reveal an inability to attend to the one act that might have helped her grow. As she begins to consider the possibility of painting seriously, she shows her work to Adèle, seeking, like a bored child, "the words and praise and encouragement that would help her to put heart into her venture" (18). Later, in an important scene in Mlle Reisz's apartment, Edna announces that she is becoming an artist. Mlle Reisz, a true artist, responds: "Ah! an artist! You have pretensions, Madame." Edna may wish to be an artist, but Mlle Reisz correctly questions Edna's will to be an artist: "The artist must possess the courageous soul" (21). Lacking that courage and "devoid of ambition," Edna works at her painting, "striving not toward accomplishment" but drawing "satisfaction from the work itself" (25). It is a beautiful sight to see a child caught up in the pleasures of the moment, without ambition or direction, but a person in this state is not an artist, not someone who must work through moments of despair and strive toward a goal. As Mlle Reisz puts it: "The bird that would soar above the level plain of tradition and prejudice must have strong wings. It is a sad spectacle to see the weaklings bruised, exhausted, fluttering back to earth." But later when Edna is asked, "Whither would you soar?" she can only respond, "I'm not thinking of any extraordinary flights. I only half comprehend [Mlle Reisz]" (27).

Will is also missing in her infatuation with Robert. When Edna returns to New Orleans in the fall, she is "still under the spell of her infatuation. . . . The thought of him [is] like an obsession, ever pressing itself upon her" (28). She is infatuated, but not in love. Love requires commitment. Edna awakens to lust, first with Robert and more obviously with Arobin, but she does not have the will to love. As she later discovers, she does not love Robert (in fact she does not even know Robert), she loves loving Robert, dreaming about him—lusting after him. She also discovers that it could have been any man: Robert or Arobin or another. As May says, "The love which is separated from will . . . is characterized by a passivity which does not in-corporate and grow with its own passion. . . . It ends in something which is not fully personal because it does not fully discriminate" (278–79).

Why is Edna, like many people today, unable to love or will? Why does she stop growing? Where did she fail? I believe Chopin provides the answer—one that coincides with May's belief—in the song "Ah, si tu savais!" Edna lacks self-awareness; she fails to recognize that she herself must choose a future course of action. For example, when her husband challenges her to stop painting and pay attention to the family, she replies, "I *feel* like painting," and when pushed again, she further admits, "I'm not a painter." Why, then, does she paint? "I don't *know*" (19; emphases added). Toward the end of the novel she recognizes a need to know herself: "One of these days . . . I'm going to pull myself together for a while and think—try to determine what character of a woman I am; for, candidly, I don't know" (27).

This lack of self-knowledge is apparent in the one form of will that Edna does exert in the story: rebellion. As May says, "Protest is half-developed will" (193). On the evening that Edna learns to swim, her husband demands that she come inside the house. She refuses, seeing "that her will had blazed up, stubborn and resistant. She could not at that moment have done other than denied and resisted" (11). Later she declines to keep up her social duties, and when challenged by her husband, she rips a handkerchief apart, throws her wedding ring on the floor, and breaks a vase. But when the maid finds the ring, "Edna held out her hand, and taking the ring, slipped it upon her finger" (17). She cannot sustain her will. Her move to a new house of her own is another act of rebellion: "Instinct had prompted her. . . . She did not know . . . but whatever came, she had resolved never again to belong to another than herself" (26). Even she must admit, "It is a caprice." These acts of rebellion, which show her growing need to become an independent being, would have been more fruitful if she had been able to understand herself. Chopin's genius may be in portraying realistically a half-developed, still groping will.

May's ideas can shed light on Edna's destruction, which is rooted in lack of self-knowledge and lack of courage. Two developments lead to her suicide: the shift from fantasy to reality in her relation with Robert and her recognition of the impending choice she must make about her relation with her children.

On the night before her suicide, Robert makes it obvious that he wants to marry Edna. Her attitude changes abruptly at the mention of marriage. She insists, "I am no longer one of Mr. Pontellier's possessions to dispose of or not. I give myself where I choose. If he were to say, 'Here, Robert, take her and be happy; she is yours,' I should laugh at you both" (36). Edna wishes to move beyond the social structures that control people. She also seems to want to avoid Arobin's version of uncommitted love. She does want to *love* Robert. Robert, however, does not want "free love" and leaves before she returns, forcing Edna to face the fact that he does not understand her awakening self. Her rejection of marriage is the most self-conscious statement thus far in the novel. She knows how she cannot live, and she must now decide how she wants to live.

Furthermore, Edna must make a decision about her children. Shortly before her suicide she visits them in the country and tells them about her new house. But when the children seek to establish their place in the new scheme of things by asking where they will sleep and where their father will sleep, she says that "the fairies" will "fix it all right" (33). Edna is still wishing and will not acknowledge her choices. But Adèle, during the birth of her child, pushes the responsibility of deciding on Edna, insisting that Edna "[t]hink of the children. . . . Oh think of the children! Remember them!" (37). After leaving Adèle, Edna recognizes the choices she must make: "One has to think of the children some time or other; the sooner the better" (38). The self-consciousness of her denial of marriage and its restrictions makes her realize that her future acts will necessarily result in having to "trample upon the lives, the hearts, the prejudices of others—but no matter—still, I shouldn't want to trample upon the little lives." How can she live with the weight of guilt produced by the mere existence of her children? Yet she can no longer ignore the issue: "She meant to think of them; that determination had driven into her soul like a death wound" (38).

During this crucial beginning of self-awareness, she lacks the courage of commitment. The lack of courage to be an artist finally becomes a lack of courage to be. She cannot commit herself to Robert because her lust for him is ultimately impersonal. Robert does not know her, nor she Robert. He is faceless. During the sleepless night before her suicide, she repeats to herself, "To-day it is Arobin; tomorrow it will be some one else. It makes no difference to me." Nor can she commit herself to a life with or without her children. She knows too much to acquiesce to "married life," yet she does not have the courage to leave her children and their expectations. As she walks toward the ocean, she thinks, "[I]t doesn't matter about Léonce Pontellier—but Raoul and Etienne! . . . The children appeared before her like antagonists who had overcome her; who had overpowered and sought to drag her into the soul's slavery for the rest of her days. But she knew a way to elude them" (39).

Her situation in the world is finally made clear to her. Edna must live without Léonce or any other man who wishes to possess her, and she must therefore disgrace her children. Having begun to be self-conscious, she must now become responsible for her actions. She must make a decision. But the self-knowledge that has been thrust on her leaves her maimed, revealing the dangerous aspect of self-consciousness. Edna cannot live in innocence any longer. Yet, as May says, "How much self-awareness can a [person] bear?" (171). In Edna's growing awareness of the available choices, the "danger of the razor-blade edge of heightened consciousness on which the creative person lives" is sadly apparent. If she had had the courage to paint, she might have been able to live. The crisis of coming to terms with Robert and with her children demands a new way of life—one that incorporates her new awareness of herself. "The need to express one's self . . . springs from a maladjustment to life, or from an inner conflict, which the [person] cannot resolve in action. . . . The solution consists not of a resolution. It consists of the *deeper and wider dimension of consciousness* to which the [artist] is carried by virtue of his wrestling with the problem" (171). But Edna cannot save herself by painting.

Does Edna consciously choose suicide? May's discussion suggests two possible interpretations. One is that the suicide is Edna's first act of self-conscious will. Having honestly faced her limitations and the choices available to her, she takes the only action that maintains her dignity as a self. She cannot live and preserve her self-identity, but she can die without giving it up. A second interpretation is that Edna refuses the responsibility of consciousness. She refuses to choose and merely retreats into infantile wishing. The language Chopin uses to describe Edna during her final hours supports this interpretation. "Mrs. Pontellier's indifference [was] so apparent. . . . I have a *notion* to go down to the beach. . . . I *might* go down and *try*—[to] dip my toes in. . . . Edna walked on down to the beach rather *mechanically*. . . . She was not thinking of these things when she walked down to the beach" (emphasis added). She puts on a bathing suit, then takes it off. Just before she drowns, she considers the fact that talking with Dr. Mandelet might have helped, "but it was too late; the shore was far behind her, and her strength was gone." As if embodying every infant's wish come true, she slips into the universal womb—the ocean, where she can go on wishing about "the spurs of the cavalry officer (clanging) as he walked across the porch. There was the hum of bees, and the musky odor of pinks filled the air" (39).

Edna rejects society's stultified Victorian will (as exemplified by her husband). And we readers relish her liberation. May says, "If you have only 'will' and no 'wish,' you have the dried-up, Victorian, neopuritan man. If you have only 'wish' and no 'will,' you have the driven, unfree, infantile person who, as an adult-remaining-an-infant, may become the robot man" (218). Whether Edna is this second person depends on how one interprets the suicide. Is it an act of will—self-conscious and in control—or the wish of a person without the courage to live a life for which she takes responsibility?

PATTERNS THAT YIELD MEANING

Characters as Foils to Edna

Barbara H. Solomon

As many students know, in literature foils are generally secondary or minor characters whose traits and behavior contrast with—and hence illuminate, enhance, or set off— the qualities and actions of the major character. Sometimes in modern fiction, especially in works dramatizing an identity crisis or the process of coming of age (i.e., in the bildungsroman), the hero or heroine may consciously measure his or her abilities or attitudes against those of another character in an attempt to gain self-knowledge or to chart a course of action.

Students familiar with Sylvia Plath's *The Bell Jar* may remember the numerous observations of Esther Greenwood about other young women with whom she would like to identify or whom she rejects. Among these are the sophisticated, sexually provocative Doreen; the innocent "Pollyanna Cowgirl" Betsy; self-confident Jody; the businesslike UN Russian interpreter; and the troubled, suicidal Joan. Esther's evaluation of each of these foils is usually quite conscious; for instance, she tells us that she stared at "the Russian girl in her double-breasted gray suit . . . and I wished with all my heart I could crawl into her and spend the rest of my life barking out one idiom after another" (61). Each judgment made by Esther helps to dramatize her dissatisfaction and her longing for a strong, uncomplicated identity.

One of the most fertile topics for classroom exploration in Kate Chopin's

The Awakening is the author's brilliant use of major and minor characters as foils for Edna Pontellier. As Edna undergoes a crisis, during her twenty-eighth year, in which her previous identity as Léonce Pontellier's submissive and passionless wife is transformed into that of a rebellious, passionate neophyte artist, she consciously judges the women around her, especially Adèle Ratignolle and Mlle Reisz, as she seeks to understand her own needs and actions. But in addition to the substantial depictions of these two characters, Chopin sketches a series of impressionistic portraits of minor characters who dramatize Edna's problems and options. These foils range from the shadowy pair of lovers who are vacationing at Grand Isle and who never speak to any of the other guests to the sensual and provocative Mariequita and, back in New Orleans, the sophisticated Mrs. Highcamp. Though each is very different, all share an important dramatic role. Through their attitudes or behavior, they illuminate the inevitable results of certain ideas and choices that occur to Edna at various times.

The lovers who appear early in the novel are always pictured by Chopin as backdrop figures. They live for each other, leaving when other characters appear and eschewing the life of the community of families that has grown up around Mrs. Lebrun's hotel. Chopin emphasizes their isolation with descriptions such as the following:

> The lovers were just entering the grounds of the *pension*. They were leaning toward each other as the water-oaks bent from the sea. There was not a particle of earth beneath their feet. Their heads might have been turned upside-down, so absolutely did they tread upon blue ether. (8)

When, late in the novel, Edna declares to Robert that she cares nothing for Léonce Pontellier and suggests that she and Robert will be able to be together, she is, in fact, suggesting that they should turn their backs on the community of family and friends who would be scandalized by such a liaison. Edna believes, or wants to believe, that she and Robert can live for each other without concern for anybody else. Her dream can be summarized by that most romantic phrase, giving up "all for love." But the relationship that Edna proposes must lead to their alienation from the comfortable Creole world to which both now very much belong. They would indeed become like the insubstantial lovers who exclude themselves from the activities of the world.

Next, two portraits of women instruct the reader about the limitations of Edna's choices. The first, Mariequita, is the "young barefooted Spanish girl" who makes the boat trip from Grand Isle to the Chênière Caminada with

Edna and Robert on the Sunday when they spend the entire day together. Chopin describes her physical appearance in some detail:

> She had a round, sly, piquant face and pretty black eyes. Her hands were small, and she kept them folded over the handle of her basket. Her feet were broad and coarse. She did not strive to hide them. Edna looked at her feet, and noticed the sand and slime between her brown toes. (12)

Edna's obvious curiosity makes Mariequita self-conscious. There is a frankly sensual quality about this girl, who knows Robert and begins to question him. When Mariequita asks whether Edna is Robert's "sweetheart," he responds, "She's a married lady, and has two children." His answer clearly begs the question, one that Robert probably has not yet asked himself. But Mariequita's rejoinder comically prefigures the serious situation that Robert and Edna must face. "Oh! well!" she says, "Francisco ran away with Sylvano's wife, who had four children. They took all his money and one of the children and stole his boat" (12). Ironically, only a few minutes later, Robert tells Edna about his plan of patching and trimming his own boat, fantasizing that he and she can go sailing together "some night in the pirogue when the moon shines." But Edna could never adopt Mariequita's casual attitude toward marriage and infidelity, much as she struggles to escape the consequences of her unfortunate marriage to Léonce. Edna may not care whether her behavior hurts her husband, but she is haunted by her fear of the harm she might cause her small sons, Etienne and Raoul.

In the final chapter Mariequita reappears just before Edna's arrival at Grand Isle. Fearing that Victor may be in love with Edna, she attempts to make him jealous. She threatens to abandon him to his fine lady friends and brags about her own attractiveness: "There were a dozen men crazy about her at the *Chênière*; and since it was the fashion to be in love with married people, why she could run away any time she liked to New Orleans with Célina's husband" (39). Mariequita's comments point up the contrast in the two women's attitudes, emphasizing the sense of entrapment that Edna increasingly comes to feel as the novel progresses.

A much more sophisticated woman, Mrs. James Highcamp serves as a second foil who dramatizes the impossibility of a certain kind of future for Edna. Early in the novel, when Léonce notices Mrs. Highcamp's calling card among the other cards of the visitors who had paid a call on one of Edna's Tuesdays at home (only to find her out for the afternoon), he comments, "[T]he less you have to do with Mrs. Highcamp, the better." Significantly, when Léonce is away and Edna has begun to live as she pleases, without regard for her husband's ideas, Edna becomes somewhat friendly with this acquaintance, dining at her house and attending the races with her and Alcée Arobin. Chopin portrays Mrs. Highcamp as a wife and mother who flirts with attractive men and makes a mockery of her marriage: "Mrs. Highcamp was a worldly but unaffected, intelligent, slim, tall blonde in the forties, with an indifferent manner and blue eyes that stared. She had a daughter who served her as a pretext for cultivating the society of young men of fashion" (25).

At the birthday dinner that Edna gives just before leaving Léonce's house for her "pigeon house," Mrs. Highcamp is seated next to Victor Lebrun. Chopin describes her demeanor: "Her attention was never for a moment withdrawn from him after seating herself at table; and when he turned to Mrs. Merriman, who was prettier and more vivacious than Mrs. Highcamp, she waited with easy indifference for an opportunity to reclaim his attention" (30).

During the course of the evening's festivities, she weaves a garland of yellow and red roses that she places on Victor's head; then she drapes her white silk scarf gracefully around him. When Mrs. Highcamp encourages Victor to sing, he chooses the song that Edna associates with her love for Robert. As Mrs. Highcamp departs, she invites Victor to call on her daughter, ostensibly so that the two young people can enjoy speaking French and singing French songs together. Victor responds that he intends to visit Mrs. Highcamp "at the first opportunity which presented itself." Obviously, under the guise of providing company for her daughter, Mrs. Highcamp intends to pursue this young man for her own needs. Even Edna recognizes the intensity of his physical attractiveness as he apologizes to her for his behavior "with caressing eyes" and a kiss that "was like a pleasing sting to her hand" (30).

Edna specifically rejects Mrs. Highcamp's way of life in the closing passages of the novel after she realizes that Robert will not return because of his Creole code of honor concerning infidelity and adultery. Without Robert, she visualizes a pattern for satisfying her sensual needs that the reader recognizes might well parallel Mrs. Highcamp's behavior with men: "[Edna] had said over and over to herself: 'To-day it is Arobin; to-morrow it will be some one else. It makes no difference to me, it doesn't matter about Léonce Pontellier—but Raoul and Etienne!' " (39). Having experienced passion and being unwilling to lead a life deprived of such experiences, Edna is also unwilling to lead a life of barely concealed subterfuge such as that of Mrs. Highcamp.

When students turn to examine the two most obvious foils for Edna in *The Awakening*, Adèle Ratignolle and Mlle Reisz, they will discover that these women are also foils for each other. Adèle is clearly delineated as one of the "mother-women" who are prevalent at Mme Lebrun's pension. During the summer, this pregnant mother of three small children busies herself cutting and sewing "night-drawers" to protect her children from winter drafts. Edna, who is attracted to this nurturing, maternal figure, cannot "see the use of anticipating and making winter night garments the subject of her summer meditations" (4). At a Saturday evening gathering for an informal children's talent show, the selfless Adèle does not join in the dancing because of her pregnancy but plays the piano so that the other guests can waltz: "She was keeping up her music on account of the children, she said; because she and her husband both considered it a means of brightening the home and making it attractive" (9).

In contrast, back in New Orleans when Edna begins to paint in earnest, she sets a high artistic standard for herself and does not treat her skill as a pleasant hobby meant to enrich family life. Edna's behavior when she retreats to her atelier to paint so enrages Léonce that he compares his wife's disregard for her responsibilities as a wife and mother to the ideal behavior of Adèle, openly criticizing Edna for not being more like her friend: "There's Madame Ratignolle; because she keeps up her music, she doesn't let everything else go to chaos. And she's more of a musician than you are a painter" (19). Edna is not at all influenced or intimidated by this criticism. She had only recently visited the Ratignolles at their home, and while she can appreciate the domestic harmony and gentle courtesy that pervades their household, she had come to the conclusion that theirs "was not a condition of life which fitted her" (18). Edna thinks of Adèle's life as one of blind contentment without passion. By analyzing her feelings about her friend's marriage and recognizing their differences, Edna comes somewhat closer to understanding her own nature. As Edna concludes that Adèle "would never have the taste of life's delirium," the thought occurs to Edna that she is not even sure of what she means by the phrase "life's delirium" (18). Edna's passage to self-knowledge is marked, then, by her negative reactions to the lives of others.

In direct contrast to Adèle, who considers the needs of her husband and children before her own inclinations and who generally seeks to please others, is Mlle Reisz, who is introduced to the reader on the evening of the children's performance at Mme Lebrun's hotel: "She was a disagreeable little woman, no longer young, who had quarreled with almost every one, owing to a temper which was self-assertive and a disposition to trample upon the rights of others" (9). Whereas Adèle had played the piano to please the guests, Mlle Reisz has contempt for this audience, and although as a mark of her favor she offers to play a selection of Edna's choice, Edna responds that "she would not dare to choose and begged that Mademoiselle Reisz would please herself in her selections" (9).

Just as Edna had been attracted to Adèle's comforting and outgoing nature, she is attracted to the strength and independence of the solitary artist. Mlle

Reisz is, of course, a source of information about Robert. But after Edna has visited this confidante, she recalls several of the pianist's observations, thinking of her as wonderfully sane. Edna describes one of their conversations to an uncomprehending Arobin:

> . . . when I left her [Mlle Reisz] to-day, she put her arms around me and felt my shoulder blades, to see if my wings were strong, she said. "The bird that would soar above the level plain of tradition and prejudice must have strong wings. It is a sad spectacle to see the weaklings bruised, exhausted, fluttering back to earth." (27)

On another occasion, Mlle Reisz had warned Edna that to succeed as an artist one "must possess the courageous soul," a soul "that dares and defies" (21). Clearly, the older woman has sacrificed concern for and commitment to others to pursue her artistic achievement. But just as Edna cannot identify with Adèle Ratignolle's domestic contentment, she cannot accept the total disregard for the needs or opinions of others that Mlle Reisz suggests is the price for becoming a true artist. Torn between her desire not to hurt her children and not to return to the empty shell of her existence as Léonce's wife, Edna cannot emulate the example of either of her friends. Their uncomplicated identities are well suited to each of them but insufficient for Edna.

Chopin's use of other women as foils for her central character fulfills three distinct functions. First, since Edna is not particularly analytical—at one point in the novel she thinks that she needs to set aside time soon to try to determine what sort of person she truly is—her interaction with foils such as Adèle and Mlle Reisz enables the reader to better compare Edna's character and goals with those of other women. Second, Chopin's sympathetic depiction of these two very different foils suggests the considerable range of women's behavior during an era in which women were frequently categorized as similar in instincts and interests: creatures in need of domestic security and comfort. And, finally, Edna's interaction with Adèle, who implores her to consider the children, and with Mlle Reisz, who encourages Edna to soar freely as an artist and to pursue her relationship with Robert, helps to convince readers that Edna's problems are insoluble given the environment, the era, and the strength of her newly discovered, uncompromising identity.

Two Settings:
The Islands and the City

Suzanne W. Jones

In the past when I taught *The Awakening*, I found that the two questions students most wanted answers to were "Why did Chopin end the novel with Edna's suicide?" and "How should I feel about Edna?" Students were torn between viewing Edna as a courageous woman and as an irresponsible mother. While some argued vehemently for one side or the other, others felt ambivalent toward Edna. Students were somewhat placated if I suggested that perhaps Kate Chopin herself was uncertain of her attitude toward Edna and that she ended the novel with suicide because she could not reconcile her own conflicting feelings. Certainly scholars such as Ruth Sullivan, Stewart Smith, and Elizabeth Fox-Genovese have noted that *The Awakening* reflects Chopin's ambivalence at every level—characters, narration, and language. How to get students to see this ambivalence as they read became my goal.

As John May suggests, the tension in the novel between freedom and restraint is evident in the two settings—the sea and the city. I discovered that if students evaluate Edna's behavior against the background of the two settings, they can most clearly see Chopin's ambivalence. Now when I teach the novel, I ask my class the question "How do you feel about Edna?" but I ask it twice—once after they have read chapters 1–16, which take place on the islands in the gulf, and again when they have read the last part of the novel, which is set in New Orleans.

The two settings allow Chopin to evaluate both the Victorian woman, whom she sees as inhibited, and the liberated woman, whom she depicts as a victim of her impulses. The two settings also enable Chopin to expose the confusion that arises out of the division between social role and personal identity and to focus on the way in which a social setting controls thought and determines identity. Chopin's use of two settings shows that she is concerned both with the psychological cost women pay when following behavior patterns that restrict their individuality and with the social cost they incur in attempting to break such patterns.

When I ask students what they think of Edna after reading the first sixteen chapters of the novel, they say that Edna seems aware of her feelings and her body for the first time. They look favorably on her awakening. A question about why Edna's awakening occurs on the island leads to a discussion of how Chopin uses setting to provoke character change. On Grand Isle Edna mixes intimately with Creoles for the first time and is thus given a chance to see the world through their eyes. In comparison to the Creoles, with their passion and candor, Edna seems inhibited. She is a shadow to herself and others not only because she is reserved but also because she masks her true self in order to play "mother-woman," a role in which women "idolized their children, worshipped their husbands, and esteemed it a holy privilege to efface themselves as individuals" (4). Since her social role conflicts with her true identity, Edna leads a "dual life—that outward existence which conforms, the inward life which questions" (7). However, because Edna's sense of self is closely identified with the expectations first of her father and then of her husband, she has not been able to accept her own intuitions as valid sources of concern. From readings in psychology, sociology, and the natural sciences, Chopin learned that people take for granted the validity of their conventions until they encounter another set of conventions as fully sanctioned as their own (Seyersted 49, 84–85). The change of setting introduces Edna to values that are different from hers and enables her to justify her feelings. Only such an awareness of the relativity of manners and morals can produce the emotional struggling that Edna has not allowed herself in New Orleans.

The self-awareness Edna gains on Grand Isle arises out of two causes. First, the conditions of her vacation largely release her from the roles of wife and mother and force her to see herself as Edna as well as Mrs. Pontellier. Second, the openness and vitality of the Creoles free her of her Kentucky Presbyterian reserve and allow her to reveal her hidden thoughts and feelings.

On the island Edna is freed from her children by the quadroon, from her husband by his work in the city, from her household duties by Mme Lebrun, and from the demands of fashionable society by her distance from New Orleans. In this setting, Edna also meets Mlle Reisz, who provides her with the model of a woman whose definition of self comes from her talents as a musician rather than from her identification with a husband and children. Unlike the dependent, self-effacing mother-woman, Mlle Reisz is independent and assertive. The night that Edna learns to swim, she gains a similar self-confidence, as well as independence from the friends who had been teaching her. I have students examine Chopin's comparison between Edna and a developing child. The feelings of pride, independence, and achievement that Edna gains from learning to swim correspond to those a baby feels when it learns to walk (10). Like a growing child, Edna is beginning "to realize her position in the universe as a human being, and to recognize her relations as an individual to the world within and about her" (6). Edna's summer on the gulf gives her a feeling of expanding horizons and unlimited possibilities that Chopin significantly has her equate with feelings she had in another setting—the expansive Kentucky bluegrass meadows of her childhood.

While Edna's liberation from her role as wife and mother gives her an awareness of herself as an individual apart from social roles, her close association with the Creoles gives her an awareness of the person she is beneath her social mask. Growing up in a strict Presbyterian household, she learned to be reserved and modest. Edna discovers in the Creoles an unfamiliar "freedom of expression" and an "absence of prudery" (4). The rebelliousness and sensuality that made Edna a sinful Presbyterian when she was young and the impulsiveness and lack of concern for the future that make her a negligent mother are behaviors seemingly accepted by the hedonistic Creoles. On Grand Isle Chopin has Edna discover the self beneath the veneer of civilization, the instincts disguised by manners, and the impulses checked by socialization.

Next I have students consider how Chopin uses Edna's sailing trip to Chênière Caminada. Even further from New Orleans than Grand Isle, this island becomes the setting where Chopin reveals the extent of Edna's transformation from civilized lady to sensual woman. When students examine the descriptions of Edna in this setting, they quickly discover Chopin's reliance on animal imagery. For Edna everything connected with this trip is instinctual. Desire prompts her to summon Robert for the first time, and once on the island she allows impulse to rule her behavior. Feeling drowsy, she leaves in the middle of the church service to nap; feeling hungry, she plucks an orange from a tree. She eats with animal-like relish, biting "a piece from the brown loaf, tearing it with her strong white teeth" (13). As Edna indulges her senses, paying attention to the animal part of her nature, she becomes aware of her body for the first time. Chopin describes Edna's new awareness as that of a preening animal.

Students are also quick to point out the fairy-tale quality of this setting. On this remote island, Edna can violate social taboos with impunity. She and Robert are free to live their fantasies: she is Sleeping Beauty and he is Prince Charming. The stories Mme Antoine tells them haunt their imaginations and color their world. Chopin gradually mixes fantasy with reality until their sail back to Grand Isle merges with the legends of the Baratarians.

After students recognize the significance of this shift in island settings, they are ready to consider why Chopin takes Edna back to New Orleans only days after her trip to Chênière Caminada. Such a move allows Chopin to test the potential of Edna's emerging self-awareness. After the freedom and spontaneity of the islands, Edna finds the regularity and restrictions of her old life stifling. She breaks out of her social confinement by ignoring the temporal and spatial boundaries that limit her existence. She resumes her vacation behavior, "going and coming as it suited her fancy, and, so far as she was able, lending herself to any passing caprice" (19).

Chopin underscores the effect of a new environment on Edna's perception by making repeated references to Edna's sight. On Grand Isle, Chopin describes her as "seeing with different eyes" (14). When Edna returns to her home on Esplanade Street, everything looks different:

> She felt no interest in anything about her. The street, the children, the fruit vender, the flowers growing there under her eyes, were all part and parcel of an alien world which had suddenly become antagonistic. (18)

The ability to see herself other than as society sees her helps Edna transcend society's point of view and dismiss Adèle's concern for Edna's reputation: "She began to look with her own eyes. . . . No longer was she content to 'feed upon opinion' when her own soul had invited her" (32). With her new perspective, Edna is free, in Mlle Reisz's terms, to "soar above the level plain of tradition and prejudice" (27).

To the long-repressed Edna, the permissiveness of the Creole society is a license for absolute freedom. Edna, however, not fully understanding their customs, misreads their gestures. The misunderstanding begins in her relationship with Adèle. Although Edna mistakes her candor for broadmindedness, Adèle, despite her sensuality and outspokenness, epitomizes the mother-woman. This misunderstanding continues in Edna's relationship with Robert. On his return to New Orleans, Robert continues to view her in a traditional way, even though she has overthrown the traditional roles. Edna, who is willing to defy society's code to be with Robert, is not willing to marry him and fall back into the role of mother-woman with its connotations of dependence and self-effacement. Because Robert considers wife the only legitimate role for a woman who loves a man, he cannot understand Edna's behavior. Thus while Edna's vacation in the islands richly develops her inward life, it creates problems in her social life. No one understands her.

The confusion that results from Edna's exposure to another way of life in the islands and her resulting attempt to redefine herself arises not only between Edna and the people around her but within Edna as well. Though the discovery of Creole customs awakens Edna to her emotions and senses, the experience does not totally erase her old patterns of behavior. Her body reveals her new self, only to be checked by old habits of mind. Realizing this complexity can help students understand Edna's contradictory behavior with Arobin in New Orleans. Often her new sensual self provokes a confrontation with him only to have her old repressed self refuse to deal with the consequences. When her accustomed ways of acting and thinking draw her in one direction and her newly awakened body and senses pull her in another, Edna, like those around her, does not know who she is. Although Edna rejects the old patterns of behavior expected of a mother-woman, she cannot free herself of her old habits of mind. She moves around the corner to a home of her own, but not out of New Orleans. Instead of defining herself in new ways, such as through her painting or her knowledge of horse racing, she still requires thoughts of a man to give her life stability. She never creates a new identity. As Chopin ominously indicates on the night that Edna learns to swim, establishing an identity apart from the one assigned by society is difficult.

But Edna's confusion only mirrors her creator's. Chopin cannot reconcile her own conflicting feelings about the traditional view of woman's role in society with the modern view of the individual personality. (She herself did not write professionally until after her husband's death, even though she had written stories before her marriage.) Chopin's ambivalence becomes clear to students when they see that the connotations of her imagery change as Edna moves from primitive islands to complex city, from self-centered vacation activities to communal relationships. In the islands, the references to animals and children make Edna seem more in touch with her emotions and her body and therefore more alive. In New Orleans such references make Edna seem unthinking, somewhat out of control, and rather immature. Thus what seems to be the realization of some truer self on the islands looks like self-indulgence and selfishness in New Orleans.

While Chopin's use of animal imagery makes Edna appear more sensual and natural in the islands, her use of the same imagery to describe Edna's behavior in the drawing rooms of New Orleans sometimes produces a different effect. For example, when Arobin appeals "to the animalism that stirred impatiently within her" (26), Edna yields to her desires, forgetting both her husband and Robert, despite her determination to do otherwise. Here Chopin suggests that without the constraint of social conventions, Edna has little control over her behavior.

Similarly, the connotation of Chopin's description of Edna as a child changes from childlike to childish as Edna moves from Grand Isle to New Orleans. Edna responds to disappointments with unproductive tantrums. To ameliorate the feeling of constriction in her marriage, she does not talk with Léonce but breaks a vase and stamps on her wedding ring. At the farewell dinner to her fictitious self—a dinner that should have been her apotheosis—Edna shatters not only a wine glass but the harmony of the evening. When forced to think about the future, Edna, like a child, thinks in terms of a storybook world. When her children grow concerned about where they and their father will sleep in her new house, she tells them that "the fairies would fix it all right" (32). Such romanticizing does not seem harmful on Chênière Caminada, but in New Orleans Chopin makes Edna's fantasies seem immature, an escape from, rather than the discovery of, reality. To quiet her feelings of despair in the city, Edna fills her time with memories of the islands. Because Edna cannot incorporate her island vision of self-fulfillment into her life in New Orleans, she loses her desire to live.

Chopin must end Edna's story with suicide because of her own inherited notions. Seeing the advantages and disadvantages of playing the traditional roles of wife and mother and of liberating oneself from such roles, Chopin cannot reconcile her conflicting feelings. When students have analyzed Chopin's use of setting and her ambivalent response to Edna in the two different settings, they can better understand the ending. I always ask them why it is appropriate that Edna commits suicide on Grand Isle and why this setting should once again evoke the environment of her childhood. It is the expanse of the sea and the liberation of the vacation setting that awaken her to possibilities but to dangers as well. Edna's longing for the freedom of her childhood, a feeling she reexperiences in the islands, contains the potential for both expansion and destruction. Edna's childlike confidence on Grand Isle produces a desire "to swim far out where no woman had swum before," but at the same time Edna overestimates her strength and has a "quick vision of death" (10), a foreshadowing of her suicide. Edna similarly overestimates her ability to defy society and its roles and traditions.

The two settings in the novel enable Chopin to expose not only the confusion that arises when a woman experiences a new place but also the way a social setting controls thought and determines identity. A study of Chopin's use of these two settings can give students an appreciation for a fine writer's skillful use of place to initiate conflict and to reveal theme.

Symbolism and Imagery in *The Awakening*

Joyce Dyer

Kate Chopin is a psychological symbolist. I try to help my students understand this when I teach *The Awakening*. If they ever leave the book without admiring Chopin's intricate use of symbols and images to project Edna Pontellier's psyche, I feel I have failed in some essential way. Without its imagery, the novel would lose much of its brightness and density, and Edna Pontellier might lose her chance of being understood.

It is not hard to convince students that Chopin's style is distinctively poetic, visual, and sensuous. In the first sentence, they are introduced to a green and yellow multilingual parrot; in the last sentence they hear the "hum of bees" and smell "the musky odor of pinks." Colors, smells, sounds, and visual images are important and prevalent throughout Chopin's 1899 novel. After reading the dinner-party sequence, one artistic student in my class a few years ago confidently said, "You know, I could paint this." And he did.

Students easily and naturally select favorite symbols. Some can almost recite the refrain of the sea after their reading is complete. ("The voice of the sea is seductive"; "The voice of the sea speaks to the soul" [6].) They are curious about the symbolic appearances of minor characters: the woman in black who says her beads; the young lovers who haunt the beaches for private spots, including the children's tent toward which they so appropriately gravitate; Mariequita, Chopin's Spanish vixen; the man in Edna's imagination who stands despondent and naked on the beach, unable to wing his way from earth. And they hear the music in the background, songs by Louis Hérold, Chopin, Wagner, and Balfe.

But what students often fail to see on their own is that Chopin's symbolism is not merely a decorative frill. It is an essential artistic component. The book depends on symbolism to define Edna's psychological dilemma and romantic sensibility; to explain the limitations and dangers of her new vision; and, finally, to help readers understand why Edna walks into the sea. What students need to learn from teachers, then, is how Chopin's symbols elaborately and meticulously connect to tell the complete and complex story of Edna Pontellier.

I begin with the sea. It is here where Edna begins her search and here where we must begin ours. The sea is the novel's central symbol of romantic possibility. It announces both the sexual and the spiritual freedom Edna hopes to achieve. The sea's touch, murmur, and odor charge Edna's sleeping sensuality. The serpentine waves embrace her, seductively. Compared to the fundamental appeal of the sea, Edna's need of Robert seems almost arbitrary. John R. May writes that the gulf, and the entire sensuous Creole setting, provides "a climate of psychological relaxation sufficient to allow

Edna's true nature to reveal itself" (1039). Most students have stepped into the ocean by the time they reach us; they will be able to recall their own memories of the physical pleasures of the sea and a hot southern sun.

Explaining the sea's spiritual content might prove a more arduous task. A knowledge of archetypes and literary tradition must be introduced in some preliminary sense. The gulf—like the woods in Hawthorne, the Mississippi River in Twain, the ocean in Melville—is a place that promises spiritual as well as physical freedom. The sea urges Edna toward limitlessness, toward transcendence, toward the romantic. As Donald Ringe recognized years ago, above all else *The Awakening* "is a powerful romantic novel" ("Romantic Imagery" 587). Its sea invites the soul "to wander for a spell in abysses of solitude" (6).

The sea, in Chopin as in Melville, is potentially all that the shore is not. Indeed, Melville's last paragraphs from "The Lee Shore" in *Moby-Dick* are symbolically equivalent to Chopin's own descriptive passages about sea and land.

> Know ye, now, Bulkington? Glimpses do ye see of that mortally intolerable truth; that all deep, earnest thinking is but the intrepid effort of the soul to keep the open independence of her sea; while the wildest winds of heaven and earth conspire to cast her on the treacherous, slavish shore?
>
> But as in landlessness alone resides the highest truth, shoreless, indefinite as God—so, better is it to perish in that howling infinite, than be ingloriously dashed upon the lee, even if that were safety! For worm-like, then, oh! who would craven crawl to land! Terrors of the terrible; is all this agony so vain? Take heart, take heart, O Bulkington! Bear thee grimly, demigod! Up from the spray of thy ocean-perishing—straight up, leaps thy apotheosis! (149)

Even some of Chopin's metaphors for the sea are remarkably like Melville's: "For worm-like, then, oh! who would craven crawl to land!" ("like worms struggling blindly toward inevitable annihilation" [19]); "Up from the spray of thy ocean-perishing" (the "Venus rising from the foam" allusion [39]); "demigod" and "apotheosis" (the gulf spirit choosing Edna as a "semi-celestial" [10]). The concept of a romantic sea—and a slavish shore—was one that both Melville and Chopin had thoroughly absorbed.

I next ask students to locate other symbols that make Chopin's direct reference to concepts such as "the unlimited" and "space and solitude" (10) emotionally comprehensible and complete. Slowly, they begin to recall images whose enormity attracted their own imaginations. The Kentucky meadow helps Edna realize how much she still longs for the opportunity to wander "idly, aimlessly, unthinking and unguided" (7). The mystic moon tempts her with its clear, bright reflection of life's promise. Without beginning or end, without shape or outline, the moon's "mystic shimmer" (9) hints at indefinite human expansion and deeply affects Edna.

The gulf spirit is a third vital symbol of the elevation Edna hopes for. Robert's lighthearted, folksy explanation of what has happened to Edna on the crucial night of her moonlit swim has serious dimensions. Superstition has it that on the twenty-eighth of every August the gulf spirit "seeks some one mortal worthy to hold him company, worthy of being exalted for a few hours into realms of the semi-celestials." And, Robert proposes, "tonight he found Mrs. Pontellier. Perhaps he will never wholly release her from the spell" (10). Edna's increasingly regal, imperious manner throughout the book confirms the prescience of Robert's remark.

But a hundred things will prevent Edna's apotheosis here on earth. Léonce represents the social conventions that Edna must persistently counter. In a speech whose language contains clear resonances of Henrik Ibsen's *Hedda Gabler* (1891) and Henry Fuller's *With the Procession* (1895), Léonce scolds Edna for neglecting Tuesday reception days: "Why, my dear, I should think you'd understand by this time that people don't do such things; we've got to observe *les convenances* if we ever expect to get on and keep up with the procession" (17).

Oaks and violets point to further limitations. The oaks appear recurrently to remind us of the essential biological connection between mothers and children. Like Lafcadio Hearn, who in *Chita* compares the Louisiana oaks to "fleeing women with streaming garments and wind-blown hair" (14–15), Chopin sees the oaks as female and maternal. Children, again and again, play croquet under their protective shade. The oaks periodically "moan as they [bend] their heads" (11) in the same way Edna suffers in her role as protector. Edna knows that Raoul and Etienne will, though innocently, "drag her into the soul's slavery for the rest of her days" (39). But she nevertheless cannot trample on their "little lives" (38) and recognizes that in this world she must do what Adèle asks: "Think of the children, Edna. Oh think of the children! Remember them!" (37).

The possibility of becoming an artist is severely compromised by the emotional and physical deformity of Mlle Reisz. She is associated with black lace and artificial violets, a flower that John B. Vickery notes has been connected to "rites of protection against harm" by J. G. Frazer (320). To be as alone as she—to be all alone—is a terrible risk. One of Edna's final fears is that she will be left alone. Although at times she appears to want just this, she often seeks the approval of friends and needs the idea of a beloved one to brighten her days. She will never exchange these things for a bunch of artificial violets.

Students will now be ready to understand a third group of symbols, a group that most powerfully conveys the book's darkest irony: that as Edna awakens to the romantic possibilities of the self, she simultaneously acquires a deeper understanding of the inevitable limitations of her new vision. These symbols, often symbol pairs, juxtapose the poignant longing of Edna with the inevitable disappointment she will come to know. They tell us that although she finally recognizes the extent of her passion, she never will be able to fulfill it. Although she longs for a beloved, a Robert who will satisfy her in every way, she grows to understand "that the day would come when he, too, and the thought of him would melt out of her existence, leaving her alone" (39). Although she dreams of becoming an artist, she lacks the courageous and solitary temperament great art demands. Although she wants to be free to do whatever she wishes, she knows her children will defeat her. She dreams, but awakens knowing her dreams will vanish. "The years that are gone seem like dreams—if one might go on sleeping and dreaming—but to wake up and find—oh! well! perhaps it is better to wake up after all, even to suffer, rather than to remain a dupe to illusions all one's life" (38), she tells Dr. Mandelet during her last walk on the streets of New Orleans.

Students can be helped to identify and appreciate ironic images. Discussing one image in some detail will make others become more visible. Mlle Reisz's alternation between the Chopin impromptu and Wagner's *Tristan und Isolde* is a good example of the way Chopin imagistically mixes romantic desire with inevitable disappointment. The impromptu, even in the quiet minor chords that open the piece, suggests the "soulful and poignant longing" (21) of a romantic like Edna. But Mlle Reisz, who knows something about the loneliness of the romantic vision, soon glides into the *Liebestod* of Isolde, the song Isolde sings before she dies in her dead lover's cold embrace.

With this preliminary introduction, students usually begin to recall other closely paired images that are needed for our understanding of Edna's dilemma. Mlle Reisz feels Edna's shoulder blades at one point, "to see if [her] wings were strong." She knows, from her own battle with convention, that the idealist has a hard time surviving: "The bird that would soar above the level plain of tradition and prejudice must have strong wings. It is a sad spectacle to see the weaklings bruised, exhausted, fluttering back to earth" (27). But Edna, walking the white gulf beaches just before her suicide swim, sees just such a bird, broken-winged, "beating the air above, reeling, fluttering, circling disabled down, down to the water" (39).

During her birthday party in chapter 30, the colors yellow and red are carefully juxtaposed in the clothing, the table setting, even the flowers that adorn the room. Yellow recalls the sun that Edna has enjoyed more and more as her days on Grand Isle have progressed. Her friends have even begun to associate her with this vital force. "Ah! here comes the sunlight!" (26) cries Mlle Reisz as Edna enters her apartment. In the Swinburne lines that Gouvernail recites after Victor's head is wreathed with a garland of yellow and red roses, we begin to learn how the red blends symbolically with the yellow: "There was a graven image of Desire / Painted with red blood on a ground of gold." Close examination of "A Cameo," the poem from which the lines are taken, shows how inextricably death and desire (or, as the poem also calls them, pain and pleasure) are linked. Bernard Koloski believes the lines have extensive implications for the novel: "behind the sometimes wild activities of the guests is the brooding presence of death" ("Swinburne Lines" 609). Indeed, the poem's last two lines depict Death standing "aloof behind a gaping grate." Part of Edna's annoyance with the decadent behavior of some of her dinner guests comes from her own awareness of the ugly and destructive side of passion, the side Swinburne reminds us of with his use of red. Will her own passion, which she now knows is unavoidable, someday make of her a Mrs. Highcamp? Is it really possible for her "spiritual vision . . . of the beloved one" to survive in the midst of a force as powerful as this?

Again and again Chopin hints at Edna's inevitable destiny: she feels victorious ("the regal woman, the one who rules, who looks on, who stands alone"), but at the same time she senses "the old ennui overtaking her" (30); Edna reads Emerson, but, as George Arms notes, she falls asleep doing so (219); she is "Venus rising from the foam" to Victor but also Aphrodite attempting to drown herself; she looks to the night, romantically hoping to find in it the sweet mystery to match her mood, but, as I have noted elsewhere, she is met instead by "eternal stars [that] mock her semi-celestial aspirations" ("Night Images" 227); the night of her mystic swim begins with a silver moon, but as Edna sits on the porch it turns to copper.

We must finally return with our students to the sea. Like Edna, we must end our search where we began it. Like Edna, we can no longer escape the sea's difficult ambiguities. It remains a romantic emblem to the end, the only place where a Venus can be born or an apotheosis occur. But what Edna knows by now is that it has its own dark ironies. True, it is the sea described for Bulkington, but it is also, as Donald Ringe knows, the sea of Melville's Pip: "it can cause, as it does to Pip . . ., an 'intense concentration of self' that can hardly be endured" ("Romantic Imagery" 583). It is this sea that even from the beginning had invited Edna "to lose [her soul] in mazes of inward contemplation" (6).

It is a sea whose promise is infused with death. Even the night of the moonlit swim Edna begins to see this connection. As she swims farther and farther out, "A quick vision of death smote her soul" (10). Lewis Leary shows that lines reminiscent of Whitman's sea in "Out of the Cradle Endlessly Rocking" occur repeatedly in Chopin's descriptions. He concludes, "she seems clearly to have intended her reader to understand from echoes of Whitman like these that death would be part of the plot" (121). Gregory L. Candela suggests that dark irony is infused in the novel through yet another tie to Whitman: "an equally strong refrain in Whitman's poem and Chopin's novel is the mockingbird's which beckons Edna" (163).

Awakening is a serious matter. For what Edna's "inward contemplation" at last has let her know is this: the only way to remain a romantic and hold onto our dreams and illusions is to die. Edna's dreams and ideals are so important to her that she refuses to give them up—in spite of the high price she has to pay. She rejects the very idea of compromise and walks into the gulf.

In the final paragraphs of the book, Edna begs for understanding. Not judgment. Mlle Reisz would have only laughed at her. Robert never understood. Maybe Dr. Mandelet would have understood, yet she knows it is too late to explore that possibility. But the novel's elaborate symbolism does, at least, allow Chopin's readers to understand. When we feel ourselves tied to the drab shore, we cannot but admire Chopin's Edna for the strength of her uncompromising dreams.

Stylistic Categories in *The Awakening*

Nancy Rogers

In addition to being a rich novel of ideas, especially for the study of such issues as the marriage contract, adultery, and the economics of woman's place, Kate Chopin's *The Awakening* offers the undergraduate student fruitful opportunities for stylistic analysis. While teaching at the University of Tübingen in West Germany, I used the novel as part of a seminar, entitled Textual Linguistics, for undergraduate English majors whose skills in literary analysis were approximately equal to those of junior or senior majors at an American college or university. The purpose of the course was to make the students more aware of language, to help them study literary discourse from a linguistic orientation. This training was especially important for my German students, working in a language other than their own, yet at the same time thoroughly competent both in using spoken English and in analyzing the written language. However, the approach is also highly appropriate and useful for American students, who are often so entranced by the analysis of character, theme, and plot or by the application of literary theory that they forget to look at language, at what the words of the text are saying or implying, at how the style, or linguistic features, affects or produces meaning.

The course met once a week for two hours; I began to prepare the students for style study by introducing them to the work of major authors in the field (Booth, Fowler, Kroeber, Leech, Lodge, Page, Searle, Spitzer, Ullmann, Watt, and Widdowson, among others). In lectures I outlined such topics as the various methods of approaching a novel (looking at isolated passages, e.g., beginnings, versus tracing significant patterns throughout a work), narrative voice, idiolect and dialect, and speech act theory and explained how to recognize and interpret such stylistic features as elegant variation or verbal-nominal style. The primary text for the course was Leech and Short's *Style in Fiction: A Linguistic Introduction to English Fictional Prose*, a fine work with an excellent choice of passages for analysis. After comparing different types of descriptive passages and studying classic stylistic writings like Ian Watt's analysis of the first paragraph of Henry James's *Ambassadors*, the students were assigned texts to analyze. All students read the entire works assigned, but pairs of them examined certain passages, usually a chapter or two of a novel, and reported their findings orally to the group. Students were reminded always to keep in mind the artistic relevance of the key linguistic traits they discovered. For the term paper, each student analyzed one or two chapters of a novel—one term we focused on Ralph Ellison's *Invisible Man*, another on Tillie Olsen's *Tell Me a Riddle*. During the last class I integrated students' findings into a style study of the entire work.

One of the texts that students did not find interesting at first was *The Awakening*, precisely because on initial investigation its style seemed extremely straightforward, unadorned, and uncomplicated. Since most of them had recently studied Joyce and Woolf, they anticipated a particularly difficult challenge—to find the "common denominator" (Spitzer's term) of Chopin's style—and one that ultimately would prove dull. That this conjecture was faulty is proved, I hope, by what follows.

I thought that it would be fruitful to analyze chapter 1 of *The Awakening*, since it posits an important dislocation of the novel: the estrangement of Edna Pontellier and her husband. The students were asked to examine lexical and grammatical categories, figures of speech, and linkages within the text. In addition, they were to analyze such other aspects of style as narrative point of view, speech and thought presentation, and conversational interaction. The observations that follow are based not only on what the students found in their initial confrontation with and probing of chapter 1 but also on the conclusions I have reached about the style of *The Awakening* through further study of both this chapter and the novel as a whole.

Lexis

In general, the vocabulary is simple, colloquial, and specific. Since Chopin is setting the stage for her novel, it is not surprising to find that most nouns are physical and concrete, establishing space, place, and characters. The preponderance of abstract nouns refer to the social and economic processes of life ("property," "society," "right," "privilege," etc.). The most obvious nominal stylistic feature is the use of words in quotes—" 'bridges,' which connected the Lebrun cottages" "the size of 'the game' "—which create a mood of informality and allow the reader to share the perceptions of the vacationers at Grand Isle. Adjectives of color, size, sound, and degree help set the scene of a small beach resort, which is further delineated by adverbs of repetition ("over and over") and mood ("lazily," "slowly," "silently," "hazily"). The quiet, intimate, hot summer atmosphere, with time for "adventure out there in the water" and for newspaper reading on shore, is conveyed through this dense lexical configuration.

The almost hothouse ambiance is also established by the verbs, which are primarily either static and intransitive or forms of the copula. Even the transitive verbs, of which there are very few, usually represent a state rather than an action; for example, instead of using the more direct "gaze" or "turned away," Chopin has Mr. Pontellier "fix his gaze" and "withdraw his glance," thus anchoring the actions in a longer span of time. Likewise, there is a scattering of reflexive verbs ("applied himself," "seated themselves," "stretched themselves"), which tend to prolong an action, adding to the lazy mood here depicted. The many nonfinite verb phrases (participles and infinitives—there are almost as many nonfinite verb forms in this chapter as there are conjugated verbs) contribute to a move away from action and toward stasis. Even the conjugated verbs are often either in the progressive aspect ("were playing," "was advancing") or use such semimodals as "kept" and thus create a feeling of continuousness and peace so overwhelming that it almost mesmerizes the reader. There are no abrupt actions, simply quiet, lengthy arrivals and departures among the main characters, with the bustling about of Mme Lebrun in the background. It is clearly a scene for reading a day-old newspaper.

Grammar

The entire chapter is built on declarative sentences, as is customary for a narrative introduction to place and personages. These sentences, which average sixteen words in length, are quite often complex, usually containing a relative clause or a verb phrase. Sentence structure is loose, a kind of construction in which trailing constituents predominate over anticipatory constituents. This structure removes suspense from a narrative and creates a sense of naturalness, directness, relaxation, ease, and informality that is perfect for the lazy days at the Lebrun resort. The most common sentence structure is the subject followed by an element such as a verb or relative clause and complemented by a participle, as in "it was the mockingbird . . . whistling," ". . . he, understanding . . . ," and "the gulf looked far away, melting. . . ." This structure, which occurs in fourteen of the sixty sentences in the chapter, adds to the feeling of suspension conveyed through the lexical features.

Figures of Speech

With only one figure of speech, this chapter typifies the naturalness and directness of Chopin's language throughout *The Awakening*. There are few rhetorical flourishes here (little rhyme, alliteration, assonance, etc.), so that a figure of speech surprises the careful reader. The quasi simile "looking at his wife as one looks at a valuable piece of personal property which has suffered some damage" thus comes forcefully to the reader's attention, bringing with it the notions of possession and economics that are central to the novel.

Cohesion

The most notable feature of cohesion (or connectives within the text) is the use of third-person pronouns to refer to the subject of the preceding sentence or paragraph. It is noteworthy that Mr. Pontellier is the subject of every paragraph except the opening two, which feature the parrot. This concentrated focus on Edna's husband becomes more significant as one reads the novel, for he subsequently figures less prominently in its events. Let us look at the elements of narrative point of view and speech and thought presentation to see how Chopin skillfully removes Mr. Pontellier from an inner, closed circle.

Narrative Stance

As is typical of nineteenth-century novels, the third-person narrator here sees all and knows what all characters are thinking. The direct description of Léonce Pontellier, who is viewed as if immobile, as if in a photograph, is sparse in detail. There are no value judgments in the description ("wore eye-glasses," "of forty," "of medium height and slender build," "stooped a little," "hair was brown and straight") of this seemingly central character. His description is in notable contrast to that of Mme Lebrun, who is depicted by such subjective adjectives as "fresh" and "pretty" and who, in comparison with Léonce, is active, interesting, and vital. Instead of seeing much of Mr. Pontellier, the reader must learn about him from what he does (smokes, reads, and leaves) and how he interacts with others (disgusted by the noise around him, mildly angry with his wife, etc.). The apparent objectivity of the narrator is undermined by the many negative verbs used to describe Mr. Pontellier's actions ("unable to read," "ceased", "stopped," "quitting") and by the irony contained in the following passage: "The parrot and the mocking-bird were the property of Madame Lebrun, and they had the right to make all the noise they wished. Mr. Pontellier had the privilege of quitting their society when they ceased to be entertaining." Wayne Booth's "secret communion" between implied author and implied reader (304) is carried out through the ironic juxtaposition of the birds, who have rights, and Mr. Pontellier, who has none. Although the narrator is not intrusive here, a certain distancing from Mr. Pontellier is clearly intended, and the reader is left with the impression of a rather boring man who is not even interesting enough to be invited to remain in the company of a pair of birds.

Speech and Thought Presentation

Even though there is little direct reported speech in this chapter, this is probably the most important stylistic category for establishing the relationships among characters in the novel. The chapter opens with a quotation in direct speech, which is notable both for being in a foreign language, French, and for being uttered by a parrot. The words "*Allez-vous-en! Allez-vous-en! Sapristi!* That's all right!" seem to be addressed to the only observer on the scene, Mr. Pontellier. The mild insult combines with the mockingbird's "maddening persistence" in whistling to force Mr. Pontellier from the birds' presence. Mr. Pontellier is thus isolated and alienated from—and even rejected by—the victors on the porch, who have all the rights while he has none. (It later becomes clear that the parrot did indeed intend to order Mr. Pontellier from his presence and that his command was a speech act, not just a repetition; this revelation occurs in chapter 9 when the parrot uses the same words to order the Farival twins away from the piano: " '*Allez-vous-en! Sapristi!*' shrieked the parrot outside the door. He was the only being present who possessed sufficient candor to admit that he was not listening to these gracious performances for the first time that summer.")

In the next instance of speech presentation, a parallel between Mr. Pontellier and the parrot is effected through the former's addressing his wife with a mild insult: "What folly! to bathe at such an hour in such heat!" The commanding insult hurled at Mr. Pontellier by the parrot had effectively alienated him and removed him from the presence of the birds. Likewise, Pontellier's insult to his wife, which is exacerbated by the exaggerated statement "You are burnt beyond recognition," sets him apart from Edna and her friend. Here Mr. Pontellier has violated a rule of conversation by stating what is patently false in a feeble attempt to make his voice heard and to make himself count in the threesome.

In the nonconversation that follows, the relationship between Edna and her husband is exposed as one in which the marriage partners communicate very poorly with each other. Throughout the exchange, Edna does not respond to Mr. Pontellier's speech acts, refusing to rise to the bait of the insult and instead laughing at and with Robert. In response to Mr. Pontellier's "What is it?" the two friends engage in an unsuccessful attempt to describe to an outsider, Edna's husband, an adventure that they have shared. Mr. Pontellier then tries to persuade Robert to accompany him to the billiards game, an invitation that is turned down. Failing to perceive the reality of the situation, that Edna and Robert prefer the company of each other, Mr. Pontellier instructs his wife, "[S]end him about his business when he bores you, Edna," making the almost classic statement of a cuckold. Once again refusing to respond to his instructions, Edna issues one of her own—"Here, take the umbrella"—and then asks a familiar question without a subject: "Coming back to dinner?" The response is a shrug of the shoulders.

In the preceding exchange of words and gestures, little communication takes place between husband and wife. In fact, the only real contact between them occurs on an unspoken level, on two occasions. In the first, Edna silently reaches for her rings, which her husband is safeguarding in his pocket, and he, understanding, gives them to her. The other occurs at the end of the chapter, when Mr. Pontellier's thoughts about whether or not he will return to dinner are conveyed by the narrator; although these thoughts remain unspoken, they are understood by his wife. Both examples illustrate the patterns established in the marriage—the symbolic giving of the rings and the social proclivities of the husband—which have obviously been repeated many times. These are fragile moorings on which to base a marriage, especially in view of the brevity of the couple's spoken exchanges and their lack of appropriate responses to each other, indicating a deadness, a loss of passion, and mere acceptance of the conventions of the marriage. The closest that Edna and her husband will come to each other in this novel is in the unspoken thought that ends their interaction in the first chapter.

This survey of stylistic categories in chapter 1 of *The Awakening* only sketches the possibilities for linking language and meaning in the novel. For example, chapter 36 is crucial for demonstrating how Chopin uses pragmatics, or speech acts, to lead Edna and Robert to the fatal question, "What do you mean?" Chapter 10, in which Edna is introduced to swimming, could be studied from the perspective of narrative point of view, as an illumination of Edna's character, of what separates her from the other city visitors to Grand Isle. Other assignments might include the following: (1) Study the linguistic manifestations of the theme of ownership throughout the novel. (2) Examine the imagery of the novel and its effects. (3) Discover when and why the narrator breaks narrational silence and intrudes in the novel. (4) Analyze the major scenes of confrontation through conversation, for example, between Edna and Mme Ratignolle (7), Edna and Mr. Pontellier (17), and Edna and Dr. Mandelet (38).

By concentrating on the linguistic features of *The Awakening*, my German students discovered that, far from being a dull exercise in stylistic analysis, this novel is rich in providing exciting avenues from language to meaning. In fact, they became so interested in the novel that they proposed translating it into German as a collective enterprise; a little research, however, showed that the task had already been accomplished. Although they were unable to undertake the translation, the students found that analysis of the novel's style was replete with insight into the heart of the text, especially into the psychological motivation of characters. It is evident that a thorough examination of the style of *The Awakening* as a whole (and of Chopin's entire fictional prose) would bolster the opinion, held by many critics, that Chopin should be regarded as a psychological realist rather than a regionalist. The psychological clues about characters and their relationships as well as the masterful buildup of atmosphere provided through the manipulation of language are glittering treasures for the student of style, who learns to appreciate the greatness of *The Awakening* on the most fundamental level, that of language.

Edna as Icarus: A Mythic Issue

Lawrence Thornton

After ten years of teaching *The Awakening* I have yet to meet a class that is not enthusiastic about Chopin's themes and sympathetic toward Edna Pontellier. Students immediately respond to Edna as a type, an Everywoman who courageously chooses death over the dishonor of submitting to marital and social conventions, and they regard the novel's powerful imagery of repression and liberation as a distant mirror of conditions facing contemporary women and minority groups. Paradoxically, this sympathy, and the ethical philosophy behind it, makes teaching *The Awakening* fairly tricky. Men and women, blacks and whites, Asians and Hispanics are so caught up in Edna's pursuit of freedom and identity that they frequently lose the critical distance necessary to understand how Edna bears a certain responsibility for her fate. Since I have encountered this problem at an open-admissions state university, a highly selective liberal arts college, and a major research institution, it seems universal enough for me to briefly discuss the means I have used to deal with it.

While there is no question that *The Awakening* is a strong political novel, it is also a subtle psychological study in the manner of *Madame Bovary*, and the challenge to the teacher lies in finding ways to synthesize these elements. One way to do this is to begin with Chopin's major symbolism, the myth of Icarus. Approaching the novel from this perspective has two advantages. First, it immediately establishes a broad context for a study of ambition and overreaching. Second, it reveals a protagonist considerably more interesting and sympathetic than she would be as a mere political victim. I present this analysis at the beginning of the two class sessions devoted to the novel. While references to the myth are scattered throughout the text, the most important appear in the two or so pages of chapter 27. This material can be covered in about thirty minutes of intensive explication.

Short as it is, chapter 27 is a dramatic high point in the novel, the place where a peculiar conversation between Edna and Alcée Arobin culminates in "the first kiss of her life to which her nature had really responded." I go through it almost line by line, beginning with the sequence of events leading up to the kiss: Edna's return from Mlle Reisz's apartment, where she admitted her love for Robert Lebrun; her letter to Léonce announcing her intention to move to the "pigeon house"; Arobin's arrival and the time they spend together before the fire while he plays with Edna's hair and she responds "sensitively."

Arobin is wonderfully presented as an archetypal roué who has only one thing on his mind. Students see this immediately and generally assume that Edna's thoughts have drifted back to Robert. I suggest that they look again and pay close attention to what Edna says. With a little help they see that she is interested in something Mlle Reisz told her earlier in the day, and they conclude that an idea has precedence over both Alcée and Robert. To emphasize the importance of this ranking in Edna's mind, I read the following passage aloud:

> One of these days . . . I'm going to pull myself together for a while and *think*—try to determine what character of woman I am; for, candidly, I don't know. By all the codes which I am acquainted with, I am a devilishly wicked specimen of the sex. But some way I can't convince myself that I am. I must *think* about it. (my italics)

Then I insist that the class underline *think* and any variation of the word they find in the chapter. Explanations will follow.

The next stop on the way to the labyrinth and Icarus is embedded in one of the novel's truly comic moments. After listening to Edna, Alcée suspects that her moral scruples may deflect his desire, so he hastily says "Don't" to her intention to "think." Full of flattery, he can tell her what "character of woman" she is, but Edna is not fooled. She knows what he will say and tells him not to bother. Then she asks, irrelevantly as far as Arobin is concerned, "Do you know Mademoiselle Reisz?" He does, indifferently, but Edna's thought has already gone considerably beyond his answer. She wants to get at an idea that has been bothering her, an idea planted by the irascible pianist: "She says queer things sometimes in a bantering way that you don't notice at the time and you find yourself *thinking* about afterward" (my italics). Arobin remains patiently beside her. Although she is not talking about him, she has not moved, and he continues playing with her hair, half listening to what he considers idle chatter, asking for an example. Edna responds:

> Well, for instance, when I left to-day, she put her arms around me and felt my shoulder blades, to see if my wings were strong, she said. "The bird that would soar above the level plain of tradition and prejudice must have strong wings. It is a sad spectacle to see the weaklings bruised, exhausted, fluttering back to earth."

Arobin accommodates his language to Mlle Reisz's rhetorical flourishes: "Whither would you soar?" he asks. Despite the leer one imagines as he speaks, it is a key question that galvanizes all the apparently casual references to flight up to this point in the novel. The question, I suggest, has to do with the nature of flight, and I ask the class to listen carefully to Edna's response: "I'm not *thinking* of any extraordinary flights. *I only half comprehend her*" (my italics).

Frustrated because the musician has got between him and the woman he desires, Arobin responds petulantly, "Why have you introduced her at a moment when I desired to talk of you?" Before going on with this exchange, I remind the class that we have reached that critical juncture in the text where Edna will, in a matter of minutes, abandon her role as obedient wife and conventional mother and become Arobin's mistress. The context of this choice, I add, has never really been closely attended to, and one learns something absolutely essential to a full understanding of the novel when the situation is clearly grasped. Again I ask the class to listen to what she says. " 'Oh! talk of me if you like,' cried Edna, clasping her hands beneath her head; 'but let me *think* of something else while you do' " (my italics). Edna is simply no longer present at the scene.

Arobin senses that something is wrong and feels jealous of her thoughts: "some way I feel as if they were wandering, as if they were not here with me." That is one of the few accurate observations Arobin is allowed. Edna "only looked at him and smiled," after which follow kisses and seduction.

Attentive students see what has happened. They quickly offer lists of images associated with flight and birds, and I encourage these observations while pointing out that Chopin has also made much of understanding, that "awakening" always partakes of both physical and intellectual knowledge. And so, after arguing that the novel is based on ideas about flight and knowledge, I remind the class that it opens with a resplendent parrot in a cage, a prototypical bird whose prison is symbolic of gulf and maze, society and conventions. With any luck the students begin to see the outlines of the mythological world Chopin has been patiently working up from the opening sentence.

Before taking on the myth directly, I spend more time discussing references to thought and knowledge scattered through the novel, noting that Chopin often breaks into the normal scenic presentation of the work and comments with all the freedom and authority of omniscience. Chapter 6 provides a dramatic illustration:

> A certain light was beginning to dawn dimly within her,—the light which, showing the way, forbids it. . . .
>
> Mrs. Pontellier was beginning to realize her position in the universe as a human being. . . .
>
> But the beginning of things, of a world especially, is necessarily vague, tangled, chaotic, and exceedingly disturbing. How few of us ever emerge from such beginnings! How many souls perish in the tumult!

I argue that the authority of this voice, the ironic tone and the sense of foreboding that hangs over these statements, is not to be confused with

Edna's thoughts. Although Edna always seems to reach for understanding, wants to see it emerge from the mist, she never fully possesses it. The hazy desire to contemplate Mlle Reisz's warning is as far as she gets.

With most classes this perception is the moment of truth. My desire all along has been to show the students how the problematics of knowledge and the mythic element of the novel dovetail in the little scene leading up to Edna's seduction. At this juncture I suggest that *The Awakening* is about "the bird that would soar above the level plain of tradition and prejudice" and about what is involved in such an escape. As Mlle Reisz knows, such soaring, such "knowledge," requires "strong wings," a synecdoche of self-knowledge—"What character of woman I am." The central issue of the musician's question, then, has to do with knowledge of the conditions that will greet Edna once she leaves the plain of tradition, that is, the labyrinth of social conventions, marriage, and motherhood that is closing around her like a vise.

The overall mythic structure of the novel can now be quickly filled in: the house on Esplanade Street, the Tuesday at home, the insistent children, the "mother-women" function as aspects of the labyrinth. The minotaur is Léonce and, more generally, marriage. Daedalus is Mlle Reisz, who flouts conventions and survives by understanding the conditions of her life and the costs and consequences of freedom and independence. In examining Edna's shoulder blades to ascertain whether Edna has the knowledge to fly, the musician is as cautious as an instructor checking a protégé's parachute before a first jump. To emphasize this point, I read from the myth and repeat Daedalus's injunction to Icarus to keep a middle course over the sea. Fly too high, I suggest, ignore what your elder says, and your wax will melt, your wings will disappear, and so will you.

I ask the class to return to our scene, reading it now with an eye not only to the relationship between Edna and Icarus but also to the motif of understanding that I argue is central to the myth, perhaps even its moral. I say that Edna has consciously made herself available to Arobin even though she knows that Mlle Reisz's warning should not be dismissed. In fact, she seems aware that her friend's image could help her understand her own nature and present condition. I emphasize that the musician's comment should be seen as a terribly dramatic sign, like the voice from the control tower warning of wind shear. Then I ask the class to look at what Edna says—"One of these days . . . I'm going to pull myself together for a while and think"—and at her saying it as Arobin is making the first gestures of his desire known to her, a desire that even to someone as relatively sheltered as Edna carries enough complications that prudence would seem to require "thinking" about what is going to happen before it does. The class agrees, and then they see, remembering her qualification—"I only half comprehend her." Out of that half knowledge tragedy strikes, albeit in slow motion. Edna, like Icarus, is enamoured of the sky. Succumbing to Arobin is like the flight up and away, but Edna does not consider the consequences her old mentor has presented in the image of the falling bird.

By the time Arobin leaves, Edna has settled for inferior knowledge inspired by his embrace. She believes she understands "the significance of life," and the cliché guides us to what Chopin wants us to think about that. Edna has sex with Arobin not out of love, or even lust, but because the act, carnal knowledge, is the equal of wings to her. She flies out of the labyrinth of tradition and prejudice, having forgotten that she was going to think, having ignored the chilling image the musician offered of the weaklings, the ignorant, "fluttering back to earth." That image of a bird falling from the sky, from its own ignorance, becomes her memento mori.

To see how all this should be regarded, we must have recourse once again to Mlle Reisz's words. "It is a sad spectacle to see the weaklings. . . ." She asks Edna point-blank whether she is strong enough to fly, that is, to endure the consequences of escape, and it is clear that Edna does not understand.

By "sad spectacle" Mlle Reisz means two things. First, spectacle: something silly, foolish, immodest, immature. Second, SPECTACLE: a mighty scene, something the observer might attend to and learn from, a tragedy. Edna and Icarus exemplify both definitions, and students begin to see how easily myth and reality join here, as through a semipermeable membrane. Edna and Icarus exist on two planes at once, I suggest. As persons, they represent the little world of an embarrassing spectacle where overreaching leads to catastrophe. As examples, however, they represent themselves center stage in the world of tragedy.

Such, in my estimation, is what Chopin has been getting at all along: *The Awakening* as exemplum. Edna Pontellier lives in a time and place where essence is confounded with role, the dancer with the dance. The self can only thrive by discarding its role and flying to freedom, to some place where one's sex is not the determinant of one's destiny. It can happen, I tell the class. We have the examples of Mlle Reisz and of Chopin herself, who maintained her distance from the crowd and carved out an identity in language.

Self-realization is never easy, and I think it is essential to help our students understand the importance of Mlle Reisz's injunction about strength and knowledge. Chopin, I conclude, tells us that escape requires careful calculation of all consequences, particularly those only half comprehended. In other words, escape in Chopin's lexicon means "thinking" about what happens afterward. Miscalculation, inattention to common sense, led Icarus to the terrible fall that Auden imagined while "the sun shone / As it had to on the white legs disappearing into the green / Water." Or, for Edna, to the sensuous touch of the sea, regrets, images of her youth, "the dusky odor of pinks."

Focusing initially on the ironic function of the Icarus references provides a context for a detailed psychological study of a woman caught between the oppressive conditions of her society and fantasies that led to a fatal choice. It is my belief that students must understand the degree of Edna's illusion at the end of the narrative as she dies with the romantic sound of the cavalry officer's spurs that return her to her adolescence. Those final lines backlight the novel as surely as Flaubert's do at the end of *Sentimental Education* when the aged Frederick and Deslauriers agree that the best time of their lives was a nonevent, an illusion. Such a comparison makes it easier to see how clearly Chopin is working in the tradition of psychological realism, a mode that questions both the nature of Edna's desires and the romantic flight she takes out of the bayou.

Edna as Psyche:
The Self and the Unconscious

Rosemary F. Franklin

The Eros and Psyche myth, especially as interpreted by the Jungian theorist Erich Neumann, helps to clarify for students some of the widely divergent interpretations of *The Awakening*. The mythic model mediates the extreme views of Edna as either consummate hero or pathetic victim. It accounts for the possible failure implied by Edna's suicide but also avoids the psychological approach that sees Edna's conflict as narrowly pathological. A view of Edna as a Psyche figure broadens her struggle to a universal and tragic one.

The Psyche myth shares the tripartite structure of the male hero myth—the departure, the labors, and the reward—but differs from that myth in the seeming passivity of Psyche's activity. Psyche is the victim of Aphrodite, who becomes jealous when the beautiful young mortal diverts worshippers from her shrines. She condemns Psyche to a "wedding" with the monster death, but Eros, Aphrodite's son and the assigned executioner, falls in love with Psyche and spirits her away to a dream palace where all her physical needs are provided. She cannot see Eros, who comes to her nightly as her lover, and he warns her not to become curious about his identity.

Psyche's life goes on in easy pleasure until her jealous stepsisters arouse her suspicions about the "monster" she sleeps with. Psyche decides to see him and kill him. In her first assertive act, she arms herself with a knife and carries an oil lamp to hold over the sleeping Eros. In the light of the lamp she clearly sees the beautiful god of love, and, startled, she drops some hot oil on him. Simultaneously, she is accidentally wounded by one of his arrows. Eros runs away and Psyche is left alone and pregnant.

This portion of the myth presents a mortal whose beauty sets her apart from the collective—the community's pressure of opinion that blocks the individual. She is alienated from her culture and singled out for punishment by the type of the Terrible Mother, who takes revenge on the female departing from the matriarchy's purely procreative goals. In his lust, Eros too would dominate Psyche and forbid her to know him beyond his dark embrace. Their symbiotic sexual and romantic love discourages individuation. But some elemental drive to awareness arouses Psyche's curiosity, and her dawning consciousness brings about the separation necessary before individuation can occur. Their wounds represent both their "fall" and their bond.

Alone, Psyche journeys out to find Eros. When she arrives at Aphrodite's palace, the goddess, now more enraged than ever because her son and the mortal have deceived her, commands Psyche to perform seemingly impossible labors. This segment of the myth suggests again that the collective

144

wants to reserve passion for its service and punish the errant individual. Psyche uncomplainingly submits to Aphrodite's commands, but several times the magnitude of the tasks makes her want to commit suicide.

In her four labors Psyche deals with superhuman powers. Told to sort a great pile of seeds, she succeeds only through the help of ants. Out of chaos potentials for growth are brought into order. The second task is to steal some wool from golden sun rams. Despondently, she thinks of drowning herself in a nearby river. But a river reed counsels her to wait until dark and pluck some of the wool from bushes the rams have brushed against. Then Aphrodite tells Psyche to take a crystal goblet and fetch the water of a torrential stream pouring from heaven to Hades. Here Zeus's eagle flies to her aid, completing this task. In these labors Psyche has received help from benevolent creatures of nature, suggestive, perhaps, of inner, instinctual resources she is developing.

But Aphrodite has grown very angry and now assigns the task that Psyche has to perform alone: go down to Hades and fetch a beauty ointment for Aphrodite. In despair Psyche thinks of suicide as the quickest way to Hades. As she climbs a tower to throw herself off, the tower speaks to her and tells her of a secret route to Hades and a ritual method to avoid destruction. One thing she must do is refuse to give aid to anyone who asks it. The desire for relationship is a strength and weakness of woman. In the struggle to find self, a woman may have to refuse to enter draining relationships. After performing her tasks as directed, Psyche is on her way back up from Hades with the ointment box when she thinks that Eros might be won over if she applied some of the cream. As she opens the box, a deathly sleep emerges and she succumbs. On the brink of triumph, she seems to fail. But Eros's love is so aroused that he flies down from his heavenly seat and removes the ointment. Thereupon he enlists Zeus's support for a marriage, Psyche is elevated to heavenly status, and the child Joy is born.

The dark palace of Eros, the impulses to suicide, Hades, and the box of beauty cream are all one—the regression of the individual to unconsciousness. What was at first perceived as comfortable pleasure is finally deathlike to the emerging ego. The labors toward individuation involve ordering, grasping, and containing diffuse and threatening psychic energy. In the myth, aid comes from without, but psychologically these helpers are inner resources whose representations progress from ants to an eagle, a tower, and finally Eros, the impulse to life instead of death. The mortal becomes queen, Aphrodite becomes the benevolent mother-in-law, and the whole character of human life is elevated as mere pleasure gives way to joy.

Edna's life traces Psyche's. As the novel opens, Edna lives in the Catholic Creole collective as a married woman and the mother of two. But, as Adèle observes, Edna is not one of the matriarchs whose role it is to regulate society for the patriarchs. Edna's Protestantism and its concomitant, the desire to strike out alone, place her apart. She first awakens to the sexuality she has suppressed, and then she begins a search for herself beyond the collective's definition. But her suicide tells us that she has failed, for reasons hard to define. The pattern of the myth aids understanding.

The "mother-women," represented by Adèle, are inhabitants of the sensual world Edna awakens to. But at the end of the novel Dr. Mandelet remarks that sensuality, the way nature provides mothers for the race, is really a trap, not an aspect of freedom. In this novel sexuality is outlawed except as it serves the matriarchal collective. Life in the palace with Eros is an unconscious one, even if pleasurable. Chapter 6, which describes the attraction and menace of the sea, indicates the burden under which Edna labors: to find the self one must go down into the darkness and reemerge, but the impulse to lose one's self there is as strong as the will to live. Eros and Thanatos are equally powerful gods in this novel. Edna's battles between waking and sleeping, learning to swim and drowning, and flying over the water and falling in are part of this mythic, psychological struggle.

Edna's struggle is more difficult than Psyche's, but it is also more true to the reality of women living in the nineteenth century. Edna is aroused to sexual awakening at the same time she first yearns for self-awakening. Psyche, in contrast, experiences sexual awakening separately in the palace of darkness. Self-awakening occurs after she is definitively separated from Eros. But Edna confuses the two, and she is thus pulled into a paradox of antagonistic awakenings. For example, she criticizes as "hopeless ennui" the fusion of two beings into one she sees in Adèle's marriage, but she fails to realize that this is the very same fusion she wishes with Robert (18).

Since *The Awakening* was published, a critical battle has been waged between those who see Edna as hero and those who see her as victim. This controversy can be depolarized in the light of the Psyche myth. Edna is both the heroine who sets out on the quest for self and the victim of the collective and of her own impulses to regress. Thus, she is a tragic heroine, surely a more interesting role than that of either hero(ine) or victim.

The question of tone relates to this issue as well. Chopin's narrative voice is both critical and sympathetic. It sets itself against Mr. Pontellier because "he could not see that [Edna] was becoming herself and daily casting aside that fictitious self which we assume like a garment with which to appear before the world" (19). But when Edna pities Adèle "for that colorless existence which never uplifted its possessor beyond the region of blind contentment," the narrator injects through indirect discourse an implied criticism of Edna's attitude: Edna thinks to herself that Adèle "would never have the taste of life's delirium. Edna vaguely wondered what she meant by 'life's delirium.' It had crossed her thought like some unsought, extraneous impression" (18). Much of the overwrought style of the novel is a parody of Edna's romanticism: Edna sees life as "a grotesque pandemonium and humanity like worms struggling blindly toward inevitable annihilation" (19). Many who criticized *The Awakening* right after its publication probably did not notice the distinction between Chopin and this parodic narrative voice, erroneously thinking that Chopin herself had succumbed to a decadent romanticism.

In many ways *The Awakening* is a critique of romantic love. Chopin understands that sometimes the animus in the woman is so strongly projected onto the beloved that she cannot perceive the real man. Mlle Reisz understands projection too as she asks Edna if she loves *Robert*. Edna responds, saying a woman does not select nor can she know why she loves (26). Even Edna, like a tragic hero, knows her weakness—succumbing to "infatuation"—because she had been infatuated as a girl with three men, and the "hopelessness" of these loves colored them "with the lofty tones of a great passion" (7). But she persists in loving Robert, especially since he is gone, and only when he returns from Mexico does she allow herself to perceive briefly that some of the romance wanes because he is with her (33).

As the stimulus to Edna's awakening, Robert is the most important Eros figure in the novel, and after he leaves for Mexico, because, like Eros, he fears the collective, Edna must begin the lonely labor to find herself. Alcée and Victor are two other faces of Eros. Alcée, the promiscuous aspect of Eros, bears a wound from a duel over love and describes himself as "a wicked, ill-disciplined boy" (25). That Edna has an affair with him even as she knows Robert is returning demonstrates that lust is a small part of her love for Robert. Victor is a more innocent Alcée. This high-spirited, youthful Eros plays the role at Edna's party, where he is draped and bedecked with roses and where Gouvernail quotes from Swinburne on desire (30). Significantly, all these men revolve around the matriarchs, who keep them more or less under control.

After Edna returns to New Orleans, she must embark on Psyche's task of developing her strengths. She resumes painting, but before art can enable her to find herself, she must deal with the moods that arise from her discontent and her romantic fantasies. Warned by Mlle Reisz, Edna needs to grow strong wings to fly above the "plain of tradition and prejudice." She engages in a "quest"—Chopin's word—to gain advice from her friends, but her quest for knowledge about her self is mixed in with her desire to gain information about Robert. Here she again traces Psyche's pattern. Instead of pursuing positive labors, however, Edna seems to be consuming psychic energy fighting despondency. Adèle's marriage depresses her, and at the Lebruns' house she almost gives up her quest when she finds Robert has not mentioned her in letters.

Edna's birthday party marks a significant moment for her. It is a private coming of age since she plans to move into the "pigeon house." The narrative voice strikes a triumphant tone as it describes her as "the regal woman, the one who rules, who looks on, who stands alone," but almost immediately despair strikes her: "she felt the old ennui overtaking her; the hopelessness which so often assailed her, which came upon her like an obsession. . . . a chill breath . . . seemed to issue from some vast cavern wherein discords wailed" (30). She thinks of the "unattainable" beloved and begins a journey down into her own Hades, dressed almost like Persephone, goddess of the underworld.

Edna's mood persists as the novel rapidly draws to a close. After she and Robert have revealed their love for each other, Robert is frightened by her determination to manage her own life because he is still very much a creature of the collective. He definitively separates from her for the second and last time. Ironically, the hold of the matriarchy over Edna is also evident as she leaves Robert to attend Adèle's delivery. Adèle's physical labor distracts Edna from the spiritual labor in which she is engaged. She leaves the "scene of torture" with Adèle's warning in her mind—"Think of the children" (37). Not only must Edna remember her duty to her present children, but she may also be thinking of some possible future children if she lives her life as a sexually liberated woman. These thoughts are amplified as Dr. Mandelet expresses his opinion that romantic love is nature's trick to secure mothers for the race. Edna's awakening to the illusion of romantic love is reinforced by Robert's departure. As the night passes, she realizes that no man will ever satisfy her restless soul. She can never return to the dark palace where perfect union with the beloved is imaginable, and she is unable to engage in the true labors to find her self. The loneliness of the solitary soul engulfs her as the powerful unintegrated contents of the unconscious win.

Because I want to avoid giving the teacher's prescription, I do not offer this approach until my students have had two days to discuss the novel. After free discussion I may summarize several of the interpretive issues that this pattern clarifies, such as Edna's propensity to sleep, the sea as symbol of both losing and finding the self, Edna's moods and aimlessness, Edna's "love" for Robert, Chopin's attitude toward Edna, and, of course, the reason for Edna's suicide. Then I pass out a chart summarizing the myth. This is an opportunity to introduce Jung and archetypal criticism to undergraduates. In courses on women in literature, summarizing feminist debate on the implications of the myth leads to lively discussion (see the references to criticism in Franklin). In a realism and naturalism course, the instructor can raise important questions about the mythopoeic qualities of a novel usually categorized as realistic.

APPENDIX

The Myth of Psyche and Eros and Archetypal Meaning

Psyche's Early Experience and Development	
	Jungian Interpretation
Psyche arouses Aphrodite's jealousy.	The "Terrible Mother," the collective, resists development of the individual.
Eros visits Psyche anonymously in the palace.	Sexual and romantic love do not further individuation.
Psyche, armed with knife and oil lamp, sees Eros.	The coming of consciousness is accompanied by suffering and separation.

Psyche's Labors	
1. Ants help her sort seeds.	Ordering the unconscious powers with the aid of intuition and insight (perhaps Eros). Benevolent nature aids the first three labors.
2. River reed tells her to gather rams' wool at night.	
3. Eagle fetches goblet of water from torrential river.	
4. Tower instructs her on her way to Hades. She is warned not to show pity.	Fourth labor is direct confrontation with the unconscious. Requires resolute ego.
Psyche fails because she opens box of beauty ointment.	Failure may be necessary to restore feminine balance.

Resolution of the Myth	
Eros rescues and marries Psyche. She is elevated to status of goddess.	Psyche attains fully conscious selfhood.
Child Joy is born.	The unconscious is no longer threatening.

A Reader-Response Approach

Elizabeth Rankin

> The cat made friends with him, and climbed into his
> lap when he smoked his cigar. He stroked her silky
> fur, and talked a little about her. He looked at Edna's
> book, which he had read; and he told her the end, to
> save her the trouble of wading through it, he said. (36)

Robert Lebrun and Edna Pontellier are readers. It is one of the things they
share with each other, one of the things they share with us as well. One
imagines them reading a book like Chopin's *The Awakening*—Edna, there
in the suburban café, absorbed in the romance of a young married woman
and her admirer, awash in the luxuriant sensuality of the images. She is not
yet halfway through the novel, but she can foresee its ending: the lovers (of
this she is certain) are doomed. There is no way for them, no hope of breaking
the bonds of convention and responsibility that tie them down. Their fate
(Edna sees this already) is tragic, but how will it come about? Robert knows.
He read this novel earlier in the summer when those scandalous French
romances were making the rounds. "She dies in the end," Robert tells her.
"Walks into the Gulf and drowns herself. It is all very sad." Edna nods. It
is what she expected. There seems to be no need to go on reading now.

Yes, they are much alike, Robert Lebrun and Edna Pontellier—much
alike and much like any first-time reader of novels. Much like our students
when they first encounter *The Awakening*, much like us when we first
encountered it years or months, maybe only weeks, ago. Students have
certain expectations when they read the novel, expectations shaped by their
culture, their knowledge, their desires. Inevitably, what they bring to the
novel influences what they find there. And so as they read, they project and
predict, hypothesize and revise, until finally the novel coheres in their
imaginations.

When I first taught *The Awakening* in my American literature survey
class, I had read it myself only once, and only weeks before. Its newness
probably inspired the approach I would take, the way I would try to share
with my students the experience of reading this enchanting, seductive, intriguing, unsettling novel.

It is often said that we do not read novels, we reread them. And, in fact,
all the traditional critical approaches to literature presume rereading. They
see reading not as a temporal but as a spatial experience, the book not as
act but as artifact. Within these approaches, the readers' part is minimal; if
they take an active role in the reading process, it is only to speculate about

150

the author's intentions. With the advent of phenomenology and reader-response criticism, though, this conventional approach has been challenged. Teachers and theorists seek out ways to validate the reading experience itself, to open it into a conscious process that empowers the reader, calls attention to the interpretive act, and reveals to us the part we play in the act of reading (Tompkins, *Reader-Response Criticism*; Suleiman and Crosman).

In one sense, reader-response criticism is not novel-specific: in revealing to the reader the dynamics of the reading process, it is teaching a habit of reading, a self-conscious approach that can be applied to the reading of any novel, any story, any poem—or any road sign or menu, for that matter. What such an approach does is open up the novel, revealing its temporal nature, its rhetorical structure, the sources of its emotional impact on the reader. With *The Awakening*, however, a reader-response approach is still more revealing. For as it exposes the dynamics of the reading process, exploding the notion of the passive, receptive reader, it also unmasks the dilemma of the novel's central character, Edna Pontellier.

In Edna's eyes, her dilemma is unresolvable. Circumscribed by the assumptions and expectations of her culture, she breaks out of the confining role of "mother-woman" in search of some more fulfilling notion of self. "I would give my life for my children," she tells Mme Ratignolle, "but I wouldn't give myself" (16). But what exactly is this self she is after? Can it be defined apart from its social context? If Edna's frantic attempts to divest herself of all obligations and bonds is any indication, she seems to think that it can. But what she does not realize is that she can no more abstract her self from the roles she plays than the reader can abstract himself or herself from the text. The complex interrelation of individual, family, social milieu, and larger culture is as much a given for Edna as the rhetorical relation between reader, writer, text, and world is for us.

This is not to say that Edna must simply accept these roles and take a passive attitude toward her fate in the world. Rather, she must find a place to stand in that world, a place that is both within her culture and outside it, just as the reader must stand both within and outside the text. The purpose of a reader-response approach to *The Awakening* is to help students see for themselves that there is such a place.

Of course a reader-response approach might take many forms, as is demonstrated by Russell Hunt and Kathleen McCormick in two fine articles in *College English*. In my classes, I begin by intervening in the reading process, asking students to stop halfway through the novel and predict where it is heading. An analysis of these predictions will reveal two things: the values and assumptions the students have brought to the text and the expectations the developing text has been shaping.

For instance, suppose that some students predict (as they inevitably do, in my classes) that Edna will leave Léonce to pursue her romantic dreams, only to become disillusioned and return to him, chastened, in the end. Such a prediction, bound to provoke disagreement, leads immediately to a consideration of a variety of possible scenarios:

1. Edna leaves Léonce, realizes her mistake, and returns, purged of her selfish romantic notions.
2. Edna leaves Léonce and finds freedom and fulfillment in a new life.
3. Edna leaves Léonce, only to find that the world outside is ugly and cold; she realizes her mistake, but too late.
4. Edna leaves Léonce, finds a brief interlude of happiness, but is forced by societal pressures to return.

Obviously, these options do not exhaust the possibilities. There are any number of other issues to consider: Will Edna run away with Robert, or on her own? Will she leave the children? What will become of her art? What fulfillment will she find in the world outside? what frustrations? If she does return, what factors will influence her decision?

To get a sense of the possibilities, the options confronting both Edna and Kate Chopin, I sometimes chart the class's predictions on the board, including at the same time variations on these possibilities that the students, for one reason or another, did not predict. A typical chart, when it is finished, might look something like the one shown here. Most reader predictions will cluster around certain nodes on the chart; these clusters offer a good place to start the discussion.

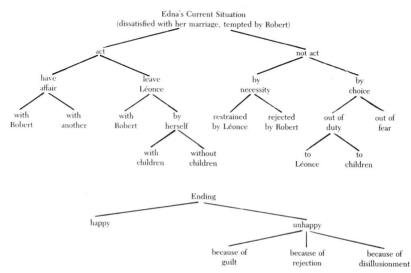

If some students expect Edna to leave Léonce and be miserable, for instance, why do others expect her to leave and find fulfillment? Have some readers read the novel more closely than others, noticed clues in the characterization or imagery that would favor one of these options? Since this is certainly possible, it is well to begin with a close examination of the text. One question might focus on Léonce's character. Is Léonce, as Edna's friends believe, the "best husband in the world"? Those who think so cite Edna's own admission that "she knew of none better," perhaps supporting their argument by pointing out the gifts he brings to Edna, the concern he shows for her welfare. In these readers' views, Léonce has good reason to be unhappy with Edna: she is immature, peevish, and generally neglectful of her children. As these traditionalists make their case, though, other students object. They cite Léonce's arrogance, his condescending attitude. They point up the irony in the narrator's paean to the virtues of the mother-women and note the contrasting imagery of the caged bird and open sea.

In the course of this discussion, some minds may change. But textual evidence alone cannot resolve these matters. Even if readers agree, finally, that Léonce is not the ideal husband and that Edna is no paragon of feminist virtue, they will still predict different endings. And having become aware of their different predictions, they will now be eager to continue reading the novel, to find out who is "wrong" and who is "right." Their desire, of course, is perfectly natural. One of the pleasures of reading, for all of us, is having our expectations fulfilled—or expertly subverted. But at this point there is more to be gained by delaying this pleasure, by further pursuing instead the original questions: What accounts for our different predictions about the novel? What factors influence our divergent expectations?

For many students, these will be difficult questions. So far, they have managed to imagine only one story—a story consistent with their working theory of the world—and their lack of life experience and previous academic training make it difficult for them to imagine any other, much less to probe the workings of their own imaginations. In this they are very much like Edna Pontellier herself, for Edna too has trouble imagining stories. When we meet her, she is in transition. Having found that she simply cannot accept the common story of her culture, a story that does not account for her feelings and needs as a woman and human being, she is trying to imagine a more inclusive alternative. But, like our students, she is limited by her lack of world experience; forced to come up with an alternative for the story she is rejecting, Edna seizes on the kind of story she is used to reading—in this instance, the romantic novel. What this story offers her is a role she finds more satisfying than that of mother-woman: the role of romantic adventuress—or tragic heroine.

Similarly, many students will reject one story (one reading of the novel) for another. Some may, in fact, follow Edna's lead, rejecting the possibility of her returning to Léonce in the end, only to substitute for this story a romantic version in which Edna runs away with Robert and finds happiness and fulfillment. Others will, however, go even further than Edna. After all, they are in an English class, and no matter what their previous pleasure-reading experience urges them to believe, they know that the happily-ever-after ending is infrequent in serious literature. Already, then, they have a perspective that Edna does not have, and from this perspective they envision an unhappy end to the story.

Interestingly, this unhappy ending usually takes a predictable form as well. In my classes, at least, students are much more likely to predict that Edna will leave Léonce, become disillusioned with her dreams, and end up alone than that she will leave Léonce, find she lacks the courage to defy society, and allow herself to be coaxed back into the stifling role of mother-woman. (The possibility that she will commit suicide seems to be almost unthinkable; in all the times I have taught the novel, only one student has predicted it—a West German swimmer, only recently arrived in this country.)

The reasons governing such expectations are varied. Perhaps as readers we too are seduced by the old romantic notion of the isolated self. We see it not only in popular fiction and drama but in the very classics of American literature that may have preceded our reading of Chopin's novel in the survey course. Or perhaps we feel that a novel should take us somewhere, that it should not simply circle back on itself (the way life does). This, in effect, is what would happen if Edna returned, out of weakness, to Léonce in the end. Other reasons may have more to do with desire than with expectations. If we want a happy ending for the novel but know we cannot realistically expect one, we may compromise our knowledge with our desire, envisioning an unhappy ending that is not yet quite final. For instance, those who believe in the traditional story that Edna has rejected may prefer the nonclosure of her being unhappy and alone because such an ending still holds out the possibility, beyond the last page of the novel, that Edna will eventually come to her senses and return.

The factors that shape our predictions for the story are fascinating—and crucial, too, for understanding this particular novel. I have said that students have trouble recognizing these factors, because they have not yet developed an ironic stance—the ability to see their worlds as another kind of fiction. Still, with the right questions, we can nurture this ironic habit. Instead of asking, "Why did you predict that Edna will find happiness with Robert?" we might ask, "What factors might influence a reader to expect such an ending?" Some of these factors, of course, are in the text, but others are in the reader—or, rather, in the complex set of attitudes, experience, and desires that inform the reading process. By helping our students to ask and answer these questions—first about other readers, then, tentatively, about themselves—we are helping them to broaden their field of vision.

I must add before closing that I am well aware of the irony of my own stance here. In talking about how to teach this novel, I presume to stand outside the text. Yet I am also within it, constructing a story about Edna Pontellier that is consistent with my theory. It is hard to say which came first: the story that I needed to imagine for Edna, to make her cohere in my imagination, or the theory that allowed me to see the form of that story. Many factors that I might explore are no doubt at work here: my feminist values, my modern literature background, the influence of colleagues steeped in poststructuralist theory—not to mention my congenital rage for order and delight in complexity. But perhaps the single most influential factor is a holdover from an earlier part of my education (some might call it a holdover from an earlier era). For me, this factor is as strong as the most naive reader's desire for a happy ending: it is the need to believe, despite all evidence to the contrary, that literature has something to teach us about how to live.

PARTICIPANTS IN SURVEY
OF *AWAKENING* INSTRUCTORS

William L. Andrews, University of Wisconsin, Madison; Kent Bales, University of Minnesota; Martha Banta, University of California, Los Angeles; Deborah J. Barrett, Houston Baptist University; Dale Marie Bauer, Miami University, Ohio; Carol M. Bensick, University of Oregon; Barbara Bilson, Santa Monica College; Lynn Z. Bloom, Virginia Commonwealth University; Thomas Bonner, Jr., Xavier University of Louisiana; Gina Burchard, Texas A&M University; Helen G. Chapin, Hawaii Pacific College; Beverly Lyon Clark, Wheaton College; Cathy N. Davidson, Michigan State University; Sara D. Davis, University of Alabama; Joan Del Fattore, University of Delaware; Maria Dittman, Marquette University; Margaret M. Dunn, Stetson University; Joyce Dyer, Western Reserve Academy; Deborah S. Ellis, Case Western Reserve University; Barbara C. Ewell, Loyola University, New Orleans; Elizabeth Fox-Genovese, Emory University; Rosemary F. Franklin, University of Georgia; Judi Gaitens, Kent State University; Marcia Gaudet, University of Southwestern Louisiana; E. Laurie George, New York Institute of Technology; Theodora R. Graham, Pennsylvania State University, Capitol Campus; Jo Ellen Jacobs, Millikin University; Elaine Jasenas, State University of New York, Binghamton; Suzanne W. Jones, University of Richmond; Karen Kalinevitch, St. Louis Community College, Florissant Valley; John M. Keeler, County College of Morris, New Jersey; M. Jimmie Killingsworth, Texas Tech University; Bernard Koloski, Mansfield University; Joyce Ladenson, Michigan State University; Andrew M. Lakritz, Miami University, Ohio; Kathleen M. Lant, California Polytechnic State University; Patricia Hopkins Lattin, University of Wisconsin Centers; Priscilla Leder, Louisiana State University, Eunice; Diane Lichtenstein, College of St. Thomas; Mary Mason, Emmanuel College, Boston; Robert McIlvaine, Slippery Rock University; Toni A. H. McNaron, University of Minnesota; Ann R. Morris, Stetson University; Patrick David Morrow, Auburn University; Merritt Moseley, University of North Carolina, Asheville; Lydia A. Panaro, Manhattan College; Mary E. Papke, University of Tennessee; Pamela L. Parker, North Harris County College, Houston; Marco Portales, University of Houston, Clear Lake; Elizabeth Rankin, University of North Dakota; James Rocks, Loyola University, Chicago; Nancy Rogers, National Endowment for the Humanities; Susan J. Rosowski, University of Nebraska, Lincoln; Margaret Schaefer, Chicago Institute for Psychoanalysis; John Schilb, Associated Colleges of the Midwest; Anne Howland Schotter, Wagner College; Kathryn Lee Seidel, University of Central Florida; Per Seyersted, University of Oslo, Norway; Ann R. Shapiro, State University of New York, Farmingdale; Peggy Skaggs, Angelo State University; Barbara H. Solomon, Iona College; B. A. St. Andrews, State University of New York, Upstate Medical Center; Patrick Sullivan, Springfield College; U. T. Summers, Rochester Institute of Technology; Evelyn Sweet-Hurd, Lake Jackson, Texas; Lawrence Thornton, University of California, Los Angeles; Emily Toth, Pennsylvania State University; Paula A. Treichler, University of Illinois, Urbana-Champaign; Nancy Walker, Stephens College; Bernice Larson Webb, University of Southwestern Louisiana.

WORKS CITED

Paperback Editions and Anthologies

The American Tradition in Literature. Ed. George Perkins et al. 6th ed. 2 vols. New York: Random, 1985.

Anthology of American Literature. Ed. George McMichael. 3rd ed. 2 vols. New York: Macmillan, 1985.

The Awakening. Ed. Margaret Culley. New York: Norton, 1976.

The Awakening. Ed. Kenneth Eble. New York: Capricorn, 1964.

The Awakening. New York: Avon, 1972.

The Awakening and Other Stories. Ed. and introd. Lewis Leary. New York: Holt, 1970.

The Awakening and Selected Short Stories. New York: Bantam, 1981.

The Awakening and Selected Stories. Ed. and introd. Sandra M. Gilbert. New York: Penguin, 1984.

The Awakening and Selected Stories. Ed. and introd. Barbara H. Solomon. New York: Signet, 1976.

The Awakening and Selected Stories. Introd. Nina Baym. New York: Modern Library, 1981.

The Norton Anthology of American Literature. Ed. Nina Baym et al. 2nd ed. 2 vols. New York: Norton, 1985.

The Norton Anthology of Literature by Women: The Tradition in English. Ed. Sandra M. Gilbert and Susan Gubar. New York: Norton, 1985.

Books and Articles

Abel, Elizabeth, Marianne Hirsch, and Elizabeth Langland, eds. *The Voyage In: Fictions of Female Development.* Hanover: UP of New England, 1983.

Allen, Priscilla. "Old Critics and New: The Treatment of Chopin's *The Awakening.*" *The Authority of Experience: Essays in Feminist Criticism.* Ed. Arlyn Diamond and Lee R. Edwards. Amherst: U of Massachusetts P, 1977. 224–38.

Arms, George. "Kate Chopin's *The Awakening* in the Perspective of Her Literary Career." *Essays on American Literature in Honor of Jay B. Hubbell.* Ed. Clarence Gohdes. Durham: Duke UP, 1967. 215–28.

Arner, Robert D. "Characterization and the Colloquial Style in Kate Chopin's 'Vagabonds.' " *Markham Review* 2 (1971): 110–12.

——, ed. *Kate Chopin.* Spec. issue of *Louisiana Studies* 14 (1975): 11–139.

———. "Kate Chopin's Realism: 'At the 'Cadian Ball' and 'The Storm.' " *Markham Review* 2 (1970): 1–4.

———. "Landscape Symbolism in Kate Chopin's *At Fault.*" *Louisiana Studies* 9 (1970): 142–53.

Bakhtin, Mikhail Mikhailovich. *The Dialogic Imagination: Four Essays.* Trans. Caryl Emerson and Michael Holquist. Austin: U of Texas P, 1981.

Bardot, Jean. "L'influence française dans la vie et l'œuvre de Kate Chopin." Thèse de doctorat, Université de Paris-IV, 1985–86.

Beauvoir, Simone de. *The Second Sex.* 1953. Trans. and ed. H. M. Parshley. New York: Vintage, 1974.

Berne, Eric. *Games People Play.* 1964. New York: Ballantine, 1978.

Berthoff, Warner. *The Ferment of Realism: American Literature, 1884–1919.* 1965. New York: Cambridge, 1981.

Bonner, Thomas, Jr. "Christianity and Catholicism in the Fiction of Kate Chopin." *In Old New Orleans.* Ed. W. Kenneth Holditch. Jackson: UP of Mississippi, 1983. 118–25.

———. "Kate Chopin: An Annotated Bibliography." *Bulletin of Bibliography* 32 (1975): 101–05.

———. *The Kate Chopin Companion.* Westport: Greenwood. Forthcoming.

———. "Kate Chopin's *At Fault* and *The Awakening*: A Study in Structure." *Markham Review* 7 (1977): 10–14.

Booth, Wayne C. *The Rhetoric of Fiction.* Chicago: U of Chicago P, 1961.

Bush, Robert. *Grace King: A Southern Destiny.* Baton Rouge: Louisiana State UP, 1983.

Butler, Harry Scott. "Sexuality in the Fiction of Kate Chopin." Diss. Duke U, 1979.

Candela, Gregory L. "Walt Whitman and Kate Chopin: A Further Connection." *Walt Whitman Review* 24 (1978): 163–65.

Candela, Joseph L., Jr. "The Domestic Orientation of American Novels, 1883–1913." *American Literary Realism 1870–1910* 13 (1980): 1–18.

Cantwell, Robert. "*The Awakening* by Kate Chopin." *Georgia Review* 10 (1956): 489–94.

Carey, Kay. *Cliffs Notes on Chopin's* The Awakening. Lincoln: Cliffs Notes, 1980.

Carnahan, Lucille. Personal interviews. Aug. 1984, Aug. 1985.

Carter, Dan T. *When the War Was Over: The Failure of Self-Reconstruction in the South 1865–1867.* Baton Rouge: Louisiana State UP, 1985.

Casale, Ottavio Mark. "Beyond Sex: The Dark Romanticism of Kate Chopin's *The Awakening.*" *Ball State University Forum* 19 (1978): 76–80.

Cash, Wilbur Joseph. *The Mind of the South.* 1941. New York: Random, 1960.

Cather, Willa. *My Mortal Enemy.* 1926. New York: Vintage, 1954.

———. Review of Chopin's *The Awakening. Leader* 8 July 1899. Rpt. in *The World and the Parish: Willa Cather's Articles and Reviews, 1893–1902.* Ed. William M. Curtin. Vol. 2. Lincoln: U of Nebraska P, 1970. 697–99.

Chase, John Churchill. *Frenchmen, Desire, Good Children, and Other Streets of New Orleans.* 3rd ed. New York: Macmillan, 1979.

Chopin, Kate. *The Awakening.* Chicago: Stone, 1899.

———. *The Complete Works of Kate Chopin.* Ed. and introd. Per Seyersted. 2 vols. Baton Rouge: Louisiana State UP, 1969.

Christ, Carol P. *Diving Deep and Surfacing: Women Writers on Spiritual Quest.* Boston: Beacon, 1980.

Cooke, Rose Terry. "Mrs. Flint's Married Experience." 1880. *"How Celia Changed Her Mind" and Selected Stories.* Ed. Elizabeth Ammons. New Brunswick: Rutgers UP, 1986. 93–130.

Culley, Margaret, ed. *The Awakening.* By Kate Chopin. New York: Norton, 1976.

———. "Kate Chopin and Recent Obscenities." *Kate Chopin Newsletter* 1 (1975): 28–29.

Davidson, Cathy N. "Chopin and Atwood: Woman Drowning, Woman Surfacing." *Kate Chopin Newsletter* 1 (1975): 6–10.

DeLouche, Ivy. Personal interview. Aug. 1984.

Dyer, Joyce. "Kate Chopin's Sleeping Bruties." *Markham Review* 10 (1980): 10–15.

———. "Night Images in the Work of Kate Chopin." *American Literary Realism 1870–1910* 14 (1981): 216–30.

Eaton, Clement. *A History of the Old South.* New York: Macmillan, 1949.

Eble, Kenneth. "A Forgotten Novel: Kate Chopin's *The Awakening.*" *Western Humanities Review* 10 (1956): 261–69. Rpt. in Culley, *The Awakening* 165–73.

Eliot, George. *Middlemarch.* 1871. Ed. Gordon S. Haight. Boston: Riverside, 1956.

Ewell, Barbara C. *Kate Chopin.* New York: Ungar, 1986.

Ezell, John Samuel. *The South since 1865.* New York: Macmillan, 1963.

Fishman, Pamela M. "Interaction: The Work Women Do." *Social Problems* 25 (1978): 397–406. Rpt. in Thorne et al. 89–101.

Fletcher, Marie. "The Southern Woman in the Fiction of Kate Chopin." *Louisiana History* 7 (1966): 117–32. Rpt. in Culley, *The Awakening* 170–73.

Fowler, Roger. *Linguistics and the Novel.* London: Methuen, 1977.

Fox-Genovese, Elizabeth. "Kate Chopin's Awakening." *Southern Studies* 18 (1979): 261–90.

———. *Within the Plantation Household.* Chapel Hill: U of North Carolina P, 1988.

Frank, Francine Wattman. "Women's Language in America: Myth and Reality." *Women's Language and Style.* Ed. Douglas Butturff and Edmund L. Epstein. Akron: L & S, 1978. 47–61.

Franklin, Rosemary F. "*The Awakening* and the Failure of Psyche." *American Literature* 56 (1984): 510–26.

Fryer, Judith. *The Faces of Eve: Women in the Nineteenth Century American Novel.* New York: Oxford UP, 1976.

Gerrard, Lisa. "The Romantic Woman in Nineteenth-Century Fiction: A Comparative Study of *Madame Bovary, La Regenta, The Mill on the Floss,* and *The Awakening.*" Diss. U of California, Berkeley, 1979.

Gilbert, Sandra M. "The Second Coming of Aphrodite: Kate Chopin's Fantasy of Desire." *Kenyon Review* 5 (1983): 42–56.

Gilbert, Sandra M., and Susan Gubar. *The Madwoman in the Attic: The Woman Writer and the Nineteenth-Century Literary Imagination.* New Haven: Yale UP, 1979.

Gilman, Charlotte Perkins. "The Yellow Wallpaper." 1892. *The Norton Anthology of American Literature.* Ed. Nina Baym et al. 2nd ed. Vol. 2. New York: Norton, 1985. 644–57.

Glasgow, Ellen. *Virginia.* New York: Doubleday, 1913.

Hall, Jacquelyn Dowd. *Revolt against Chivalry: Jessie Daniel Ames and the Women's Campaign against Lynching.* New York: Columbia UP, 1979.

Hearn, Lafcadio. *Chita: A Memory of Last Island.* 1889. Chapel Hill: U of North Carolina P, 1969.

Henley, Nancy M. "Power, Sex, and Nonverbal Communication." *Berkeley Journal of Sociology* 18 (1973–74): 1–26. Rpt. in Thorne et al. 184–203.

Hernandez, Leona S. Personal interviews. Aug. 1984, Aug. 1985

Holland, Dorothy Garesché. *The Garesché, De Bauduy and Des Chapelles Families: History and Genealogy.* St. Louis: Schneider, 1963.

Holman, C. Hugh, and William Harmon. *A Handbook to Literature.* 5th ed. New York: Macmillan, 1986.

House, Elizabeth Balkman. "*The Awakening*: Kate Chopin's 'Endlessly Rocking Cycle.'" *Ball State University Forum* 20 (1979): 53–58.

Howell, Elmo. "Kate Chopin and the Creole Country." *Louisiana History* 20 (1979): 209–19.

———. "Kate Chopin and the Pull of Faith: A Note on 'Lilacs.'" *Southern Studies* 18 (1979): 103–09.

Hunt, Russell A. "Toward a Process-Intervention Model in Literature Teaching." *College English* 44 (1982): 345–57.

Inge, Tonette Bond. "Kate Chopin." *American Woman Writers: Bibliographical Essays.* Ed. Maurice Duke et al. Westport: Greenwood, 1983. 47–69.

James, Henry. *The Golden Bowl.* Harmondsworth, Eng.: Penguin, 1966.

James, William. *The Principles of Psychology.* Vol. 1. 1890. New York: Dover, 1950.

Jasenas, Elaine. "The French Influence in Kate Chopin's *The Awakening.*" *Nine-teenth-Century French Studies* 4 (1976): 312–22.

Jones, Anne Goodwyn. *Tomorrow Is Another Day: The Woman Writer in the South, 1859–1936.* Baton Rouge: Louisiana State UP, 1981.

Jones, Ann Rosalind. "Writing the Body: Toward an Understanding of *l'Ecriture Féminine.*" *Feminist Studies* 7 (1981): 247–63. Rpt. in Showalter, *New Feminist Criticism* 361–77.

Jones, Suzanne W. "Place, Perception, and Identity in *The Awakening.*" *Southern Quarterly* 25 (1987): 108–19.

Justus, James H. "The Unawakening of Edna Pontellier." *Southern Literary Journal* 10 (1978): 107–22.

Kelley, Mary. *Private Woman, Public Stage: Literary Domesticity in Nineteenth-Century America.* New York: Oxford, 1984.

King, Edward. "Old and New Louisiana." *Scribner's Monthly* 7 (Nov. 1873): 1–32; (Dec. 1873): 129–60.

Klinkowitz, Jerome. *The Practice of Fiction in America: Writers from Hawthorne to the Present.* Ames: Iowa State UP, 1980.

Kolodny, Annette. "A Map for Rereading: Gender and the Interpretation of Literary Texts." Showalter, *New Feminist Criticism* 46–62.

Koloski, Bernard J. "The Structure of Kate Chopin's *At Fault.*" *Studies in American Fiction* 3 (1975): 89–95.

———. "The Swinburne Lines in *The Awakening.*" *American Literature* 45 (1974): 608–10.

Kraditor, Aileen S. *The Ideas of the Woman Suffrage Movement: 1890–1920.* 1971. New York: Norton, 1981.

Kramer, Cheris. "Excessive Loquacity: Women's Speech as Represented in American Etiquette Books." Speech Communication Assn. Conference, Austin, 10–12 July 1975.

———. "Women's Speech: Separate but Unequal." *Quarterly Journal of Speech* 60 (1974): 14–24. Rpt. in Thorne et al. 43–56.

Kroeber, Karl. *Styles in Fictional Structure: The Art of Jane Austen, Charlotte Brontë, George Eliot.* Princeton: Princeton UP, 1971.

Lakoff, Robin Tolmach. "Women's Language." *Women's Language and Style.* Ed. Douglas Butturff and Edmund L. Epstein. Akron: L & S, 1978. 139–58.

Lattin, Patricia Hopkins. "Kate Chopin's Repeating Characters." *Mississippi Quarterly* 33 (1979–80): 19–37.

Lauter, Paul, ed. *Reconstructing American Literature: Courses, Syllabi, Issues.* Old Westbury: Feminist, 1983.

Leary, Lewis. *American Literature: A Study and Research Guide.* New York: St. Martin's, 1976.

———. Introduction. The Awakening *and Other Stories by Kate Chopin.* New York: Holt, 1970. iii–xviii.

———. "Kate Chopin and Walt Whitman." *Walt Whitman Review* 16 (1970): 120–21. Rpt. in Culley, *The Awakening* 195–99.

———. "Kate Chopin's Other Novel." *Southern Literary Journal* 1 (1968): 60–74.

Leech, Geoffrey N., and Michael H. Short. *Style in Fiction: A Linguistic Introduction to English Fictional Prose.* London: Longman, 1981.

Levine, Robert S. "Circadian Rhythms and Rebellion in Kate Chopin's *The Awakening.*" *Studies in American Fiction* 10 (1982): 71–81.

Lodge, David. *The Language of Fiction: Essays in Criticism and Verbal Analysis of the English Novel.* New York: Columbia UP, 1966.

Luthi, Max. *Once upon a Time: On the Nature of Fairy Tales.* New York: Ungar, 1970.

Marks, Elaine. "Women and Literature in France." *Signs: Journal of Women in Culture and Society* 3 (1978): 832–42.

May, John R. "Local Color in *The Awakening.*" *Southern Review* 6 (1970): 1031–40. Rpt. in Culley, *The Awakening* 189–95.

May, Rollo. *Love and Will.* New York: Norton, 1969.

Mayer, Charles W. "Isabel Archer, Edna Pontellier, and the Romantic Self." *Research Studies* [Washington State U] 47 (1979): 89–97.

McCord, Louisa Susannah. "Enfranchisement of Women." *Southern Quarterly Review* ns 5 (1852): 322–41. Rpt. in *All Clever Men, Who Make Their Way: Critical Discourse in the Old South.* Ed. Michael O'Brien. Fayetteville: U of Arkansas P, 1982. 337–56.

McCormick, Kathleen. "Theory in the Reader: Bleich, Holland, and Beyond." *College English* 47 (1985): 836–50.

McQuade, Donald, et al., eds. *The Harper American Literature.* 2 vols. New York: Harper, 1987.

Melville, Herman. *Moby-Dick.* 1851. Ed. Charles Feidelson, Jr. New York: Bobbs, 1964.

Mills, Elizabeth Shown. *Chauvin dit Charleville.* Mississippi State: Mississippi State U, 1976.

Moers, Ellen. *Literary Women.* New York: Doubleday, 1976.

Neumann, Erich. *Amor and Psyche: The Psychic Development of the Feminine; A Commentary on a Tale by Apuleius.* Trans. Ralph Manheim. 1956. Princeton: Princeton UP, 1971.

O'Brien, Sharon. "The Limits of Passion: Willa Cather's Review of *The Awakening.*" *Women and Literature* 3 (1975): 10–20.

Page, Norman. *Speech in the English Novel.* London: Longman, 1973.

Pattee, Fred Lewis. *The Development of the American Short Story: An Historical Survey.* New York: Harper, 1923.

Phelps, Elizabeth Stuart. "The Angel over the Right Shoulder." 1852. *Images of Women in Literature.* Ed. Mary Anne Ferguson. 4th ed. Boston: Houghton, 1986. 43–50.

Plath, Sylvia. *The Bell Jar.* 1963. New York: Bantam, 1975.

Potter, Richard H. "Kate Chopin and Her Critics: An Annotated Checklist." *Missouri Historical Society Bulletin* 26 (1970): 306–17.

Rankin, Daniel S. *Kate Chopin and Her Creole Stories.* Philadelphia: U of Pennsylvania P, 1932.

Rich, Adrienne. "It Is the Lesbian in Us. . . ." *On Lies, Secrets, and Silence: Selected Prose 1966–1978.* New York: Norton, 1979. 199–202.

———. "Women and Honor: Some Notes on Lying." *On Lies, Secrets, and Silence: Selected Prose 1966–1978.* New York: Norton, 1979. 185–94.

Ringe, Donald A. "Cane River World: Kate Chopin's *At Fault* and Related Stories." *Studies in American Fiction* 3 (1975): 157–66.

———. "Romantic Imagery in Kate Chopin's *The Awakening*." *American Literature* 43 (1972): 580–88.

Roberts, Edgar V. *Writing Themes about Literature*. Englewood Cliffs: Prentice, 1969.

Rocks, James E. "Kate Chopin's Ironic Vision." *Revue de Louisiane/Louisiana Review* 1 (1972): 11–20.

Rosen, Kenneth M. "Kate Chopin's *The Awakening*: Ambiguity as Art." *Journal of American Studies* 5 (1971): 197–99.

Rosowski, Susan J. "The Novel of Awakening." *Genre* 12 (1979): 313–32. Rpt. in Abel, Hirsch, and Langland 49–68.

———. *The Voyage Perilous: Willa Cather's Romanticism*. Lincoln: U of Nebraska P, 1986.

Sattel, Jack W. "Men, Inexpressiveness, and Power." Thorne et al. 118–24.

Schuyler, William. "Kate Chopin." *Writer* 7 (1894): 115–17. Rpt. in Seyersted and Toth 115–19.

Scott, Anne Firor. *The Southern Lady: From Pedestal to Politics, 1830–1930*. Chicago: U of Chicago P, 1970.

Searle, John R. *Speech Acts: An Essay in the Philosophy of Language*. London: Cambridge UP, 1969.

Seyersted, Per. *Kate Chopin: A Critical Biography*. Baton Rouge: Louisiana State UP; Oslo: Universitetsforlaget, 1969.

Seyersted, Per, and Emily Toth, eds. *A Kate Chopin Miscellany*. Natchitoches: Northwestern State UP; Oslo: Universitetsforlaget, 1979.

Shaffner, Randolph P. *The Apprenticeship Novel: A Study of the "Bildungsroman" as a Regulative Type in Western Literature*. New York: Lang, 1984.

Showalter, Elaine, ed. *The New Feminist Criticism: Essays on Women, Literature, and Theory*. New York: Pantheon, 1985.

Simpson, Lewis P. Foreword. Arner, *Kate Chopin* 5–10.

Skaggs, Peggy. *Kate Chopin*. Boston: Twayne, 1985.

———. " 'The Man-Instinct of Possession': A Persistent Theme in Kate Chopin's Stories." *Louisiana Studies* 14 (1975): 277–85.

———. "Three Tragic Figures in Kate Chopin's *The Awakening*." *Louisiana Studies* 13 (1974): 345–64.

Smith-Rosenberg, Carroll. "The Female World of Love and Ritual: Relations between Women in Nineteenth-Century America." *Signs: Journal of Women in Culture and Society* 1 (1975): 1–29.

Spacks, Patricia Meyer. *The Female Imagination*. New York: Knopf, 1975.

Spangler, George. "Kate Chopin's *The Awakening*: A Partial Dissent." *Novel* 3 (1970): 249–55.

164   Works Cited

Spitzer, Leo. *Linguistics and Literary History: Essays in Stylistics.* Princeton: Princeton UP, 1948.

Springer, Marlene, ed. *Edith Wharton and Kate Chopin: A Reference Guide.* Boston: Hall, 1976.

———. "Kate Chopin: A Reference Guide Updated." *Resources for American Literary Study* 11 (1981): 280–303.

"St. Louis Convents." *Missouri Republican* 30 June 1868: 2.

"St. Louis Woman Who Has Won Fame in Literature." *Post-Dispatch* [St. Louis] 26 Nov. 1899, sec. 4: 1.

Stone, Robert. *Children of Light.* 1986. New York: Ballantine, 1987.

Suleiman, Susan R., and Inge Crosman, eds. *The Reader in the Text: Essays in Audience and Interpretation.* Princeton: Princeton UP, 1980.

Sullivan, Ruth, and Stewart Smith. "Narrative Stance in Kate Chopin's *The Awakening.*" *Studies in American Fiction* 1 (1973): 62–75.

Taylor, Helen, ed. *Kate Chopin Portraits.* London: Women's, 1979.

Thorne, Barrie, Cheris Kramarae, and Nancy Henley, eds. *Language, Gender and Society.* Rowley: Newbury, 1983.

Thornton, Lawrence. "*The Awakening*: A Political Romance." *American Literature* 52 (1980): 50–66.

Tompkins, Jane P. "*The Awakening*: An Evaluation." *Feminist Studies* 3 (1976): 22–29.

———, ed. *Reader-Response Criticism: From Formalism to Post-Structuralism.* Baltimore: Johns Hopkins UP, 1980.

Toth, Emily. "Bibliography of Writings on Kate Chopin." Seyersted and Toth 212–61.

———. "The Independent Woman and 'Free' Love." *Massachusetts Review* 16 (1975): 647–64.

———. *Kate Chopin.* New York: Atheneum. Forthcoming.

———. "Timely and Timeless: The Treatment of Time in *The Awakening* and *Sister Carrie.*" *Southern Studies* 16 (1977): 271–76.

Treichler, Paula A. "The Construction of Ambiguity in *The Awakening*: A Linguistic Analysis." *Women and Language in Literature and Society.* Ed. Sally McConnell-Ginet, Ruth Borker, and Nelly Furman. New York: Praeger, 1980. 239–57.

Ullmann, Stephen. *Style in the French Novel.* London: Cambridge UP, 1957.

Van Sittert, Barbara Culver. "Social Institutions and Biological Determinism in the Fictional World of Kate Chopin." Diss. Arizona State U, 1975.

Veblen, Thorstein. *The Theory of the Leisure Class.* 1899. New York: Penguin, 1979.

Vickery, John B. *The Literary Impact of* The Golden Bough. Princeton: Princeton UP, 1973.

Walker, Nancy. "Feminist or Naturalist: The Social Context of Kate Chopin's *The Awakening.*" *Southern Quarterly* 17 (1979): 95–103.

Waters, Julia Breazeale. Personal interview. Aug. 1984.

Watt, Ian. "The First Paragraph of *The Ambassadors*: An Explication." *Essays in Criticism* 10 (1960): 250–74.

Welter, Barbara. *Dimity Convictions: The American Woman in the Nineteenth Century*. Athens: Ohio UP, 1976.

Welty, Eudora. "Place in Fiction." *South Atlantic Quarterly* 55 (1956): 57–72. Rpt. in *The Eye of the Story: Selected Essays and Reviews*. New York: Random, 1978. 116–33.

Wheeler, Otis B. "The Five Awakenings of Edna Pontellier." *Southern Review* 11 (1975): 118–28.

Widdowson, H. G. *Stylistics and the Teaching of Literature*. London: Longman, 1975.

Williamson, Joel. *The Crucible of Race: Black-White Relations in the American South since Emancipation*. New York: Oxford, 1984.

Wilson, Edmund. *Patriotic Gore: Studies in the Literature of the American Civil War*. 1962. Boston: Northeastern UP, 1984.

Wilson, Maryhelen. "Kate Chopin's Family: Fallacies and Facts, Including Kate's True Birthdate." *Kate Chopin Newsletter* 2 (1976–77): 25–31.

———. Personal interview. May 1985.

———. "Woman's Lib in Old St. Louis: 'La Verdon.' " *St. Louis Genealogical Society* 14.4 (no year): 139–40.

Wolff, Cynthia Griffin. "Thanatos and Eros: Kate Chopin's *The Awakening*." *American Quarterly* 25 (1973): 449–72. Rpt. in Culley, *The Awakening* 206–18.

Wood, Ann Douglas. "The Literature of Impoverishment: The Woman Local Colorists in America 1865–1914." *Women's Studies* 1 (1972): 3–45.

Ziff, Larzer. *The American 1890s: Life and Times of a Lost Generation*. New York: Viking, 1966.

Zimmerman, Don. H., and Candace West. "Sex Roles, Interruptions and Silences in Conversation." Thorne et al. 105–29.

Zlotnick, Joan. "A Woman's Will: Kate Chopin on Selfhood, Wifehood, and Motherhood." *Markham Review* 3 (1968): 1–5.

Films and Videotapes

The Awakening: A Novel by Kate Chopin [excerpts, 15 min.]. Dir. Paul Lally. Children's Television International, 1980. Available on film or tape from the Indiana University AV Center, Bloomington, IN 47405-5901.

The Bostonians. Dir. James Ivory. Merchant-Ivory Productions for Rank and Rediffusion Films, 1984.

A Doll's House. Dir. Joseph Losey. World Film Series, 1973.

The End of August [*The Awakening*, feature length]. Dir. Bob Graham. Quartet, 1982. Available on tape from video stores.

The Joy That Kills [Chopin's "The Story of an Hour"]. Dir. Tina Rathborne. Cypress Films in association with Mark/Jett Productions, 1984. Available from the Louisiana Humanities Resource Center, University of Southwestern Louisiana, PO Box 40396, Lafayette, LA 70504.

Kate Chopin's "The Story of an Hour." Dir. Marita Simpson. Ishtar, 1982. Available on film or tape from Ishtar Films, Box 51, Patterson, NY 12563.

INDEX

Abel, Elizabeth, 12, 27
Aeschylus, 35, 39
Allen, Priscilla, 14
Angelou, Maya, 87
Aristotle, 88
Arms, George, 14, 15, 130
Arner, Robert D., 14, 15
Atwood, Margaret, 14, 29, 87
Austen, Jane, 87

Bakhtin, Mikhail, 22, 47–49, 52
Balfe, Michael William, 17, 126
Balzac, Honoré de, 30
Bardot, Jean, 66
Bauer, Dale Marie, 10, 22
Baym, Nina, 5
Beaulieu, Jean Marie, 64
Beauvoir, Simone de, 12
Behra, Robert, 66
Berne, Eric, 105
Berthoff, Warner, 11, 14, 81
Blackwell, Elizabeth, 5
Bonner, Thomas, Jr., 15, 16, 23
Booth, Wayne C., 132, 135
Breazeale, Phanor, 60
Brend, Ruth M., 54
Brontë, Charlotte, 7, 87
Brooks, Cleanth, 99
Brown, Rita Mae, 87
Browning, Robert, 105
Burtt, H. E., 56
Bush, Robert, 36
Butler, Harry Scott, 84
Butler, Samuel, 27

Candela, Gregory L., 14, 81, 131
Candela, Joseph L., Jr., 14
Cantwell, Robert, 14
Carey, Kay, 18
Carnahan, Lucille, 63, 64
Carter, Dan T., 36
Casale, Ottavio Mark, 14, 81
Cash, Wilbur Joseph, 12
Cassatt, Mary, 17
Cather, Willa, 3, 14, 21, 29, 30–31, 32, 65
Cézanne, Paul, 17
Charleville, Victoria Verdon, 61, 62
Chase, John Churchill, 69

Chopin, Frédéric, 16, 24, 126, 129
Chopin, Jane, 66
Chopin, Jean, 65
Chopin, Lélia, 63
Chopin, Marie Therese, 66
Chopin, Oscar, 63, 67, 68, 88
Chopin, Oscar, Jr., 64
Chopin, Tom, 66
Christ, Carol P., 12
Cixous, Hélène, 59
Conrad, Joseph, 98
Cooke, Rose Terry, 11
Crane, Stephen, 44, 84, 98, 102
Crosman, Inge, 151
Culley, Margaret, 3, 5, 17, 65, 94, 96, 97

Davidson, Cathy N., 14
Davis, Rebecca Harding, 103
Delacroix, Eugène, 17
DeLouche, Ivy, 64
Dewing, Thomas Wilmer, 17
Dickerson, Wayne, 53
Disney, Walt, 28
Dix, Dorothy (Elizabeth Gilmer), 3, 9, 11, 96
Doctorow, E. L., 104
Dostoyevsky, Fyodor, 107
Douglas, Ellen, 87
Dreiser, Theodore, 83, 84, 102
Dunn, Margaret M., 17, 23
Dyer, Joyce, 10, 15, 24

Eaton, Clement, 12, 70
Eble, Kenneth, 3, 6, 13, 96
Eliot, George, 32
Eliot, T. S., 107
Ellison, Ralph, 132
Emerson, Ralph Waldo, 81, 82, 130
Ewell, Barbara C., 10, 13, 14, 15, 23
Ezell, John Samuel, 68, 69

Faris, Wilson, 67
Faulkner, William, 39, 44, 104
Fishman, Pamela M., 57
Flaubert, Gustave, 12, 21, 29, 30, 102, 143
Fletcher, Marie, 12, 14

Fonda, Jane, 18
Fowler, Roger, 132
Fox-Genovese, Elizabeth, 10, 14, 22, 36, 39, 41, 120
Frank, Francine Wattman, 54, 55, 56
Franklin, Rosemary F., 14, 18, 21, 24, 148
Frazer, James George, 128
Freeman, Mary E. Wilkins, 87
Freud, Sigmund, 28, 96, 105
Fryer, Judith, 12
Fuller, Henry Blake, 128

Garesché, Kitty, 62
Garland, Hamlin, 84, 102
Geller, Robert, 18
George, E. Laurie, 10, 21, 22
Gerrard, Lisa, 82
Gilbert, Sandra M., 4–5, 6, 12, 14
Gilman, Charlotte Perkins, 5, 9, 11, 34, 35, 38, 49, 52, 96, 103, 105
Glasgow, Ellen, 37
Gleser, Goldine C., 55
Goethe, Johann Wolfgang von, 27
Gottschalk, Louis A., 55
Graham, Bob, 18
Gubar, Susan, 12

Hall, Jacquelyn Dowd, 38
Harmon, William, 27
Hart, John Seely, 99
Hawkins, Joy, 17
Hawthorne, Nathaniel, 81, 82, 101, 127
Hearn, Lafcadio, 70, 128
Heilbrun, Carolyn G., 12
Henley, Nancy M., 56
Hernandez, Leona S., 64
Hérold, Louis, 17, 126
Hill, Rebecca, 87
Hirsch, Marianne, 12, 27
Holland, Dorothy Garesché, 62
Holman, C. Hugh, 27
Hoover, John Neal, 66
House, Elizabeth Balkman, 81
Howell, Elmo, 15, 81
Howells, William Dean, 44, 84
Hugo, Victor, 102
Hunt, Russell A., 151
Hurston, Zora Neale, 87
Hutchinson, Ward, 22, 48–49, 50, 52

Ibsen, Henrik, 12, 18, 35, 39, 128
Inge, Tonette Bond, 15
Irigaray, Luce, 59
Ivory, James, 18

Jacobs, Jo Ellen, 10, 21, 23
James, Henry, 18, 26, 48, 82, 84, 98, 132
James, William, 22, 48, 49, 50, 52
Jasenas, Elaine, 14
Jewett, Sarah Orne, 87
Jones, Ann Rosalind, 53
Jones, Anne Goodwyn, 12, 14
Jones, Suzanne W., 14, 24
Jong, Erica, 32, 87
Joyce, James, 27, 133
Jung, Carl Gustav, 24, 105, 144
Justus, James H., 14

Kelley, Mary, 12
King, Edward, 69–70
King, Grace, 36
Klinkowitz, Jerome, 84–85
Kolodny, Annette, 12
Koloski, Bernard J., 15, 46, 130
Kraditor, Aileen S., 36, 38
Kramer (Kramarae), Cheris, 53, 54, 57
Kristeva, Julia, 59
Kroeber, Karl, 132

Laing, Ronald David, 28
Lakoff, Robin Tolmach, 54, 55
Lakritz, Andrew M., 10, 22
Lally, Paul, 17
Landis, Carney, 56
Landis, M. H., 56
Langland, Elizabeth, 12, 27
Lattin, Patricia Hopkins, 4, 14, 15, 21, 22, 44
Lauter, Paul, 13, 99
Leary, Lewis, 5, 6, 14, 15, 81, 82, 99, 130–31
Leech, Geoffrey N., 132
Lessing, Doris, 87
Levine, Robert S., 14
Lodge, David, 132
Losey, Joseph, 18
Luthi, Max, 28

Macy, John, 99
Manet, Edouard, 17
Marks, Elaine, 22, 53, 59
Maugham, Somerset, 27
Maupassant, Guy de, 16, 34, 77
May, John R., 14, 102, 120, 126
May, Rollo, 23, 107–08, 110–13
Mayer, Charles W., 14
McConnell-Ginet, Sally, 54
McCord, Louisa Susannah, 36
McCormick, Kathleen, 151

McCoy, Mildred, 16
McQuade, Donald, 7
Melville, Herman, 81, 82, 101, 127, 130
Miller, Nancy, 12
Mills, Elizabeth Shown, 61
Moers, Ellen, 12
Morris, Anne R., 17, 23
Morrison, Toni, 7, 87

Neumann, Erich, 144
Norris, Frank, 84, 102

O'Brien, Sharon, 14
O'Flaherty, Eliza, 61, 64
O'Flaherty, George, 62
O'Flaherty, Thomas, 61
Olsen, Tillie, 132

Page, Norman, 132
Papke, Mary E., 4, 15, 22–23
Pattee, Fred Lewis, 66
Percy, William Alexander, 39
Phelps, Elizabeth Stuart, 11
Plath, Sylvia, 87, 114
Plato, 107
Poe, Edgar Allan, 82
Pollard, Percival, 96
Porcher, Frances, 65
Potter, Richard H., 15
Prendergast, Maurice, 17

Rankin, Daniel S., 4, 13, 61, 62, 63, 96
Rankin, Elizabeth, 18, 24–25
Raphael, 30
Rathborne, Tina, 17
Renoir, Pierre-Auguste, 17
Rhys, Jean, 87
Rich, Adrienne, 58
Rilke, Rainer Maria, 107
Ringe, Donald A., 14, 15, 81, 127, 130
Roberts, Edgar V., 105
Robinson, Lillian, 12
Rocks, James E., 15
Rogers, Nancy, 10, 24
Rosen, Kenneth M., 14
Rosowski, Susan J., 10, 21, 32, 82

Sartre, Jean-Paul, 107
Sattel, Jack W., 56
Schuyler, William, 62
Scott, Anne Firor, 12, 36
Searle, John R., 132

Seyersted, Per, 3, 9, 11, 13, 15, 16, 34,
   35, 36, 38, 60, 61, 62, 63, 65, 67, 68,
   70, 73, 84, 102, 121
Shaffner, Randolph P., 27, 33
Shakespeare, William, 30, 35, 39
Short, Michael H., 132
Showalter, Elaine, 12
Simpson, Lewis P., 82, 83
Simpson, Marita, 17
Sisley, Alfred, 17
Skaggs, Peggy, 10, 13, 14, 15, 23
Smedley, Agnes, 32
Smith, Sidney, 99
Smith, Stewart, 14, 120
Smith-Rosenberg, Carroll, 12
Solomon, Barbara H., 4, 14, 15, 24, 74
Spacks, Patricia Meyer, 12
Spangler, George, 14
Spitzer, Leo, 132, 133
Springer, Marlene, 15
Stanton, Elizabeth Cady, 5, 35
Stocker, Erik, 66
Stone, Robert, 16
Stowe, Harriet Beecher, 82
Suleiman, Susan R., 151
Sullivan, Ruth, 14, 120
Sweet-Hurd, Evelyn, 3, 23
Swinburne, Algernon, 46, 130, 147

Tarbell, Edmund Charles, 17
Taylor, Helen, 5, 6, 15
Thoreau, Henry David, 82
Thornton, Lawrence, 14, 21, 24
Tillett, Wilbur Fisk, 96
Tolstoy, Leo, 12, 107
Tompkins, Jane P., 14, 151
Toth, Emily, 10, 13, 15, 16, 22, 38, 60,
   62, 63, 65, 67, 84
Treichler, Paula A., 57, 59, 89
Twain, Mark, 26, 83, 84, 99, 127

Ullmann, Stephen, 132

Van Sittert, Barbara Culver, 84
Veblen, Thorstein, 3, 9, 11, 22, 48, 49,
   50, 52
Vickery, John B., 128

Wagner, Richard, 16, 24, 30, 70, 126, 129
Walker, Nancy, 10, 14, 22, 39
Waters, Julia Breazeale, 61, 63, 64
Watkins, John, 55
Watt, Ian, 132

Welter, Barbara, 12
Welty, Eudora, 12, 87
West, Candace, 56
Wharton, Edith, 15, 49, 87
Wheeler, Otis B., 14, 82
Whitman, Walt, 14, 43, 44, 81, 82, 83, 131
Widdowson, H. G., 132
Williamson, Joel, 38
Wilson, Colin, 107
Wilson, Edmund, 13
Wilson, Maryhelen, 61, 66

Wolfe, Thomas, 27
Wolff, Cynthia Griffin, 3, 9, 13, 28, 96
Wolkenfeld, Suzanne, 96, 97
Wollstonecraft, Mary, 87
Wood, Ann Douglas, 12
Woolf, Virginia, 87, 133

Ziff, Larzer, 3, 11, 14, 34, 49
Zimmerman, Don H., 56
Zlotnick, Joan, 14, 81